A Roman Women Reader

$\mathcal{BC}$ LATIN Readers

Series Editor:
Ronnie Ancona, Hunter College and CUNY Graduate Center

These Readers provide well annotated Latin selections written by experts in the field, to be used as authoritative introductions to Latin authors, genres, topics, or themes for intermediate or advanced college Latin study. Their relatively small size (approximately 600 lines) makes them ideal to use in combination. Each volume includes a comprehensive introduction, bibliography for further reading, Latin text with notes at the back, and complete vocabulary. Nineteen volumes are available. Check our website for more information: www.BOLCHAZY.com.

A Roman Women Reader

Selections from the Second Century BCE through the Second Century CE

Sheila K. Dickison
and Judith P. Hallett

Bolchazy-Carducci Publishers, Inc.
Mundelein, Illinois USA

Series Editor: Ronnie Ancona

Volume Editor: Laurie Haight Keenan

Cover Design & Typography: Adam Phillip Velez

A Roman Women Reader
Selections from the Second Century BCE through the Second Century CE

Sheila K. Dickison and Judith P. Hallett

Bolchazy-Carducci Publishers, Inc.
1570 Baskin Road
Mundelein, Illinois 60060
www.bolchazy.com

Printed in the United States of America
2015
by United Graphics

ISBN 978-0-86516-662-2

Library of Congress Cataloging-in-Publication Data

A Roman women reader : selections from the second century BCE through the second
century CE / [compiled by] Sheila K. Dickison and Judith P. Hallett.
    pages cm -- (BC Latin readers)
  ISBN 978-0-86516-662-2 (pbk. : alk. paper) 1. Women--Literary collections. 2. Latin
language--Readers. 3. Latin literature. I. Dickison, Sheila K. (Sheila Kathryn), 1942-
compiler. II. Hallett, Judith P., 1944- compiler.
  PA6118.W66R66 2014
  870.9'3522--dc23

                                                                        2014043544

Contents

List of Illustrations

Preface

This Latin reader on Roman women features a series of relatively brief selections from a wide range of Latin prose and poetic writings. They date from the second and first century BCE to the first and second century CE, thereby spanning the so-called Roman "classical" era. In introducing each of these passages, we have sought to provide both its literary and historical context as well as to indicate what we regard as its significance. We have assembled this array of Latin texts— composed by a diverse group of Roman authors writing in a variety of literary genres—into a single Latin *Reader* with several objectives in mind. First and foremost, this volume tries to familiarize college and university-level Latin language and literature students with important evidence about women, as individuals and as members of larger social entities, in classical Roman society. It also endeavors to highlight themes and conventions that inform women's literary representations in Latin texts. These passages come from works that for the most part do not figure in standard Latin textbooks for students at the intermediate and advanced levels, nor in Latin language and literature courses devoted to such canonical authors as Catullus, Cicero, Caesar, Vergil, Horace, Ovid, and Livy.

We would like to thank our editors, Ronnie Ancona and Laurie Haight Keenan, for the "Latin *TLC*" (*tempus, labor, cura*) they have lavished upon this complex undertaking; the anonymous readers for Bolchazy-Carducci Publishers; and various colleagues and students—Lauri Dabbieri, Donald Lateiner, Victoria Pagán, Elizabeth Settoducato, Marilyn Skinner—for their support and assistance. We dedicate this volume to the memory of four remarkable women who taught us as undergraduates: Frances Norwood and Mary E. White of the University of Toronto, and Barbara P. McCarthy and Margaret E. Taylor of Wellesley College. The rigorous linguistic and literary training, close attention to textual and grammatical detail, and above all joy in engagement with classical texts that they valued and imparted have energized and sustained us throughout our scholarly and professional lives.

SHEILA K. DICKISON AND JUDITH P. HALLETT

Introduction

A substantial body of scholarship published over the past four decades testifies to the growing academic interest in the topic of Roman women, validating research into women's lives and textual depictions as a major sub-field in classical studies. Both the sheer volume and high quality of these publications on Roman women have themselves suggested—to our editors as well as to ourselves—a need for sharing the results of such research beyond the circle of scholarly specialists, most immediately to college and university students capable of reading, in the original Latin, the texts that this research seeks to illuminate. We hope, too, that this volume conveys the intellectual excitement that we ourselves have experienced in engaging with these texts in the course of undertaking and benefiting from this research.

The close focus in this volume on our Latin textual evidence for Roman women's lived experiences and literary representations also prompts questions that readers might wish to pose of the Latin selections presented here, so as to make further connections among them. One such question is how the literary genre of a given work affects its portrayal of women. Taking generic factors into account may help elucidate the misogynistic sentiments often voiced by works of satire, poetic invective, and oratory.

Another important question is how and why elite Roman men who write about contemporary women from their own social milieu depict these women as simultaneously "other," utterly different from men as a group, and yet "same," praiseworthy for sharing publicly displayed traits and qualities with their male kinsmen. Yet another is how words written by Roman women themselves both counter and confirm popular male stereotypes about women.

A few words on the women who figure in the Latin texts we have chosen. Several of them are actual historical figures: Clodia Metelli, Fulvia, the emperor Nero's mother Agrippina the Younger, and the Pompeian benefactress Eumachia among them. Some of these historical figures, such as Fulvia and Agrippina—are sufficiently prominent to rate mention by a variety of ancient sources. Others are obscure individuals whose lives are only recorded by a single text.

To be sure, we have incorporated a few portraits of fictional female figures by such Latin authors as Plautus and Petronius, as well as purported descriptions of actual Roman women that would seem to contain fictional elements, also by well-known Latin writers such as Horace, Propertius, and Juvenal. These texts are noteworthy for offering memorable portraits of Roman female stereotypes, or for their vivid dramatization of issues faced by actual women in their relationships as wives and mothers, friends and lovers. Or both. Our main focus, however, is on historical figures: women represented as contemporary Romans by the writers who describe them, usually during the time period in which these women were alive, but occasionally later. For example, our only source for the funeral speeches delivered by Julius Caesar to honor his dead female kinswomen during the first half of the first century BCE is Suetonius' biography of Caesar, written in the early second century CE, while our most dramatic account of how Agrippina the Elder met her death in the mid-first century CE is by Suetonius' coeval Tacitus.

Many of the Roman women featured in our selections speak in the first person in these texts: some evidently in their own words, some in words attributed to them by male writers. Indeed, our volume accords special attention to the words of the four Roman women from the classical period whose writings have survived to the present day; namely, the second century BCE noblewoman Cornelia; the late first century BCE elegiac poet Sulpicia, whose verses celebrate an illicit love affair with a younger man; another love poet from the first century CE, also, coincidentally, named Sulpicia, whose verses celebrate her passion for her husband; and Claudia Severa, wife of a military officer stationed at the British fort of Vindolanda ca. 100 CE.

Some scholars have questioned the authenticity of Cornelia's letter to her son, and challenged the female authorship of five or more of the eleven elegiac poems associated with the earlier Sulpicia. But even if these writings may not actually be by these women, they provide valuable evidence about how Roman women of the classical period were thought, at the time, to have expressed themselves in writing. What is more, much testimony about classical Roman society indicates that women read and wrote letters and literature, suggesting that a substantial body of female-authored work from the ancient Roman world has been irretrievably lost. We hope that our *Roman Women Reader* will serve as a powerful reminder that some Roman women were actively engaged, as readers and producers of texts, with the written as well as the spoken word.

We have chosen Latin texts that spotlight Roman women of different ages and at different stages of their lives, most of which depict their interactions with men and women from both within and outside of their households. So, too, the women featured in these texts come from different social classes and different geographic locales. Both domestic tasks and public pursuits, cultural and political, loom large among their activities. These texts also portray women of very different social backgrounds as sharing certain concerns, chief among them that of performing satisfactorily and successfully in their familial roles as wives and mothers—in marriage, childbearing, and childrearing.

Some of the texts describe, at times graphically, women's erotic desire and activity outside the realm of legitimate marriage. Including such texts in our purview is, we believe, entirely appropriate for a collection of readings designed for Latin learners at the college and university level, in contrast to Latin textbooks that are also, and often primarily, directed at secondary school students. The readings we have selected are, after all, designed specifically to furnish Latin students with a comprehensive and accurate picture of what our sources relate about the images and realities of women in Roman antiquity. Furthermore, along with acknowledging the maturity and cultural sophistication of our intended student audience, this Reader attempts to respond to their curricular needs and academic experiences in a variety of other ways.

Most obviously—and in contrast to the exemplary intermediate Latin Reader on Roman women by Raia, Luschnig, and Sebesta, which is aimed primarily at Latin students in secondary school and lower-level college courses—this Reader is designed for somewhat more advanced Latin classes. It will be of special value to students coping with the complexities of the ancient Latin language, and comprehending its development over a period of several centuries. We have selected, for example, a number of texts from the second and early first centuries BCE, written in "archaic" Latin, several inscriptions among them. In organizing these texts, we have adopted a chronological rather than a thematic perspective, too. We would like to illustrate to our readers that Latin underwent major linguistic changes over the centuries that comprise the classical Roman period, when Rome itself evolved from a republican form of government into an empire; we also seek to foreground "intertextual" allusions by later authors to the language as well as the themes of their predecessors in their depictions of Roman women.

So, too, in addition to selecting inscriptions and other passages for inclusion, we have chosen several texts that college-level students might encounter, but only in English translation, outside their Latin classes in courses on Greco-Roman civilization, and more specifically in courses on women and gender in classical antiquity. Indeed, our volume resembles in a major regard such sourcebooks assigned for these courses in translation as MacLachlan's *Women in Ancient Rome* (2013). Its discussions introducing and contextualizing the individual Latin passages try to indicate, where possible, how the passage in question reflects generally held Roman cultural attitudes and common social practices. Notes to the passages themselves, while concerned with matters of Latin grammar and literary style, attempt to do the same.

Finally, this volume accords attention to certain aspects of Roman women's cultural images that are awarded pride of place in the ancient sources themselves. Among the themes that recur in the passages that we have selected are the negative representation of women's sexual desire and agency, and the concomitant tendency by Roman authors to portray women who behave self-assertively in the public sphere as also engaging in conduct of a sexually transgressive nature. The sources we have included on Fulvia, Clodia Metelli, and the younger Agrippina perhaps provide the most vivid examples of such representations, although the characterization by the younger Cato of Papirius Praetextatus' politically meddling, concupiscent mother belongs in this category as well. Another recurring motif is the depiction of self-assertive Roman mothers as at the center of dysfunctional family relationships potentially destructive to their male children. Here, again, the portrayal of Agrippina the Younger immediately comes to mind, along with what our sources imply about Papirius Praetextatus' mother and even Cornelia, mother of the Gracchi. These emphases, too, make this collection of Latin readings distinctive from a pedagogical as well as linguistic and literary perspective.

We recognize that our readers may wish to learn more not only about the extant testimony on Roman women themselves, but also about how scholars interpret Latin literary representations of women, than this volume can possibly share. Consequently, we encourage them to read from the works cited in our bibliography (below). Many of the scholarly works it lists have shaped our own readings of the texts included in this volume, and suggest further directions for investigating these and other texts.

ᴖᴗ *Suggested reading*

Adams, J. N. *The Latin Sexual Vocabulary*. Baltimore, MD: The Johns Hopkins University Press, 1982.

Astin, Alan E. *Cato the Censor*. Oxford: Clarendon Press, 1978.

Babcock, Charles L. "The Early Career of Fulvia." *American Journal of Philology* 86 (1965) 1–32.

Beard, Mary. *Pompeii*. London: Profile Books, 2008.

———. "The Sexual Status of Vestal Virgins." *Journal of Roman Studies* 70 (1980) 12–27.

Brunn, Christer. "Water for Roman Brothels: Cicero 'Cael.' 34." *Phoenix* 51 (1997) 364–73.

Cahoon, Leslie. "The Bed as Battlefield: Erotic Conquest and Military Metaphors in Ovid's *Amores*." *Transactions of the American Philological Association* 118 (1988) 297–307.

Carlon, Jacqueline. *Pliny's Women: Constructing Virtue and Creating Identity in the Roman World*. Cambridge: University Press, 2009.

Carp, T. "Two Matrons of the Late Republic." *Women's Studies* 8 (1981) 189–200.

Champlin, Edward. *Nero*. Cambridge, MA: Harvard University Press, 2003.

Conte, Gian Biagio. *Latin Literature: A History*. Baltimore and London: Johns Hopkins University Press, 1994.

Cooley A. E., and M. G. L. Cooley. *Pompeii: A Source Book*. London and New York: Routledge, 2004.

Courtney, Edward. *A Companion to Petronius*. Oxford: University Press, 2001.

———. *A Commentary on the Satires of Juvenal*. London: Athlone Press., 1980.

Delia, Diana. "Fulvia Reconsidered." In *Women's History and Ancient History*, pp. 197–217. Edited by Sarah B. Pomeroy. Chapel Hill and London: University of North Carolina Press, 1991.

Dickison, Sheila K. "Juvenal's Sixth Satire and the Imperial Ideology of Marriage." In *Rome and her Monuments: Essays on the City and Literature of Rome in Honor of Katherine A. Geffcken*, pp. 603–17. Edited by Sheila K. Dickison and Judith P. Hallett. Wauconda, IL: Bolchazy-Carducci Publishers, 2000.

———. "Women in Rome." In *Civilization of the Ancient Mediterranean: Greece and Rome*, Vol. III, pp. 1319–32. Edited by Michael Grant and Rachel Kitzinger. New York: Charles Scribner's Sons, 1988.

Dixon, Suzanne. "Conclusion: The Allure of 'La dolce Vita' in Ancient Rome." In *Reading Roman Women: Sources, Genres and Real Life*, pp. 133–56. London: Duckworth, 2001.

———. *The Roman Mother*. Norman and London: University of Oklahoma Press, 1988.

Dobbins, John J. "Problems of Chronology, Decoration and Urban Design in the Forum at Pompeii." *American Journal of Archaeology* 98 (1994) 629–94.

Dutsch, Dorota. *Female Discourse in Roman Comedy: On Echoes and Voices.* Oxford: Oxford University Press, 2008.

Ecce Romani III: A Latin Reading Program. From Republic to Empire, 4th ed. Boston: Pearson Prentice Hall, 2009.

Fantham, E., H. P. Foley, N. B. Kampen, S. B. Pomeroy, and H. A. Shapiro. *Women in the Classical World: Image and Text.* Oxford and New York: Oxford University Press, 1994.

Franklin, James L. Jr. *POMPEIS DIFFICILE EST: Studies in the Political Life of Imperial Pompeii.* Ann Arbor: University of Michigan Press, 2001.

Geffcken, Katherine A. *Comedy in the PRO CAELIO.* Leiden: E. J. Brill, 1973. Reprinted with an appendix on the *In Clodium et Curionem.* Wauconda, IL: Bolchazy-Carducci Publishers, 1995.

Ginsburg, Judith. *Representing Agrippina: Constructions of Female Power in the Early Empire.* Oxford and New York: Oxford University Press, 2006.

Habinek, Thomas N. *The Politics of Latin Literature: Writing, Identity and Empire in Ancient Rome.* Princeton, NJ: Princeton University Press, 1998.

Hallett, Judith P. "Contextualizing the Text: The Journey to Ovid." *Helios* 17 (1990) 187–211.

——. "Cornelia and Her Maternal Legacy" and "Fulvia, Mother of Iullus Antonius." *Helios* 33.2 (2006, special issue on Roman mothers, edited by Judith P. Hallett) 119–47 and 149–64.

——. "Human Connections and Paternal Evocations: Two Elite Roman Women Writers and the Valuing of Others." In *Valuing Others in Classical Antiquity,* pp. 353–73. Edited by Ralph Rosen and Ineke Sluiter. Leiden: Brill, 2010.

——. "Martial's Sulpicia and Propertius' Cynthia." *Classical World* 86.2 (1992) 99–123.

———. "*Perusinae Glandes* and the Changing Image of Augustus." *American Journal of Ancient History* 2 (1977) 151–71.

———. "Women as 'Same' and 'Other' in [the] Classical Roman Elite." *Helios* 16.1 (Spring 1989) 59–78.

———. "Women Writing in Rome and Cornelia, Mother of the Gracchi," "The Eleven Elegies of the Augustan Poet Sulpicia," "The Fragment of Martial's Sulpicia," and "The Vindolanda Letters from Claudia Severa," pp. 13–24, 45–65, 85–92, 93–99. In *Women Writing Latin: From Roman Antiquity to Early Modern Europe,* Volume 1: "Women Writing Latin in Roman Antiquity, Late Antiquity, and the Early Christian Era." Edited by Laurie J. Churchill, Phyllis R. Brown, and Jane E. Jeffrey. Routledge: London and New York, 2002.

Hallett, Judith P., and Marilyn B. Skinner. *Roman Sexualities*. Princeton: University Press, 1997.

Halporn, James W., Martin Ostwald, and Thomas G. Rosenmeyer. *The Meters of Greek and Latin Poetry.* Indianapolis: Hackett, 1994.

Hemelrijk, Emily A. *MATRONA DOCTA. Educated Women in the Roman Elite from Cornelia to Julia Domna.* London and New York: Routledge, 2004.

Hopkins, M. K. "The Age of Roman Girls at Marriage." *Population Studies* 18 (1965) 309–27.

Lateiner, D., Barbara K. Gold, and Judith Perkins, eds. *Roman Literature, Gender and Reception: DOMINA ILLUSTRIS.* New York and Abingdon, UK: Routledge, 2013.

MacLachlan, Bonnie. *Women in Ancient Rome: A Sourcebook.* London and New York: Bloomsbury Press, 2013.

McGlathery, Daniel B. "Petronius' Tale of the Widow of Ephesus and Bakhtin's Material Bodily Lower Stratum." *Arethusa* 31 (1998) 313–36.

Moeller, Walter O. *The Wool Trade in Ancient Pompeii.* Leiden: E. J. Brill, 1976.

Nagle, Betty Rose. *The Poetics of Exile: Program and Polemic in the* TRISTIA *and* EPISTULAE EX PONTO *of Ovid*. Bruxelles: Latomus, 1980.

Norwood, Frances. "The Riddle of Ovid's *Relegatio*." *Classical Philology* 58 (1963) 150–63.

Osgood, Josiah. *Turia: A Roman Woman's Civil War*. Oxford: Oxford University Press, 2014.

Parker, Holt. "Other Remarks on the Other Sulpicia." *Classical World* 86.1 (1992) 89–95.

———. "Why Were the Vestals Virgins? Or the Chastity of Women and the Safety of the Roman State." *American Journal of Philology* 125.4 (2004) 563–601.

Pryzwansky, Molly M. *Feminine Imperial Ideals in the 'Caesares' of Suetonius*. ProQuest Document on-line. Duke University Dissertation, 2008.

Raia, Ann, Cecilia Luschnig, and Judith L. Sebesta, *The World of Roman Women: A Latin Reader*. Newburyport, MA: Focus Press, 2005.

Richlin, Amy. "Sulpicia the Satirist." *Classical World* 86.2 (1992) 125–40.

———. "The Fragments of Terentia." In *Roman Literature, Gender and Reception:* DOMINA ILLUSTRIS, pp. 93–118. Edited by D. Lateiner, Barbara K. Gold, and Judith Perkins. New York and Abingdon, UK: Routledge, 2013.

Saller, Richard P. "*Pater Familias*, *Mater Familias* and the Gendered Semantics of the Roman Household." *Classical Philology* 94 (1999) 182–97.

Salzman, M. R. "Cicero, the *Megalenses* and the Defense of Caelius." *American Journal of Philology* 103 (1982) 299–304.

Shackleton Bailey, D. R., ed. "Appendix III." In *Cicero's Letters to Atticus*, Vol. V, pp. 404–13. Cambridge: University Press. 1966.

Shelton, Jo-Ann. "Pliny the Younger and the Ideal Wife." *Classica et Mediaevalia* 41 (1990) 163–86.

———. *The Women of Pliny's Letters*. London and New York: Routledge, 2013.

Sherwin-White, A. N. *The Letters of Pliny: A Historical and Social Commentary*. Oxford: Clarendon Press, 1966.

Skinner, Marilyn. "Clodia Metelli." *Transactions of the American Philological Association* 113 (1983) 273–87.

———. *Clodia Metelli: The Tribune's Sister*. Oxford: University Press, 2011.

Staples, Ariadne. *From Good Goddess to Vestal Virgins: Sex and Category in Roman Religion*. London and New York: Routledge, 1997.

Stevenson, Jane. *Women Latin Poets: Language, Gender and Authority from Antiquity to the Eighteenth Century*. Oxford and New York: Oxford University Press, 2005.

Tatum, W. J. *Publius Clodius Pulcher*. Chapel Hill and London: University of North Carolina Press, 1999.

Treggiari, Susan. *Terentia, Tullia and Publilia: The Women of Cicero's Family*. London and New York: Routledge, 2007.

Walcott, P. "On Widows and Their Reputation in Antiquity." *Symbolae Osloenses* 66 (1991) 5–26.

Wallace-Hadrill, Andrew. *Suetonius: The Scholar and His Caesars*. New Haven: Yale University Press, 1984.

Warmington, B. H. *Nero: Reality and Legend*. New York: W. W. Norton, 1969.

Wildfang, Robin Lorsch. *Rome's Vestal Virgins: A Study of Rome's Vestal Priestesses in the Late Republic and Early Empire*. London and New York: Routledge, 2006.

Will, Elizabeth Lyding. "Women in Pompeii." *Archaeology* 32 (1979) 34–43.

Williams, Craig A. *Roman Homosexuality*. 2nd ed. Oxford: University Press, 2010.

Zanker, Paul. *Pompeii: Public and Private Life*. Cambridge, MA: Harvard University Press, 1998.

Latin Text

- Note that consonantal *v* rather than intervocalic *u* is used throughout this Reader. For consistency, an initial capital letter is used at the beginning of sentences in all the Latin texts.

- The texts listed below are used except for the following specific divergences from the text and punctuation:

  Reading 3, Cornelius Nepos, Fragment 59:
  Line 19: *superest* for Teubner *restat*
  Line 23: *insistere* for Teubner *desistere*
  Line 28: *pudet* for Teubner *pudebit*

✣ *Latin text credits*

1. Plautus, *Casina* 147–211: *Plautus Casina*, ed. W. T. MacCary and M. M. Willcock. Cambridge University Press, 1978.

2. Marcus Porcius Cato, *De Agri Cultura* 143: *Cato and Varro On Agriculture*, ed. and transl. William Davis Hooper, rev. Harrison Boyd Ash. Loeb Classical Library: Harvard University Press, 1935.

3. Cornelius Nepos, Fragment 59; Livy, *Ab Urbe Condita* 30.12.11–18 and 15.1–8: (1) *Nepotis vitae cum fragmentis*, ed. P. K. Marshall. Teubner, 1977. (2) *Ab Urbe Condita*, Vol. 4, ed. R. S. Conway and S. K. Johnson. Oxford Classical Texts: Oxford at the Clarendon Press, 1914.

4. Aulus Gellius, *Noctes Atticae* 1.23.1: *The Attic Nights of Aulus Gellius*, ed. and transl. John C. Rolfe. Loeb Classical Library: Harvard University Press, 1927.

5. *CIL* I.2.2161; I.2.1837: *Remains of Old Latin IV: Archaic Inscriptions*, ed. and transl. E. H. Warmington. Loeb Classical Library: Harvard University Press, 1940, repr. 1967.

6. *CIL* I.2.1570; I.2.1732; VI.18324: (1 and 2) *Remains of Old Latin IV: Archaic Inscriptions*, ed. and transl. E. H. Warmington. Loeb Classical Library: Harvard University Press, 1940, repr. 1967. (3) *Carmina Sepulcralia Latina*, ed. J. Cholodniak. University of Michigan Online, 1897.

7. Suetonius, *Divus Julius*, 6: *Suetonius,* Vol. I, ed. and transl. J. C. Rolfe, intro. K. R. Bradley. Loeb Classical Library: Harvard University Press, 1913, rev. and repr. 1998.

8. Cicero, *Pro Caelio* 33–36; Cicero *Ad Atticum* 12.38a and 42 excerpts: (1) *M. Tulli Ciceronis Pro M. Caelio Oratio*, ed. R.G. Austin, 3rd ed. Oxford University Press, 1960. (2) *Cicero's Letters to Atticus*, Vol. 5, ed. D. R. Shackleton Bailey. Cambridge University Press, 1966.

9. Cicero, *Philippics*, passim; Martial, 11.20: (1) Cicero, *Orationes: Pro Milone, Pro Marcello, Pro Ligario, Pro Rege Deiotaro, Philippicae I–XIV*, 2nd ed., ed. A. C. Clark. Oxford University Press, 1918; (2) J. P. Hallett, "*Perusinae Glandes* and the Changing Image of Augustus," *American Journal of Ancient History* 2 (1977) 151–77; (3) Martial, *Epigrams* Vol. III: Books 11–14, ed. and trans. D. R. Shackleton Bailey. Loeb Classical Library: Harvard University Press, 1993.

10. Horace, *Satires*, 1.2.37–134 excerpts: Horace, *Satires, Epistles, Ars Poetica*, transl. H. R. Fairclough. Loeb Classical Library: Harvard University Press, 1929, repr. 1970.

11. Tibullus 3.8–18 passim; *AE* 1928.73: (1) *Catullus, Tibullus, Pervigilium Veneris*, second ed. rev. G. P. Goold. Loeb Classical Library: Harvard University Press, 1988. (2) Jane Stevenson, *Women Latin Poets: Language, Gender and Authority from Antiquity to the Eighteenth Century.* Oxford University Press, 2005. (3) *M. Tulli Ciceronis Epistulae*, Vol. I: *Epistulae ad Familiares*, ed. L. C. Purser. Oxford University Press, 1901.

12. Propertius 4.8: *Propertius,* ed. and transl. H. E. Butler. Loeb Classical Library: Harvard University Press, 1912, repr. 1967.

13. Ovid, *Tristia*, 3.7: *Ovid Tristia Ex Ponto*, ed. and transl. Arthur Leslie Wheeler, rev. G. P. Goold. Loeb Classical Library: Harvard University Press, 1988.

14. Petronius, *Satyricon*, 111–12: *Petronii Arbitri Satyricon Reliquiae*, ed. Konrad Mueller. Teubner, 1995.

15. Suetonius, *Nero*, 34: *Suetonius*, Vol. II, ed. and transl. J. C. Rolfe, intro. K. R. Bradley. Loeb Classical Library: Harvard University Press, 1913, rev. and repr. 1998.

16. *CIL* X.810 and 813: *Corpus Inscriptionum Latinarum*, Vol. X, ed. T. Mommsen. Walter de Gruyter, 1883.

17. Pliny, *Letters*, 4.19 and 8.10, excerpts: *C. Plini Caecili Secundi Epistularum Libri Novem*, ed. Mauritius Schuster. Teubner, 1952.

18. Sulpicia's Poetry; Martial 10.35 and 38: (1) Judith P. Hallett, "The Fragment of Martial's Sulpicia," pp. 85–92, in *Women Writing Latin: From Roman Antiquity to Early Modern Europe*, Vol. 1: "Women Writing Latin in Roman Antiquity, Late Antiquity, and the Early Christian Era," ed. Laurie J. Churchill, Phyllis R. Brown, and Jane E. Jeffrey. Routledge, 2002. (2) *Martial Epigrams*, Vol. II, ed. and transl. Walter C. A. Ker. Loeb Classical Library: Harvard University Press, 1961.

19. *Tabula Vindolanda* 2.291 and 2.292: Judith P. Hallett, "The Vindolanda Letters from Claudia Severa," pp. 97–98, in *Women Writing Latin: From Roman Antiquity to Early Modern Europe*, Vol. 1: "Women Writing Latin in Roman Antiquity, Late Antiquity, and the Early Christian Era," ed. Laurie J. Churchill, Phyllis R. Brown, and Jane E. Jeffrey. Routledge, 2002.

20. Juvenal, *Satires* 6. 161–171: *A. Persi Flacci et D. Iuni Iuvenalis Saturae*, ed. W. V. Clausen. Oxford University Press, 1959.

21. Aulus Gellius, *Noctes Atticae* 1.12: *The Attic Nights of Aulus Gellius*, ed. and transl. John C. Rolfe. Loeb Classical Library: Harvard University Press, 1927.

ᢏ 1 *Plautus,* CASINA *147–60, 170–77, 184–211*

PARDALISCA Prandium iusserat senex sibi parari.   147

CLEOSTRATA St!

Tace atque abi; neque paro neque hodie coquetur.

Quando is mi et filio advorsatur suo   150

5   animi amorisque causa sui,

flagitium illud hominis,

ego illum fame,

ego illum siti,

maledictis, malefactis amatorem ulciscar. . . .   155

10   flagiti persequentem,

stabulum nequitiae.

Nunc huc meas fortunas eo questum ad vicinam. . . .   161–62

CL. Myrrhina, salve.   170–71

MYRRHINE Salve, mecastor. Sed quid tu es tristis, amabo?

15   CL. Ita solent omnes quae sunt male nuptae;   174–75

domi et foris aegre quod sit satis semper est. . . .   176–77

MY. Amo te, atque istuc expeto scire quid sit.   184–85

CL. Pessumis me modis despicatur domi.

MY. Hem, quid est? Dic idem (nam pol hau satis meo

20   corde accepi querellas tuas), opsecro.

CL. Vir me habet pessumis despicatam modis,

nec mihi ius meum optinendi optio est.   190

MY. Mira sunt, vera si praedicas, nam viri

ius suom ad mulieres optinere haud queunt.

25 CL. Quin mihi ancillulam ingratiis postulat,

quae mea est, quae meo educata sumptu siet,

vilico suo se dare;   195

sed ipsus eam amat. MY. Opsecro,

tace. CL. Nam hic nunc licet dicere:

30 nos sumus. MY. Ita est; unde ea tibi est?

Nam peculi probam nihil habere addecet

clam virum, et quae habet, partum ei haud commode est,   200

quin viro aut subtrahat aut stupro invenerit.

Hoc viri censeo esse omne quicquid tuom est.

35 CL. Tu quidem advorsum tuam amicam omnia loqueris.

MY. Tace sis, stulta, et mi ausculta.

Noli sis tu illi advorsari;   205

sine amet, sine quod lubet id faciat, quando tibi nil   206-7

domi delicuom est.

40 CL. Satin sana es? Nam tuquidem advorsus tuam istaec

rem loquere. MY. Insipiens,   208-9

semper tu huic verbo vitato abs tuo viro. CL. Cui

verbo? MY. I foras, mulier.   210-11

❧ 2 Marcus Porcius Cato, DE AGRI CULTURA 143

Vilicae quae sunt officia, curato faciat. Si eam tibi   1

dederit dominus uxorem, ea esto contentus. Ea te metuat

facito. Ne nimium luxuriosa siet. Vicinas aliasque

mulieres quam minimum utatur neve domum neve ad

5 sese recipiat. Ad cenam nequo eat neve ambulatrix siet.

Rem divinam ni faciat neve mandet, qui pro ea faciat,

iniussu domini aut dominae. Scito dominum pro tota
familia rem divinam facere. Munda siet; villam   2
conversam mundeque habeat; focum purum
10 circumversum cotidie, priusquam cubitum eat, habeat.
Kalendis, Idibus, Nonis, festus dies cum erit, coronam in
focum indat, per eosdemque dies lari familiari pro copia
supplicet. Cibum tibi et familiae curet uti coctum habeat.
Gallinas multas et ova uti habeat. Pira arida, sorba, ficos,   3
15 uvas passas, sorba in sapa et pira et uvas in doliis et mala
strutea, uvas in vinaciis et in urceis in terra obrutas et
nuces Praenestinas recentes in urceo in terra obrutas
habeat. Mala Scantiana in doliis et alia quae condi solent
et silvatica, haec omnia quotannis diligenter uti condita
20 habeat. Farinam bonam et far suptile sciat facere.

ᐺ 3 *Cornelius Nepos, Fragment 59; Livy, AB URBE CONDITA 30.12.11–18 and 15.1–8*

Cornelius Nepos, Fragment 59

Verba ex epistula Corneliae Gracchorum matris ex libro
Cornelii Nepotis de Latinis Historicis excerpta.

1. Dices pulchrum esse inimicos ulcisci. Id neque maius
neque pulchrius cuiquam atque mihi esse videtur, sed si
5 liceat re publica salva ea persequi. Sed quatenus id fieri non
potest, multo tempore multisque partibus inimici nostri non
peribunt atque, uti nunc sunt, erunt potius quam res publica
profligetur atque pereat.

(Eadem alio loco.)

10 2. Verbis conceptis deierare ausim, praeterquam qui
Tiberium Gracchum necarunt, neminem inimicum tantum
molestiae tantumque laboris, quantum te ob has res, mihi
tradidisse; quem oportebat omnium eorum, quos antehac
habui liberos, partis eorum tolerare atque curare, ut quam
15 minimum sollicitudinis in senecta haberem, utique
quaecumque ageres, ea velles maxime mihi placere, atque
uti nefas haberes rerum maiorum adversum meam
sententiam quicquam facere, praesertim mihi cui parva pars
vitae superest. Ne id quidem tam breve spatium potest
20 opitulari, quin et mihi adversere et rem publicam profliges?
Denique quae pausa erit? Ecquando desinet familia nostra
insanire? Ecquando modus ei rei haberi poterit? Ecquando
desinemus et habentes et praebentes molestiis insistere?
Ecquando perpudescet miscenda atque perturbanda re
25 publica? Sed si omnino id fieri non potest, ubi ego mortua
ero, petito tribunatum; per me facito quod lubebit, cum ego
non sentiam. Ubi mortua ero, parentabis mihi et invocabis
deum parentem. In eo tempore non pudet te eorum deum
preces expetere, quos vivos atque praesentes relictos atque
30 desertos habueris? Ne ille sirit Iuppiter te ea perseverare, nec
tibi tantam dementiam venire in animum. Et si perseveras,
vereor ne in omnem vitam tantum laboris culpa tua recipias
uti in nullo tempore tute tibi placere possis.

Livy, *Ab Urbe Condita* 30.12.11–18

Intranti vestibulum in ipso limine Sophoniba, uxor   11
Syphacis, filia Hasdrubalis Poeni, occurrit; et cum
in medio agmine armatorum Masinissam insignem
cum armis tum cetero habitu conspexisset, regem
5 esse, id quod erat, rata genibus advoluta eius
'Omnia quidem ut possis' inquit 'in nobis di   12
dederunt virtusque et felicitas tua; sed si captivae
apud dominum vitae necisque suae vocem supplicem
mittere licet, si genua, si victricem attingere dextram,
10 precor quaesoque per maiestatem regiam, in qua   13
paulo ante nos quoque fuimus, per gentis
Numidarum nomen, quod tibi cum Syphace
commune fuit, per huiusce regiae deos, qui te
melioribus ominibus accipiant quam Syphacem hinc
15 miserunt, hanc veniam supplici des ut ipse   14
quodcumque fert animus de captiva tua statuas
neque me in cuiusquam Romani superbum et crudele
arbitrium venire sinas. Si nihil aliud quam Syphacis   15
uxor fuissem, tamen Numidae atque in eadem
20 mecum Africa geniti quam alienigenae et externi
fidem experiri mallem: quid Carthaginiensi ab
Romano, quid filiae Hasdrubalis timendum sit vides.   16
Si nulla re alia potes, morte me ut vindices ab
Romanorum arbitrio oro obtestorque.' Forma erat   17
25 insignis et florentissima aetas. Itaque cum modo
genua modo dextram amplectens in id ne cui Romano
traderetur fidem exposceret propiusque blanditias   18

iam oratio esset quam preces, non in misericordiam
modo prolapsus est animus victoris, sed, ut est genus
30 Numidarum in venerem praeceps, amore captivae
victor captus.

Livy, *Ab Urbe Condita* 30.15.1–8

Masinissae haec audienti non rubor solum   1
suffusus sed lacrimae etiam obortae; et cum se
quidem in potestate futurum imperatoris dixisset
orassetque eum ut quantum res sineret fidei suae
5 temere obstrictae consuleret—promisisse enim se in   2
nullius potestatem eam traditurum—ex praetorio in
tabernaculum suum confusus concessit. Ibi arbitris   3
remotis cum crebro suspiritu et gemitu, quod facile ab
circumstantibus tabernaculum exaudiri posset,
10 aliquantum temporis consumpsisset, ingenti ad   4
postremum edito gemitu fidum e servis unum vocat,
sub cuius custodia regio more ad incerta fortunae
venenum erat, et mixtum in poculo ferre ad
Sophonibam iubet ac simul nuntiare Masinissam   5
15 libenter primam ei fidem praestaturum fuisse quam
vir uxori debuerit: quoniam eius arbitrium qui possint
adimant, secundum fidem praestare ne viva in
potestatem Romanorum veniat. Memor patris
imperatoris patriaeque et duorum regum quibus
20 nupta fuisset, sibi ipsa consuleret.

Hunc nuntium ac simul venenum ferens   6
minister cum ad Sophonibam venisset, 'Accipio,'   7

inquit, 'nuptiale munus, neque ingratum, si nihil
maius vir uxori praestare potuit. Hoc tamen nuntia,
25 melius me morituram fuisse si non in funere meo
nupsissem.' Non locuta est ferocius quam acceptum   8
poculum nullo trepidationis signo dato impavide
hausit.

❧ 4 *Aulus Gellius, Noctes Atticae 1.23*

Historia de Papirio Praetextato dicta scriptaque est a
M. Catone in oratione qua usus est *Ad Milites contra
Galbam*, cum multa quidem venustate atque luce
atque munditia verborum. Ea Catonis verba huic
5   prorsus commentario indidissem, si libri copia fuisset
id temporis, cum haec dictavi. Quod si non virtutes
dignitatesque verborum, sed rem ipsam scire quaeris,
res ferme ad hunc modum est. Mos antea senatoribus
Romae fuit in curiam cum praetextatis filiis introire.
10 Tum, cum in senatu res maior quaepiam consultata eaque
in diem posterum prolata est placuitque ut eam rem
super qua tractavissent ne quis enuntiaret priusquam
decreta esset, mater Papirii pueri, qui cum parente
suo in curia fuerat, percontata est filium quidnam in
15 senatu patres egissent. Puer respondit tacendum esse
neque id dici licere. Mulier fit audiendi cupidior;
secretum rei et silentium pueri animum eius ad
inquirendum everberat; quaerit igitur compressius
violentiusque. Tum puer, matre urgente, lepidi atque

20 festivi medacii consilium capit. Actum in senatu dixit,
    utrum videretur utilius exque republica esse unusne
    ut duas uxores haberet, an ut una apud duos nupta
    esse. Hoc illa ubi audivit, animus compavescit, domo
    trepidans egreditur, ad ceteras matronas perfert.
25 Venit ad senatum postridie matrum familias caterva.
    Lacrimantes atque obsecrantes orant una potius ut
    duobus nupta fieret quam ut uni duae. Senatores,
    ingredientes in curiam, quae illa mulierum
    intemperies et quid sibi postulatio istaec vellet,
30 mirabantur. Puer Papirius in medium curiae
    progressus, quid mater audire institisset, quid ipse
    matri dixisset, rem, sicut fuerat, denarrat. Senatus
    fidem atque ingenium pueri exosculatur, consultum
    facit uti posthac pueri cum patribus in curiam ne
35 introeant, praeter ille unus Papirius, atque puero
    postea cognomentum honoris gratia inditum
    "Praetextatus" ob tacendi loquendique in aetate
    praetextae prudentiam.

ᴄᴏ 5 *Corpus Inscriptionum Latinarum I.2.2161 and I.2.1837*

CIL I.2.2161

C. Paguri C. l. Gelotis
Hospes resiste et tumulum hunc excelsum aspic[e],
quo continentur ossa parvae aetatulae.
Sepulta haec sita sum verna quoius aetatula;

5   gravitatem officio et lanificio praestitei.

    Queror fortunae cassum tam iniquom et grave.

    Nomen [s]i quaeras, exoriatur Salviae.

    Valebis hospes. Opto ut seis felicior.

CIL I.2.1837

    Posilla Senenia Quart. f., Quarta Senenia C. l.

    Hospes, resiste et pa[rite]r scriptum perlig[e]:

    matrem non licitum ess[e uni]ca gnata fruei,

    quam nei esset credo nesci[o qui] inveidit deus.

5   Eam quoniam haud licitum [est v]eivam a matre ornarie[r],

    post mortem hoc fecit aeq[uo]m extremo tempore;

    decoravit eam monumento quam deilexserat.

✎ 6 CORPUS INSCRIPTIONUM LATINARUM I.2.1570; I.2.1732; and VI.18324

CIL I.2.1570

    P. Larcius P. l. Neicia. Saufeia [Gaiae] l. Thalea.

    L. Larcius. P. f. Rufus. P. Larcius, P. f.

    Brocchus. Larcia P. [Gaiae.] l. Horaea.

    Boneis probata inveisa sum a nulla proba.

5   Fui parens domineis senibus, huic autem opsequens,

    ita leibertate illei me hic me decoraat stola.

    A pupula annos veiginti optinui domum

    omnem. Supremus fecit iudicium dies,

    mors animam eripuit, non veitae ornatum apstulit.

CIL I.2.1732

Tu qui secura spatiarus mente viator
et nostri voltus derigis inferieis,
si quaeris quae sim, cinis en et tosta favilla,
ante obitus tristeis Helvia Prima fui.
5 Coniuge sum Cadmo fructa Scrateio,
concordesque pari viximus ingenio.
Nunc data sum Diti longum mansura per aevum,
deducta et fatali igne et aqua Stygia.

CIL VI.18324

d. m. Flaviae Dionysiadis
Hic iacet exiguis Dionysia flebilis annis,
extremum tenui quae pede rupit iter,
cuius in octava lascivia surgere messe
5 coeperat et dulces fingere nequitias.
Quod si longa tuae mansissent tempora vitae,
doctior in terris nulla puella foret!
Vixit annis VII m. XI diebus XV: fecit
Annia Isias vernae suae b. m.

∿ 7 *Suetonius, DIVUS JULIUS 6*

Quaestor Iuliam amitam uxoremque Corneliam
defunctas laudavit e more pro rostris. Et in amitae
quidem laudatione de eius ac patris sui utraque
origine sic refert: "Amitae meae Iuliae maternum
5 genus ab regibus ortum, paternum cum diis

inmortalibus coniunctum est. Nam ab Anco Marcio
sunt Marcii Reges, quo nomine fuit mater, a Venere
Iulii, cuius gentis familia est nostra. Est ergo in genere
et sanctitas regum, qui plurimum inter homines
10   pollent, et caerimonia deorum, quorum ipsi in
potestate sunt reges."
In Corneliae autem locum Pompeiam duxit
Quinti Pompei filiam, L. Sullae neptem; cum
qua deinde divortium fecit adulteratam
15   opinatus a Publio Clodio, quem inter publicas
caerimonias penetrasse ad eam muliebri veste
tam constans fama erat, ut senatus quaestionem
de pollutis sacris decreverit.

ᴖ 8 Cicero, PRO CAELIO 33–36; AD ATTICUM 12.38a and 42, excerpts

Cicero, Pro Caelio 33–36

Sed tamen ex ipsa quaeram prius utrum me secum   33
severe et graviter et prisce agere malit, an remisse et
leniter et urbane. Si illo austero more ac modo, aliquis
mihi ab inferis excitandus est ex barbatis illis, non hac
5   barbula qua ista delectatur sed illa horrida quam in
statuis antiquis atque imaginibus videmus, qui
obiurget mulierum et qui pro me loquatur ne mihi
ista forte suscenseat. Exsistat igitur ex hac ipsa familia
aliquis ac potissimum Caecus ille; minimum enim
10   dolorum capiet qui istam non videbit. Qui profecto, si
exstiterit, sic aget ac sic loquetur: 'Mulier, quid tibi

cum Caelio, quid cum homine adulescentulo, quid
cum alieno? Cur aut tam familiaris fuisti ut aurum
commodares, aut tam inimica ut venenum timeres?
15 Non patrem tuum videras, non patruum, non avum,
non proavum, non abavum, non atavum audieras   34
consules fuisse; non denique modo te Q. Metelli
matrimonium tenuisse sciebas, clarissimi ac fortissimi
viri patriaeque amantissimi, qui simul ac pedem
20 limine extulerat, omnis prope civis virtute, gloria,
dignitate superabat? Cum ex amplissimo genere in
familiam clarissimam nupsisses, cur tibi Caelius tam
coniunctus fuit? Cognatus, adfinis, viri tui familiaris?
Nihil eorum. Quid igitur fuit nisi quaedam temeritas
25 ac libido? Nonne te, si nostrae imagines viriles non
commovebant, ne progenies quidem mea, Q. illa
Claudia, aemulam domesticae laudis in gloria
muliebri esse admonebat, non virgo illa Vestalis
Claudia quae patrem complexa trimphantem ab
30 inimico tribuno plebei de curru detrahi passa non est?
Cur te fraterna vitia potius quam bona paterna et
avita et usque a nobis cum in viris tum etiam in
feminis repetita moverunt? Ideone ego pacem Pyrrhi
diremi ut tu amorum turpissimorum cotidie foedera
35 ferires, ideo aquam adduxi ut ea tu inceste uterere,
ideo viam munivi ut eam tu alienis viris comitata
celebrares?

Sed quid ego, iudices, ita gravem personam   35
induxi ut verear ne se idem Appius repente convertat

40 et Caelium incipiat accusare illa sua gravitate
    censoria? Sed videro hoc posterius atque ita, iudices,
    ut vel severissimis disceptatoribus M. Caeli vitam me
    probaturum esse confidam. Tu vero, mulier—iam
    enim ipse tecum nulla persona introducta loquor—si
45 ea quae facis, quae dicis, quae insimulas, quae
    moliris, quae arguis, probare cogitas, rationem tantae
    familiaritatis, tantae consuetudinis, tantae
    coniunctionis reddas atque exponas necesse est.
    Accusatores quidem libidines, amores, adulteria,
50 Baias, actas, convivia, comissationes, cantus,
    symphonias, navigia iactant, idemque significant nihil
    se te invita dicere. Quae tu quoniam mente nescio qua
    effrenata atque praecipiti in forum deferri
    iudiciumque voluisti, aut diluas oportet ac falsa esse
55 doceas aut nihil neque crimini tuo neque testimonio
    credendum esse fateare.

       Sin autem urbanius me agere mavis, sic   36
    agam tecum. Removebo illum senem durum ac paene
    agrestem; ex his igitur sumam aliquem ac potissimum
60 minimum fratrem qui est in isto genere urbanissimus;
    qui te amat plurimum, qui propter nescio quam,
    credo, timiditatem et nocturnos quosdam inanis
    metus tecum semper pusio cum maiore sorore
    cubitabat. Eum putato tecum loqui: 'Quid
65 tumultuaris, soror? Quid insanis?'
    Quid clamorem exorsa verbis parvam rem

magnam facis? Vicinum adulescentulum aspexisti;
candor huius te et proceritas, voltus oculique
pepulerunt; saepius videre voluisti; fuisti non
70 numquam in isdem hortis; vis nobilis mulier illum
filium familias patre parco ac tenaci habere tuis copiis
devinctum. Non potes; calcitrat, respuit, repellit, non
putat tua dona esse tanti. Confer te alio. Habes hortos
ad Tiberim ac diligenter eo loco paratos quo omnis
75 iuventus natandi causa venit; hinc licet condiciones
cotidie legas; cur huic qui te spernit molesta es?

Cicero, *Ad Atticum* 12.38a

Dated 7 May, 45 BCE

<Cicero Attico Sal.>

. . . Heredes Scapulae si istos hortos, ut scribis tibi
Othonem dixisse, partibus quattuor factis liceri
cogitant, nihil est scilicet emptori loci; sin venibunt,
5 quid fieri possit videbimus. Nam ille locus Publicianus
qui est Treboni et Cusini erat ad me adlatus. Sed scis
aream esse. Nullo pacto probo. Clodiae sane placent,
sed non puto esse venalis. De Drusi hortis, quamvis
ab iis abhorreas, ut scribis, tamen eo confugiam nisi
10 quid inveneris. Aedificatio me non movet. Nihil enim
aliud aedificabo nisi id quod etiam si illos non
habuero.

Cicero, *Ad Atticum* 12.42

Dated 10 May 45 BCE

<Cicero Attico Sal.>

Scripsi<sti> tamen nescio quid de Clodia. Ubi
ergo ea est aut quando ventura? Placet mihi res sic ut
secundum Othonem nihil magis. Sed neque hanc
5   vendituram puto (delectatur enim et copiosa est) et
illud alterum quam sit difficile te non fugit. Sed,
obsecro, enitamur ut aliquid ad id quod cupio
excogitemus.

✎ 9 *Cicero, PHILIPPICS 2.77–78, 5.11, 6.4;
CORPUS INSCRIPTIONUM LATINARUM
XI.6721.305.14; Martial 11.20*

Cicero, *Philippics* 2.77–78

At videte levitatem hominis. Cum hora diei   77
decima fere ad Saxa rubra venisset, delituit in
quadam cauponula atque ibi se occultans perpotavit
ad vesperum: inde ciso celeriter ad urbem advectus
5   domum venit capite involuto. Ianitor, 'Quis tu?' 'A
Marco tabellarius.' Confestim ad eam deducitur cuius causa
venerat, eique epistulam tradidit. Quam cum illa
legeret flens—erat enim scripta amatorie; caput autem
litterarum sibi cum illa mima posthac nihil futurum;
10 omnem se amorem abiecisse illim atque in hanc
transfudisse—cum mulier fleret uberius, homo
misericors ferre non potuit, caput aperuit, in collum

invasit. O hominem nequam! Quid enim aliud dicam?

Magis proprie nihil possum dicere. Ergo, ut te

15 catamitum, nec opinato cum te ostendisses, praeter

spem mulier aspiceret, idcirco urbem terrore

nocturno, Italiam multorum dierum metu

perturbasti? Et domi quidem causam amoris   78

habuisti, foris etiam turpiorem ne L. Plancus praedes

20 tuos venderet.

Cicero, *Philippics* 5.11

Calebant in interiore aedium parte totius rei publicae

nundinae; mulier sibi felicior quam viris auctionem

provinciarum regnorumque faciebat; restituebantur

exsules quasi lege sine lege; quae nisi auctoritate senatus

5 rescinduntur, quoniam ingressi in spem rei publicae

recuperandae sumus, imago nulla liberae civitatis

relinquetur.

Cicero, *Philippics* 6.4

Quid enim ille umquam arbitrio suo fecit? Semper eo

tractus est quo libido rapuit, quo levitas, quo furor,

quo vinolentia; semper eum duo dissimilia genera

tenuerunt, lenonum et latronum; ita domesticis

5 stupris, forensibus parricidiis delectatur, ut mulieri

citius avarissimae paruerit quam senatui populoque

Romano.

CIL XI.6721.305.14

FULVIAE LANDICAM PETO

PETO OCTAVIAI CULUM

SALVE, OCTAVI FELAS

OCTAVI LAXE

5   *L. ANTONI CALVE ET FULVIA, CULUM PANDITE.*

Martial 11.20

Caesaris Augusti lascivos, livide, versus
    sex lege, qui tristis verba Latina legis,
'Quod futuit Glaphyran Antonius, hanc mihi poenam
    Fulvia constituit, se quoque uti futuam.
5   Fulviam ego ut futuam? Quid si me Manius oret
    pedicem, faciam? Non puto, si sapiam.
"Aut futue, aut pugnemus" ait. Quid quod mihi vita
    carior est ipsa mentula? Signa canent!'
Absolvis lepidos nimirum, Auguste, libellos.
10   qui scis Romana simplicitate loqui.

ᴄ᷉ *10 Horace, Satires 1.2.37–40, 77–82, 116– 19, 127–34*

Audire est operae pretium, procedere recte   37

qui moechis non voltis, ut omni parte laborent,

utque illis multo corrupta dolore voluptas

atque haec rara cadat dura inter saepe pericla. . . .   40

5   Quare, ne paeniteat te,   77

desine matronas sectarier, unde laboris

plus haurire mali est quam ex re decerpere fructus.

Nec magis huic inter niveos viridisque lapillos   80

(sit licet hoc, Cerinthe, tuum) tenerum est femur aut crus

10   rectius, atque etiam melius persaepe togatae est. . . .

Tument tibi cum inguina, num, si   116

ancilla aut verna est praesto puer, impetus in quem

continuo fiat, malis tentigine rumpi?

Non ego: nam parabilem amo Venerem facilemque. . . .   119

15   Nec vereor ne, dum futuo, vir rure recurrat,

ianua frangatur, latret canis, undique magno

pulsa domus strepitu resonet, vepallida lecto

desiliat mulier, miseram se conscia clamet,   130

cruribus haec metuat, doti deprensa, egomet mi.

20   Discincta tunica fugiendum est et pede nudo,

ne nummi pereant aut puga aut denique fama.

Deprendi miserum est . . .

11 *Tibullus 3.9, 3.13, 3.14, 3.16; L'ANNÉE EPIGRAPHIQUE 1928.73; Cicero, AD FAMILIARES 4.5*

Tibullus (Sulpicia) 3.9

Parce meo iuveni, seu quis bona pascua campi

   seu colis umbrosi devia montis aper,

nec tibi sit duros acuisse in proelia dentes;

   incolumem custos hunc mihi servet Amor.

5 Sed procul abducit venandi Delia cura.

   O pereant silvae deficiantque canes!

Quis furor est, quae mens densos indagine colles

   claudentem teneras laedere velle manus?

Quidve iuvat furtim latebras intrare ferarum

10   candidaque hamatis crura notare rubis?

Sed tamen, ut tecum liceat, Cerinthe, vagari,

   ipsa ego per montes retia torta feram,

ipsa ego velocis quaeram vestigia cervi

   et demam celeri ferrea vincla cani.

15 Tunc mihi, tunc placeant silvae, si, lux mea, tecum

   arguar ante ipsas concubuisse plagas;

tunc veniat licet ad casses, inlaesus abibit,

   ne veneris cupidae gaudia turbet, aper.

Nunc sine me sit nulla venus, sed lege Dianae,

20   caste puer, casta retia tange manu

et quaecumque meo furtim subrepit amori,

   incidat in saevas diripienda feras.

At tu venandi studium concede parenti.

et celer in nostros ipse recurre sinus.

Tibullus (Sulpicia) 3.13

Tandem venit amor, qualem texisse pudori
    quam nudasse alicui sit mihi fama magis.
Exorata meis illum Cytherea Camenis
    attulit in nostrum deposuitque sinum.
5 Exsolvit promissa Venus: mea gaudia narret
    dicetur si quis non habuisse sua.
Non ego signatis quicquam mandare tabellis,
    ne legat id nemo quam meus ante, velim,
sed peccasse iuvat, vultus componere famae
10 taedet: cum digno digna fuisse ferar.

Tibullus (Sulpicia) 3.14

Invisus natalis adest, qui rure molesto
    et sine Cerintho tristis agendus erit.
Dulcius urbe quid est? An villa sit apta puellae
    atque Arretino frigidus amnis agro?
5 Iam, nimium Messalla mei studiose, quiescas:
    non tempestivae saepe, propinque, viae.
Hic animum sensusque meos abducta relinquo,
    arbitrio quam vis non sinit esse meo.

Tibullus (Sulpicia) 3.16

Gratum est, securus multum quod iam tibi de me
    permittis, subito ne male inepta cadam.
Sit tibi cura togae potior pressumque quasillo
    scortum quam Servi filia Sulpicia:
5 sollicti sunt pro nobis, quibus illa doloris,
    ne cedam ignoto, maxima causa, toro.

AE [*L'Année Epigraphique*] 1928.73

Epitaph of Petale Sulpicia. Rome, ca. 20 BCE.

    Sulpiciae cineres lectricis cerne viator
       quoi servile datum nomen erat Petale.
    Ter denos numero quattuor plus vixerat annos
       natumque in terris Aglaon ediderat.
5 Omnia naturae bona viderat arte vigebat
       splendebat forma, creverat ingenio.
    Invida fors vita longinquom degere tempus
       noluit hanc fatis defuit ipse colus.

Cicero, *Ad Familiares* 4.5

    Quid autem fuit quod illam hoc tempore ad
    vivendum magno opere invitare posset? Quae res,
    quae spes, quod animi solacium? Ut cum aliquo
    adulescente primario coniuncta aetatem gereret?
5 Licitum est tibi, credo, pro tua dignitate ex hac
    iuventute generum deligere, cuius fidei liberos tuos te
    tuto committere putares. An ut ea liberos ex sese
    pareret, quos cum florentis videret laetaretur, qui rem

a parente traditam per se tenere possent, honores
10 ordinatim petituri essent in re publica, in amicorum
negotiis libertate sua usuri?

❧ 12 *Propertius 4.8.51–88*

Nec mora, cum totas resupinat Cynthia valvas,   51
   non operosa comis, sed furibunda decens.
Pocula mi digitos inter cecidere remissos,
   pallueruntque ipso labra soluta mero.
5 Fulminat illa oculis et quantum femina saevit,   55
   spectaclum capta nec minus urbe fuit.
Phyllidos iratos in vultum conicit ungues:
   territa vicinas Teia clamat aquas.
Lumina sopitos turbant elata Quirites,
10   omnis et insana semita nocte sonat.   60
Illas direptisque comis tunicisque solutis
   excipit obscurae prima taberna viae.
Cynthia gaudet in exuviis victrixque recurrit
   et mea perversa sauciat ora manu,
15 imponitque notam collo morsuque cruentat,   65
   praecipueque oculos, qui meruere, ferit.
Atque ubi iam nostris lassavit bracchia plagis,
   Lygdamus ad plutei fulcra sinistra latens
eruitur, geniumque meum protractus adorat.
20   Lygdame, nil potui: tecum ego captus eram.   70
Supplicibus palmis tum demum ad foedera veni,
   cum vix tangendos praebuit illa pedes,
atque ait 'admissae si vis me ignoscere culpae,

accipe, quae nostrae formula legis erit.

25 Tu neque Pompeia spatiabere cultus in umbra,   75

Nec cum lascivum sternet harena Forum.

Colla cave inflectas ad summum obliqua theatrum,

aut lectica tuae se det aperta morae.

Lygdamus in primis, omnis mihi causa querelae,

30   veneat et pedibus vincula bina trahat.'   80

Indixit legem: respondi ego 'Legibus utar.'

Riserat imperio facta superba dato.

Dein quemcumque locum externae tetigere puellae,

suffiit, ac pura limina tergit aqua,

35 imperat et totas iterum mutare lucernas,   85

terque meum tetigit sulpuris igne caput.

Atque ita mutato per singula pallia lecto

respondi, et noto solvimus arma toro.

✎ 13 Ovid, TRISTIA 3.7.1–4, 21–30

Vade salutatum, subito perarata, Perillam,

littera, sermonis fida ministra mei.

Aut illam invenies dulci cum matre sedentem,

aut inter libros Pieridasque suas.   4

. . . .

5 Sed vereor, ne te mea nunc fortuna retardet,   21

postque meos casus sit tibi pectus iners.

Dum licuit, tua saepe mihi, tibi nostra legebam;

saepe tui iudex, saepe magister eram:

aut ego praebebam factis modo versibus aures,   25

10   aut, ubi cessares, causa ruboris eram.

Forsitan exemplo, quo me laesere libelli,

    tu metuis poenae fata secunda meae.

Pone, Perilla, metum; tantummodo femina nulla

    neve vir a scriptis discat amare tuis.   30

◌ 14 *Petronius, SATYRICON 111–12, excerpts*

'Matrona quaedam Ephesi tam notae erat   111

pudicitiae, ut vicinarum quoque gentium feminas ad

spectaculum sui evocaret. Haec ergo cum virum

extulisset, non contenta vulgari more funus passis

5 prosequi crinibus aut nudatum pectus in conspectu

frequentiae plangere, in conditorium etiam prosecuta

est defunctum, positumque in hypogaeo Graeco more

corpus custodire ac flere totis noctibus diebusque

coepit. . . . Assidebat aegrae fidissima ancilla,

10 simulque et lacrimas commodabat lugenti et

quotienscumque defecerat positum in monumento

lumen renovabat. Una igitur in tota civitate fabula

erat, solum illud affulsisse verum pudicitiae

amorisque exemplum omnis ordinis homines

15 confitebantur, cum interim imperator provinciae

latrones iussit crucibus affigi secundum illam

casulam, in qua recens cadaver matrona deflebat.

Proxima ergo nocte cum miles, qui cruces asservabat

ne quis ad sepulturam corpus detraheret, notasset sibi

20 [et] lumen inter monumenta clarius fulgens et

gemitum lugentis audisset, vitio gentis humanae

concupiit scire quis aut quid faceret. Descendit igitur

in conditorium, visaque pulcherrima muliere primo
quasi quodam monstro infernisque imaginibus
25 turbatus substitit. Deinde ut et corpus iacentis
conspexit et lacrimas consideravit faciemque
unguibus sectam, ratus scilicet id quod erat,
desiderium extincti non posse feminam pati, attulit
in monumentum cenulam suam coepitque hortari
30 lugentem ne perseveraret in dolore supervacuo. . . .
At illa ignota consolatione percussa laceravit
vehementius pectus ruptosque crines super corpus
iacentis imposuit. Non recessit tamen miles, sed
eadem exhortatione temptavit dare mulierculae
35 cibum, donec ancilla vini odore corrupta primum
ipsa porrexit ad humanitatem invitantis victam
manum, deinde refecta potione et cibo expugnare
dominae pertinaciam coepit et . . . inquit . . .

"Id cinerem aut manes credis sentire sepultos?

40 Vis tu reviviscere? Vis discusso muliebri errore, quam
diu licuerit, lucis commodis frui? ipsum te iacentis
corpus admonere debet ut vivas." Nemo invitus audit,
cum cogitur aut cibum sumere aut vivere. Itaque
mulier aliquot dierum abstinentia sicca passa est
45 frangi pertinaciam suam, nec minus avide replevit se
cibo quam ancilla quae prior victa est.

Ceterum scitis quid plerumque soleat temptare   112
humanam satietatem. Quibus blanditiis impetraverat
miles ut matrona vellet vivere, isdem etiam
50 pudicitiam eius aggressus est. Nec deformis aut
infacundus iuvenis castae videbatur, conciliante
gratiam ancilla ac subinde dicente:

"Placitone etiam pugnabis amori?"

Quid diutius moror? Ne hanc quidem partem corporis
55 mulier abstinuit, victorque miles utrumque persuasit.
Iacuerunt ergo una non tantum illa nocte qua nuptias
fecerunt, sed postero etiam ac tertio die, praeclusis
videlicet conditorii foribus, ut quisquis ex notis
ignotisque ad monumentum venisset, putaret
60 expirasse super corpus viri pudicissimam uxorem. . . .
Itaque unius cruciarii parentes ut viderunt laxatam
custodiam, detraxere nocte pendentem supremoque
mandaverunt officio. At miles circumscriptus dum
desidet, ut postero die vidit unam sine cadavere
65 crucem, veritus supplicium, mulieri quid accidisset
exponit: nec se expectaturum iudicis sententiam, sed
gladio ius dicturum ignaviae suae. Commodaret modo
illa perituro locum et fatale conditorium <commune>
familiari ac viro faceret. mulier non minus misericors
70 quam pudica "Nec istud" inquit "dii sinant, ut eodem
tempore duorum mihi carissimorum hominum duo
funera spectem. Malo mortuum impendere quam

vivum occidere." Secundum hanc orationem iubet ex
arca corpus mariti sui tolli atque illi quae vacabat
75 cruci affigi. Usus est miles ingenio prudentissimae
feminae, posteroque die populus miratus est qua
ratione mortuus isset in crucem.'

∾ 15 *Suetonius, NERO 34*

Matrem facta dictaque sua exquirentem acerbius   1
et corrigentem hactenus primo gravabatur, ut invidia
identidem oneraret quasi cessurus imperio
Rhodumque abiturus, mox et honore omni et
5   potestate privavit abductaque militum et
Germanorum statione contubernio quoque ac Palatio
expulit; neque in divexanda quicquam pensi habuit,
summissis qui et Romae morantem litibus et in
secessu quiescentem per convicia et iocos terra
10 marique praetervehentes inquietarent.

Verum minis eius ac violentia territus perdere   2
statuit; et cum ter veneno temptasset sentiretque
antidotis praemunitam, lacunaria, quae noctu super
dormientem laxata machina deciderent, paravit. Hoc
15 consilio per conscios parum celato solutilem navem,
cuius vel naufragio vel camarae ruina periret,
commentus est atque ita reconciliatione simulata
iucundissimis litteris Baias evocavit ad sollemnia
Quinquatruum simul celebranda; datoque negotio
20 trierarchis, qui liburnicam qua advecta erat velut

fortuito concursu confringerent, protraxit convivium
repetentique Baulos in locum corrupti navigii
machinosum illud optulit, hilare prosecutus atque in
digressu papillas quoque exosculatus.

25 Reliquum temporis cum magna trepidatione   3
vigilavit opperiens coeptorum exitum. Sed ut diversa
omnia nandoque evasisse eam comperit, inops
consilii L. Agermum libertum eius salvam et
incolumem cum gaudio nuntiantem, abiecto clam
30 iuxta pugione ut percussorem sibi subornatum arripi
constringique iussit, matrem occidi, quasi
deprehensum crimen voluntaria morte vitasset.

Adduntur his atrociora nec incertis auctoribus: ad   4
visendum interfectae cadaver accurrisse, contrectasse
35 membra, alia vituperasse, alia laudasse, sitique interim
oborta bibisse. Neque tamen conscientiam sceleris,
quanquam et militum et senatus populique
gratulationibus confirmaretur, aut statim aut
umquam postea ferre potuit, saepe confessus
40 exagitari se materna specie verberibusque Furiarum
ac taedis ardentibus. Quin et facto per Magos sacro
evocare Manes et exorare temptavit. Peregrinatione
quidem Graeciae et Eleusinis sacris, quorum
initiatione impii et scelerati voce praeconis
45 summoventur, interesse non ausus est.

∾ 16 *CORPUS INSCRIPTIONUM LATINARUM*
   X.810 and 813

CIL X.810

EVMACHIA L F SACERD PVBL NOMINE SVO ET
M NVMISTRI FRONTONIS FILI CHALCIDICVM
CRYPTAM PORTICVS CONCORDIAE
AVGVSTAE PIETATI SVA PEQVNIA FECIT
5 EADEMQVE DEDICAVIT

CIL X.813

EVMACHIAE L F
SACERD PVBL
FVLLONES

∾ 17 *Pliny,* LETTERS *4.19 and 8.10, excerpts*

Pliny, *Letter* 4.19, excerpt

C. PLINIUS [CALPVRNIAE] HISPVLLAE SVAE S.
... non dubito maximo tibi gaudio fore, cum
cognoveris dignam patre, dignam te, dignam avo
evadere. Summum est acumen, summa frugalitas:
5 amat me, quod castitatis indicium est.
Accedit his studium litterarum, quod ex mei
caritate concepit. Meos libellos habet, lectitat,
ediscit etiam. Qua illa sollicitudine, cum videor
acturus, quanto, cum egi, gaudio adficitur!
10 Disponit, qui nuntient sibi, quem adsensum,

quos clamores excitarim, quem eventum iudicii
tulerim. Eadem, si quando recito, in proximo
discreta velo sedet laudesque nostras
avidissimis auribus excipit. Versus quidem
15 meos cantat etiam formatque cithara, non
artifice aliquo docente, sed amore, qui magister
est optimus.
His ex causis in spem certissimam adducor
perpetuam nobis maioremque in dies futuram
20 esse concordiam. . . . Vale.

Pliny, *Letter* 8.10, excerpt

C. PLINIVS FABATO PROSOCERO SVO S.
Quo magis cupis ex nobis pronepotes videre, hoc
tristior audies neptem tuam abortum fecisse, dum se
praegnantem esse puellariter nescit, ac per hoc
5 quaedam custodienda praegnantibus omittit, facit
omittenda. Quem errorem magnis documentis
expiavit in summum periculum adducta. Igitur, ut
necesse est graviter accipias senectutem tuam quasi
paratis posteris destitutam, sic debes agere dis gratias,
10 quod ita tibi in praesentia pronepotes negaverunt, ut
servarent neptem, illos reddituri, quorum nobis spem
certiorem haec ipsa quamquam parum prospere
explorata fecunditas facit. . . . Vale.

❧ 18 Sulpicia; Martial 10.35 and 10.38

Sulpicia

Si me cadurci restitutis fasciis
nudam Caleno concubantem proferat.

Martial 10.35

Omnes Sulpiciam legant puellae
uni quae cupiunt viro placere;
omnes Sulpiciam legant mariti
uni qui cupiunt placere nuptae.
5   Non haec Colchidos adserit furorem,
diri prandia nec refert Thyestae;
Scyllam, Byblida nec fuisse credit:
sed castos docet et probos amores,
lusus delicias facetiasque.
10 Cuius carmina qui bene aestimarit,
nullam dixerit esse nequiorem,
nullam dixerit esse sanctiorem.
Tales Egeriae iocos fuisse
udo crediderim Numae sub antro.
15 Hac condiscipula vel hac magistra
esses doctior et pudica, Sappho:
sed tecum pariter simulque visam
durus Sulpiciam Phaon amaret.
Frustra: namque ea nec Tonantis uxor
20 nec Bacchi nec Apollinis puella
erepto sibi viveret Caleno.

Martial 10.38

O molles tibi quindecim, Calene,
quos cum Sulpicia tua iugales
indulsit deus et peregit annos!
O nox omnis et hora, quae notata est
5   caris litoris Indici lapillis!
O quae proelia, quas utrimque pugnas
felix lectulus et lucerna vidit
nimbis ebria Nicerotianis!
Vixisti tribus, o Calene, lustris:
10 aetas haec tibi tota conputatur
et solos numeras dies mariti.
Ex illis tibi si diu rogatam
lucem redderet Atropos vel unam,
malles quam Pyliam quater senectam.

∾ 19 *Tabula Vindolanda 2.291 and 2.292*
Tab. Vindol. 2.291

Claudia Severa to Sulpicia Lepidina

    i

Cl(audia). Severa Lepidinae [suae
    [sa]l[u]tem
iii Idus Septembr[e]s soror ad diem
sollemnem natalem meum rogo
5   libenter facias ut venias
ad nos iucundiorem mihi

    ii

[diem] interventu tuo factura si

    s

Cerial[em t]uum saluta Aelius meus.

10 et filiolus salutant

    sperabo te soror

[By a second hand]

vale soror anima

mea ita valeam

karissima et have

[Back, by the first hand]

15 Sulpiciae Lepidinae

    Cerialis

    a S[e]vera

Tab. Vindol. 2.292

Claudia Severa to Sulpicia Lepidina

    i

    salutem

ego soror sicut tecum locuta fueram et promiseram

ut peterem a Broccho et venirem at te peti

et res[po]ndit mihi <i>ta corde semp[er li]citum una

    ii

5 quomodocumque possim

    at te pervenire sunt enim

    necessaria quaedam qua[e]

    iii

    rem meum epistulas meas

accipies quibus scies quid

10   sim actura haec nobis

v

....

ra eram et Brigae mansura

Cerialem tuum a me saluta

[Back, by a second hand]

[val]e m soror

karissima et anima

15   ma desideratissima

[Back, by the first hand]

Sulpiciae Lepidi

nae Ceria[li]s

a Severa Brocchi

⁓ 20 *Juvenal*, SATIRES *6. 161–71*

'Nullane de tantis gregibus tibi digna videtur?'   161

Sit formonsa, decens, dives, fecunda, vetustos

porticibus disponat avos, intactior omni

crinibus effusis bellum dirimente Sabina,

5   rara avis in terris nigroque simillima cycno,   165

quis feret uxorem cui constant omnia? Malo,

malo Venustinam quam te, Cornelia, mater

Gracchorum, si cum magnis virtutibus adfers

grande supercilium et numeras in dote triumphos.

10   Tolle tuum, precor, Hannibalem victumque Syphacem   170

in castris et cum tota Carthagine migra.

❧ 21　*Aulus Gellius, Noctes Atticae 1.12, excerpts*

Qui de virgine capienda scripserunt, quorum
diligentissime scripsit Labeo Antistius, minorem
quam annos sex, maiorem quam annos decem natam,
negaverunt capi fas esse; item quae non sit patrima et
5　matrima; item quae lingua debili sensuve aurium
deminuta aliave qua corporis labe insignita sit; item
quae ipsa aut cuius pater emancipatus sit, etiamsi
vivo patre in avi potestate sit; item cuius parentes
alter ambove servitutem servierunt aut in negotiis
10　sordidis versantur. . . .

Virgo autem Vestalis simul est capta atque in atrium
Vestae deducta et pontificibus tradita est, eo statim
tempore sine emancipatione ac sine capitis minutione
e patris potestate exit et ius testamenti faciundi
15　adipiscitur.

De more autem rituque capiundae virginis litterae
quidem antiquiores non extant, nisi quae capta prima
est a Numa rege esse captam. . . .

Nam si quis honesto loco natus adeat pontificem
20　maximum atque offerat ad sacerdotium filiam suam,
cuius dumtaxat salvis religionum observationibus
ratio haberi possit, gratia Papiae legis per senatum fit.

'Capi' autem virgo propterea dici videtur, quia
pontificis maximi manu prensa ab eo parente in cuius
25 potestate est, veluti bello capta, abducitur. In libro
primo Fabii Pictoris, quae verba pontificem maximum
dicere oporteat, cum virginem capiat, scriptum est. Ea
verba haec sunt: 'Sacerdotem Vestalem, quae sacra
faciat quae ius siet sacerdotem Vestalem facere pro
30 populo Romano Quiritibus, uti quae optima lege fuit,
ita te, Amata, capio.'

Plerique autem 'capi' virginem solam debere dici
putant. Sed flamines quoque Diales, item pontifices et
augures 'capi' dicebantur. . . .

35 'Amata' inter capiendum a pontifice maximo
appellatur, quoniam quae prima capta est hoc fuisse
nomen traditum est.

Commentary

∾ 1 *Plautus,* CASINA *147–60, 170–77, 184–211*
A humorous view of women's roles and lived realities

The comedies of Titus Maccius Plautus, our earliest Latin literary works to have survived in complete form, date from ca. 205 to 184 BCE. Plautus adapted them from Greek comedies written in the late fourth and third centuries BCE by such playwrights as Menander and Diphilus. Known as *fabulae palliatae,* "stories in Greek dress," they take place in the Greek past rather than in Plautus' Roman present.

Nevertheless, through their exuberant, imaginative use of the Latin language, and their frequent allusions to contemporary cultural practices and concerns, Plautus' plays seek to elicit what has aptly been called "Roman laughter": a vibrant brand of comic humor that evidently appealed to a diversely constituted urban audience of slaves, foreigners, and women as well as freeborn citizen males. The following scene from the *Casina,* Plautus' final play, provides a memorable example of his distinctively Roman and humorous way of writing, here about women's roles and lived realities. Its discussion of how wives should deal with wayward husbands is seasoned with Roman legal language, and powerfully depicts the challenges women faced in Roman marriages.

Plautus appears to have acted in his own comedies, along with an all-male theatrical troupe. Men, therefore, performed the parts of Cleostrata and Myrrhine, the two wealthy Athenian matrons who voice their opposing views of appropriate wifely conduct in this scene. Audiences no doubt found it especially amusing to watch male actors in female dress debate the proper behavior of a wife, in this instance one whose elderly husband mistreats her by lusting after a young female slave. What is more, this wife, Cleostrata, has reared this slave, the title character Casina, as her own daughter, and their own son desires Casina as well.

The words delivered by the male actor in the role of Myrrhine, telling Cleostrata that respectable wives must silently endure such treatment from their husbands, must have occasioned abundant laughter. Yet in the course of the play Myrrhine abandons her conservative Roman views about appropriate wifely conduct. Eventually Myrrhine joins Cleostrata and two household slaves—Pardalisca, an older woman, and Chalinus, a young man who lusts after Casina himself—in plotting to starve and humiliate not only Cleostrata's wayward husband but her own as well.

Plautus composed his comedies in a variety of Latin meters. This scene is a *canticum*, "sung verses," and metrically complex in form; many of the words, as noted below, have a distinctive musical quality.

147   **senex** = Lysidamus, Cleostrata's husband

        sibi "for himself"

149   **neque hodie coquetur** (impers. pass., fut. tense) "nor will cooking take place today"

150   **quando** here "since"

151   **causa** abl., with the objective genitives *animi amorisque* "for the sake of his pleasure and his passion"

152   **flagitium illud hominis** "that disgrace of a human being," in apposition to *is*, which refers to her husband. *Hominis* is gen. of description.

153–55 **ego illum fame, / ego illum siti, / maledictis, malefactis amatorem ulciscar** Note the repetition of *ego illum* and the coupling, without connectives (asyndeton), of two words beginning with *male-*, sound effects that add to the musical quality of Cleostrata's words.

160 **stabulum nequitiae** "stable of misbehavior," a metaphor associating Lysidamus with animal-like lust

161-62 **meas fortunas . . . questum** "to complain about my misfortunes." *Questum* is the supine of *queror*, expressing purpose.

172 **mecastor** Only women in Roman comedy swear by the Greek god Castor.

quid here "why"

174 **ita solent . . . nuptae** "all women who have married unhappily are in the habit of being sad"

domi est "both in their home and outside it there is always some sort of thing that is upsetting enough." *Domi* (here and at 186) is locative, as is *foris* at 186.

aegre quod sit satis rel. clause of characteristic

184-85 **scire quid sit** "to know the sort of thing it is," rel. clause of characteristic

186 **pessumis** = *pessimis*

me . . . despicatur "there is contempt shown for me in my house," transitive impers. pass. This construction is parallel to more common impersonal constructions such as *me taedet* and *me pudet.*

187 **dic idem** "say the same thing, i.e., say it again"

pol Characters of both genders in Roman comedy swear by the god Pollux, Castor's twin brother.

meo corde = *in meo corde*

190 **nec mihi ius meum optinendi optio est** *Optinendi* (= *obtinendi*) is a gen. gerund governed by *optio;* the two words are placed side by side to create a pun of sorts: "I have no option of obtaining my legal rights."

191 **mira sunt** "these are strange things you say"

192 **suom** = *suum*

[nam viri] ius suom ad mulieres optinere haud queunt "for men are barely able to obtain their legal rights where women are concerned." The prep. *ad* can mean "in regard to," "in the case of." Myrrhine's joke, claiming that women are actually more powerful than men although they lack men's legal rights, epitomizes her initially unsympathetic attitude toward Cleostrata's plight, an attitude that will change drastically over the course of the comedy.

193–95 **mihi** = belonging to me, an idea emphasized in 194 with *mea* and *meo*

postulat governs the indirect statement *vilico suo se dare* in 195, "he demands that he himself give [my little slave girl] to his own farm overseer."

meo sumptu "at my expense," reminds us that a respectable Roman woman could and did own property and have funds of her own apart from those of her husband, despite Myrrhine's claim below.

siet = *sit*

196 **ipsus** = *ipse*

198 **nos sumus** "we are alone"

unde ea tibi est "by what authority is she yours?"

199 **peculi . . . nihil** "nothing of private property," i.e., "no property of her own," partitive gen.

probam "respectable woman"

200–201 **et quae habet, partum ei haud commode est, quin viro aut subtrahat aut stupro invenerit** "and as for a woman who has such property, it was not appropriately secured by her, but that she is the sort who has either removed it from her husband or managed to get it by taking money for her sexual favors"

quin . . . subtrahat . . . invenerit subordinate clauses with the subjunctive, governed by *quin* in a clause of prevention. The pf. pass. pple. *partum*, here meaning "secured," "obtained," is a gendered pun, since it can also mean "having given birth to."

202 **hoc viri censeo esse omne quicquid tuom est** "I reckon that every item that is yours belongs to your husband." *Hoc omne* is the antecedent of *quidquid.*

tuom = *tuum*

203 **advorsum** = *adversum.* In using the prep. *advorsum,* "against," here; *advorsari,* a verb from the same Latin root in 205; and the adv. *advorsus* in 207 to describe the opposition between herself and Myrrhine, Cleostrata's words create what is known as a *figura etymologica,* "etymological figure": the use in close proximity of several words, often representing different parts of speech, from the same Latin root. These words also recall her earlier use of *advorsari* to describe the opposition between her husband and son. "Adversarial relationships" between individuals play a prominent role in the *Casina*'s dramatic action.

204, 205 **sis** = *si vis*

206 **sine amet, sine . . . faciat** "let him love, let him do" [that which pleases him]. *Amet* and *faciat* are either hortatory subjunctives intensified by *sine,* or indirect commands governed by *sine,* with *ut* omitted.

lubet = *libet*

207–8 **satin** = *satisne*

tuquidem = *tu + quidem*

tuam . . . rem "your own property," "your own interests [as a wife]"

istaec = *ista,* "these [unkind] things"

208 **loquere** = *loqueris*

209 **abs** = *ab*

vitato "avoid in the future," fut. imperative

huic verbo = *i foras,* actually two words

210 **i foras, mulier** "get out of my house, woman," a Roman legal formula for divorce

✑ 2 Marcus Porcius Cato, DE AGRI CULTURA 143

Cato on the duties appropriate for female slaves working as housekeepers on a Roman country estate

Authorities often refer to Marcus Porcius Cato, whose long life extended from 234 to 149 BCE, as "Cato the Elder." They do so to distinguish him from his identically named great-grandson, whom the defeat of the Roman republican cause drove to suicide in 46 BCE. Cato the Elder—a gifted orator, successful military and political leader, and authority on Italian history, Roman jurisprudence, and farming—was a prolific writer. Yet only the text of his treatise *De Agri Cultura*, "On Agriculture," our earliest extant example of connected Latin prose, survives intact.

Cato based the *De Agri Cultura* on his own experience and expectations, and composed it as a manual, offering practical advice and detailed directions for readers who managed farms. This passage provides a rare and fascinating glimpse of the working conditions that he imposed, and believed should be imposed, upon female slaves serving as housekeepers, *vilicae*, on a Roman estate. This description of the duties appropriate to a *vilica* is addressed by the master to his male slave, the *vilicus*, "estate manager," who oversees the property, and may be given this woman as a bedmate. Cato lists not only the domestic and religious responsibilities of the *vilica*, but also the social restrictions to which she must submit. His advice and directions to his addressee are precise, concise, and commanding; they make frequent use of both the imperative mood and the jussive subjunctive, another Latin construction employed to issue orders.

1   **vilicae quae sunt officia, curato faciat** Translate as *curato ut vilica faciat officia quae sunt ei*. The unusual word order of the sentence emphasizes that this paragraph will address the duties of the housekeeper, just as an earlier paragraph was directed to the farm manager. Note that *vilicae* is the first word, in the dat. (of possession), since she and her duties constitute the subject of this discussion.

curato fut. imperative in the third person sing., followed by the subjunctive, in either a substantive clause of purpose ([*ut*] *vilica faciat*) or an indirect command. Future imperatives occur in a command with a clear reference to future time; substantive clauses of purpose are used as the objects of verbs denoting an action directed toward the future. The male farm manager to whom this advice is addressed is presumably a slave. He is the subject of *curato* in this sentence, the subject of *esto,* and referred to by the pron. *tibi* (in the next sentence), and also the subject of *facito* in the sentence after that.

2   **dederit** fut. pf. tense

uxorem "as a wife, monogamous female bed partner." Roman slaves did not have the legal right to marry. If both the farm manager and the *vilica* are slaves, then *uxor* implies that the *vilica* is expected to limit her sexual favors to one bed partner.

ea with *contentus*, "satisfied with her"

esto fut. imperative of *sum, esse, fui, futurus*

2–3   **ea te metuat facito** Translate as *facito ut ea te metuat.*

3   **facito** fut. imperative, followed by a substantive clause of result

siet = *sit*; *ne . . . siet* is a jussive subjunctive, with the *vilica* as the subject.

4   **utatur** jussive subjunctive. In later, classical Latin this verb always takes an object in the abl. case, but earlier authors often use it with the acc. Cato's advice has the clear intention of limiting the housekeeper's social interactions with others.

4–5   **neve domum neve ad sese** "neither to her home nor to her quarters." Note Cato's repeated insistence that she avoid social relationships with other women, presumably because they would waste time she should be devoting to her household tasks, and fill her head with information (on, e.g., sexual matters, working conditions in other households) of which he would prefer her to be unaware.

5   **sese recipiat, eat, siet** jussive subjunctives with the *vilica* as their subject

6   **rem divinam ni faciat neve mandat** "let her not engage in religious worship, nor entrust": jussive subjunctive, with *vilica* as the subject

    qui pro ea faciat Understand *sua officia ei qui pro ea faciat*, "her duties to the sort of person who would perform them in her stead": rel. clause of characteristic.

7   **scito** third person sing. fut. imperative, "let her know," with the *vilica* as the subject, followed by indirect statement with *dominum* as its subject. The verb *scio* regularly uses the fut. imperative instead of the pres.

    pro "on behalf of, representing"

8-10   **siet, habeat, habeat** jussive subjunctives. *Eat* is a subjunctive in an anticipatory clause with *priusquam*. All have the *vilica* as their subject.

10   **cubitum eat** supine of *cubo* with *eo*: "goes to sleep"

10-11   **Kalendis, Idibus, Nonis, festus dies cum erit** Note the lack of connective words (asyndeton) to describe these significant ritual days in the Roman calendar: the first days of each month (*Kalendis*), the days marking the "middle" of the month (*Idibus*), the days halfway between the first and middle of each month (*Nonis*), and whenever else holidays occur.

12-13   **indat a**nd **supplicet** are jussive subjunctives; *vilica* is their subject.

    per eosdem . . . dies "during those same days"

    pro copia "as the opportunity presents itself"

13   **curet uti . . . habeat** jussive subjunctive governing a substantive clause of result; *vilica* is the subject of both.

14   **Gallinas . . . uti habeat** substantive clause of result governed by *curet* in the previous sentence; *vilica* is the subject of both verbs.

    pira arida, sorba . . . Note again the asyndeton (lack of connectives) in this enumeration of the many fruits and nuts that the *vilica* (subject of *habeat*) should store up, and precise details of how and where she should store them; it is striking that grapes and nuts are to be placed in pots buried in the ground, presumably to preserve them in a more thoroughly dried state than the fruits stored in liquid.

19   **haec omnia** all of the items described in this sentence: *mala Scantiana, alia quae condi solent, et silvatica*

19-20   **uti condita habeat** governed by *curato*, understood

20   **suptile** = *subtile*

        sciat jussive subjective; *vilica* is the subject.

        farina flour used in making pastry, which seems to be more finely ground-up *far*

ꙮ 3 *Cornelius Nepos, Fragment 59; Livy, AB URBE CONDITA 30.12.11–18 and 15.1–8*

Cornelia's stern advice to her son, Gaius Gracchus; an African queen's heroic example

Cornelius Nepos, Fragment 59

In a work now lost to us, entitled *On Latin Historians* and written in the mid-first century BCE, the historian and biographer Cornelius Nepos quotes two passages from a letter written by "Cornelia mother of the Gracchi." As his words indicate, his Roman readers chiefly remembered this Cornelia, a Roman noblewoman of the second century BCE, as the mother of the populist political leaders Tiberius Sempronius Gracchus and Gaius Sempronius Gracchus. Both were assassinated by political foes while serving as tribunes of the people: Tiberius in 133 and Gaius in 121 BCE. Yet Cornelia was also remembered as the daughter of the general and statesman Publius Cornelius Scipio Africanus. The Romans celebrated Scipio for defeating Hannibal at Zama, and thereby ending Rome's second war against the North African city of Carthage, in 202 BCE.

Several ancient sources testify to Cornelia's importance within and beyond the circle of her wealthy and politically powerful family. They also recall her devotion to her offspring. The first-century CE moralist Valerius Maximus relates what is probably the best known anecdote about her in chapter 4.4 of his *Memorable Deeds and Sayings*. He reports that when a woman staying at Cornelia's villa on the Bay of Naples insisted on displaying her own very beautiful jewelry, Cornelia detained her in conversation until her two sons came home from school, and then proclaimed, "These are *my* jewels." Both Cicero in the first century BCE and the oratorical authority Quintilian over a century later also credit Cornelia for her sons' eloquence in speaking. Indeed, Cicero claims at *Brutus* 211 that Tiberius and Gaius Gracchus were "nurtured not so much in Cornelia's bosom as in her speech." Since both Cicero and Quintilian refer to her letters as proof of her superior communications skills, this particular letter may well have inspired Cicero's laudatory comment. Addressed to her son Gaius, it is likely to have been written in 124 BCE. In it Cornelia seeks to dissuade him from seeking the office of tribune, which his elder brother Tiberius had held when his enemies murdered him eight years earlier.

No extant Roman author other than Nepos quotes the fragments of this letter directly. Certain features of this letter have also disconcerted many modern scholars. Chief among them are the self-absorption and self-assertiveness of its first-person speaker, and the raw, often angry, emotions voiced. These expressions of rage and entitlement differ strongly from modern notions of how an admirable mother speaks to a child. As a result, there are those who question Cornelia's authorship of this letter and even the female gender of the author.

Nevertheless, both the arguments and emotional mode of persuasion employed by this elite, privileged Roman mother to influence the political conduct of her adult son are recalled by later speeches in various Augustan writers. Perhaps the most noteworthy is the speech that Livy assigns at 2.40 of his history to Veturia, mother of the legendary traitor Coriolanus. These similarities suggest that Cornelia's words may well have struck a Roman audience as entirely appropriate under the circumstances, and that Livy may have sought to echo Cornelia's letter, and invoke her as a model, in his portrait of Veturia (Hallett, *Women Writing Latin from Roman Antiquity*, 14–18).

1   **Cornelii Nepotis** As Cornelius Nepos shared his *nomen* with Cornelia and her family of birth, the Cornelii Scipiones, it is possible that he was a distant relation, or at least sought to claim a kindred relationship.

2   **Latinis Historicis** historians who wrote in the Latin language

3   **dices pulchrum esse** "you will say that it is a beautiful thing." Indirect statement; *pulchrum*, a neuter substantive, is the predicate acc. of *inimicos ulcisci*. The late seventh- /sixth-century BCE Greek poet Sappho begins one of her most famous poems, fragment 16 Lobel-Page, by noting different opinions on what is "the most beautiful thing in the world." After acknowledging that some propose a fleet of ships, others armies on both horseback and foot, she offers her own opinion that the most beautiful thing is "whatever one loves." Cornelia may be alluding to Sappho's lyrics. Like Sappho, in this letter she challenges conventional male, political and military, notions about what is abstractly beautiful, repeating the compar. form *pulchrius* along with *maius* in the next sentence to emphasize her differing viewpoint.

id = *inimicos ulcisci*

4   **cuiquam atque mihi** "to anyone more than to me." *Atque* is used in the sense of "than" here after the comparatives, *maius* and *pulchrius*.

4–5   **si liceat** "if it should be permitted," pres. subjunctive with if-clause in fut. less vivid condition

5   **re publica salva** abl. absolute, "while the state remains safe"

     ea "these things," again, *inimicos ulcisci*

     id = *inimicos ulcisci re public salva*

6   **multo tempore** Although one might expect *longo tempore*, its use allows the repeated, anaphoric *multo tempore multisque partibus*.

     multis . . . partibus here "for many reasons"

7   **uti nunc sunt** "as things now are." Supply *ea* ("things, events") as the subject of *sunt* and *erunt*.

7–8   **potius quam . . . profligetur atque pereat** "rather than that
the state may be overwhelmed and perish." *Potius quam* governs the pres. subjunctive because it describes assumed action.
While *atque* means "than" in Cornelia's second sentence, here
it carries its more customary meaning of "and," in an allitera-
tive phrase.

9   **eadem** = *in eadem epistula*

alio loco = *in alio loco* (= passage)

10   **ausim** = *audeam*, archaic pf. subjunctive of semi-deponent
audeo, audere, ausus sum. In this potential subjunctive construction both pres. and pf. subjunctives refer without dis-
tinction to fut. time ("I would dare").

praeterquam Understand *eos qui Tiberium Gracchum necarunt.*

11   **necarunt** = *necaverunt*

neminem = *nullum*. Understand *neminem inimicum tantum
molestiae tantumque laboris mihi tradidisse quantum te mihi
tradidissse.*

11–12 **tantum molestiae tantumque laboris** partitive genitives, in
an anaphoric phrase coordinated with *quantum*

12   **ob has res** his candidacy for the tribunate. Note that Cornelia
is likening Gaius to an *inimicus*, the word that she used earlier
for the foes against whom Gaius wishes to take vengeance.
She also emphasizes his similarity to his personal enemies by
referring to his brother's killers, and mentioning his brother
by name, as the only individuals who have caused her more
difficulties than he has.

13–14 **quem oportebat . . . tolerare** Understand *quem* ("you for
whom") *oportebat tolerare partis omnium eorum liberorum
quos antehac habui. Liberos*, here the antecedent of the rel.
pron. *quos*, has been attracted into the case of the rel. pron.

14   **partis** = *partes* "responsibilities"

14–17 **curare ut . . . haberem, utique . . . ea velles, . . . uti nefas haberes** substantive clauses of result

16 **quaecumque ageres** "whatever sort of thing you did"; rel. clause of characteristic

ea = *quaecumque ageres*

17 **nefas haberes** "you would consider it an act of sacrilege"

rerum maiorum Understand with *quicquam*, "anything of rather great matters," "anything of rather serious significance."

19-20 **ne id quidem . . . opitulari** Understand *ne id spatium quidem, tam breve, potest opitulari.*

19 **spatium** = *spatium temporis*

20 **quin . . . adversere** (= *adverseris*) **. . . profliges** "help to prevent you from opposing . . . and destroying," impf. subjunctives in clause of prevention with *quin*. With the phrase *rem publicam profliges*, Cornelia echoes her statement in the first excerpt, *potius quam res publica profligetur*, claiming that failure to take vengeance on one's enemies is preferable to having the state destroyed. Here, however, she equates opposing her wishes with destroying the state, as well as representing Gaius as likely to engage in what she has previously characterized as the worst possible sort of political behavior.

21 **ecquando** The anaphora created by the series of four rhetorical questions beginning with *ecquando* suggests that Cornelia composed the letter with an ear to oral delivery: dictating its words to a slave (male or female) "reader," assuming that a slave reader would read it to Gaius as well.

22 **ecquando modus ei rei haberi poterit** "when will a limit be able to be placed on this matter?"

22-23 **ecquando desinemus et habentes et praebentes molestiis insistere?** "when will we cease insisting on troubles, both suffering them and causing them?"

24-25 **miscenda atque perturbanda re publica** gerundive in abl. of cause construction, "as a result of disrupting and disturbing our country." Supply the acc. *nos* as the persons affected with *perpudescet.*

26   **petito, facito** second person sing. fut. imperatives of *petere*
      and *facere*

      lubebit = *libebit*

28   **deum parentem** either "parent god," with both words in the
      acc. sing., or "parent of gods," with *deum* in the gen. pl., an
      alternative form of *deorum*, as it is in the next sentence. If
      deum is in the acc. sing., and Cornelia is referring to her own
      deified identity after her death, it is significant that she envi-
      sions herself as acquiring masculine, or at least as losing femi-
      nine, gender. It is, however, possible that "by parent god" she
      is referring to one of Gaius' deceased elder male relations: her
      late husband Tiberius Sempronius Gracchus, or her late father
      Publius Cornelius Scipio Africanus. If we are to understand
      the phrase as referring to the "parent of the gods," Cornelia
      presumably refers to Jupiter, particularly Jupiter Optimus
      Maximus, with whom her father claimed a special, close rela-
      tionship, as she mentions Jupiter two sentences later.

      eorum deum gen. pl.; Gaius' dead ancestors, including herself

29-30 **quos vivos atque praesentes relictos atque desertos habueris**
      "whom, when they were alive and on hand, were of the sort
      you considered abandoned and deserted"

      habueris pf. subjective, rel. clause of characteristic

30   **ne ille sirit Iuppiter te ea perseverare** optative subjunctive,
      expressing a wish; negative is *ne*, "may that Jupiter not allow
      you to continue in those actions . . . nor to allow such great
      insanity to come into your mind."

      sirit = *siverit*, pf. subjunctive of *sino*, with the force of the pres.
      tense

      ille "that Jupiter," perhaps a reference to Jupiter Optimus
      Maximus. Several of the words used by Cornelia to invoke Ju-
      piter here resemble those that the historian Livy, at 28.28.11,
      claims her father, Scipio Africanus, uttered to his mutinous
      soldiers, also when contrasting his mortal frailty to the du-
      rability of the Roman state, in 206 BCE: *Ne istuc Iuppiter*

> *Optimus Maximus sirit, urbem auspicato dis auctoribus in aeternum conditam hic fragili et mortali corpori aequalem esse,* "May Jupiter Optimus Maximus not allow henceforth that the city of Rome—founded with due auspices and the favor of the gods to endure forever—live no longer than my own, weak mortal body."

32 **vereor ne . . . recipias** pres. subjunctive in fear clause, "I fear that you may receive"

tantum laboris echoing her earlier phrase, "so much trouble"

culpa tua abl. of cause, "by your own fault"

33 **uti** = *ut . . . possis*; result clause with *tantum*

tempore tute tibi placere possis Note the alliteration of *p* and *t*, again suggesting that these words were written for reading aloud.

Livy, *Ab Urbe Condita* 30.12.11–18 and 15.1–8

The Roman moral example of an African queen: Livy's Sophoniba

In Book 30 of his *Ab Urbe Condita*, written soon after 19 BCE, the moralizing Roman historian Titus Livius, to whom we refer as Livy, recounts the final years of the Second Punic War. Waged against the North African imperial power of Carthage from 218 to 201 BCE, this conflict culminated in a series of military achievements by the Roman general Publius Cornelius Scipio, beginning with his invasion of Africa in 204 BCE. To recognize these accomplishments, Rome awarded Scipio the *cognomen* Africanus, making him its first commander-in-chief honored by the name of the nation he had vanquished.

Prior to his victory over the the Carthaginian general Hannibal at Zama in 202 BCE, Scipio had forged an alliance with Masinissa, who ruled the North African kingdom of Numidia, located in what is Algeria (and part of Tunisia) today. Together they had defeated Syphax, chief of a western Numidian tribe known as the Masaesylii. Syphax had sought to ally himself with the Carthaginians, rather than the Romans. He sealed the alliance by wedding the daughter of a Carthaginian leader named Hasdrubal, the son of Gisco. Although this woman's name was Saphanba'al, some ancient Greco-Roman authors call her Sophonisba; to Livy she is Sophoniba. Our earliest source on her, the second-century BCE Greek historian Polybius, reports that it was in fact she who persuaded Syphax to support the Carthaginians against the Romans; various other sources even claim that her father had first promised her to Masinissa.

Livy's account represents Sophoniba as pleading with Masinissa not to hand her over to the Romans after the defeat of her husband Syphax. Masinissa, Livy asserts, was so smitten by her youthful beauty and persuasive, charming words that he, the captor, became enamoured of and wed Sophoniba, his captive. Nevertheless, since Scipio insisted that she be surrendered, Sophoniba—according to Livy—drank a cup of poison, provided to her by Masinissa himself, taking her own life rather than be paraded in Scipio's triumphal procession.

Sophoniba's suicide calls to mind the conduct of two other African queens celebrated in the literary texts of Livy's day. One is the legendary Carthaginian queen Dido, represented in Vergil's *Aeneid* as predicting on her deathbed that a Carthaginian leader, presumably Scipio's foe Hannibal, would one day arise to avenge her. The other is the Egyptian Cleopatra. Livy's contemporary Horace describes her in *Odes* 1.37, composed soon after the battle of Actium in 31 BCE, as "drinking in" snake poison, and nobly facing death rather than being paraded in Augustus' Roman triumph. Horace also depicts Cleopatra's courageous embrace of death as "not womanly": that is, adhering to the standards of conduct expected of Roman males.

Similarly, Livy seems to portray the foreign Sophoniba as a role model, exceptional in her resolve and patriotism, for Roman men and women alike. Among actual women of earlier times who may have considered Sophoniba, at least as Livy characterizes her, a moral example, was Scipio's own daughter Cornelia. In the letter to her younger son Gaius Gracchus included immediately above, Cornelia fiercely faults his personal sentiments and political conduct that might harm the Roman state.

Livy's Book 30 is also roughly contemporary with Augustus' marriage and moral legislation, which provided incentives for marriage, and severely punished women's marital infidelity. Thus Livy's depiction of the foreign Sophoniba as loyal wife, valuing country over life, may have held particular resonance for his audience.

Livy, *Ab Urbe Condita* 30.12.11–18

1   **intranti** refers to Masinissa, dat. object of *occurrit.*

2–4   **cum . . . conspexisset** *cum* circumstantial clause, with Sophoniba as its subject

3–4   **insignem cum armis tum cetero habitu** "conspicuous not only because of his weapons but also the rest of his clothing"

4–5   **regem esse, id quod erat, rata** indirect statement with pf. act. pple. of *reor*, "having thought that he was a king, which he in fact was"

5   **genibus advoluta** having fallen onto her knees as a suppliant

6–7   **'omnia quidem ut possis . . . in nobis di dederunt virtusque et felicitas tua'** "the gods, your manly excellence, and your good fortune have granted that you certainly are powerful in respect to all things over us." *Dederunt ut* governs a substantive clause of result; *omnia* is an acc. of respect. Note the three nouns describing the basis of Massinissa's power: the gods, human merit, and luck.

7   **captivae** dat. with *licet*; separated by the phrase *apud dominum vitae necisque suae*, "in the presence of the man who controls her life and death." *Vitae* and *necis* are objective genitives.

9   **si genua, si victricem attingere dextram** Understand *si licet attingere genua, si licet victricem dextram*. In the protasis, or "if-clause," of this complex conditional sentence, *licet* governs two infinitives, *mittere* and *attingere*; *attingere* has two direct objects, *genua* and *dextram*; *si* occurs three times to emphasize the parallelism of *genua* and *dextram* as objects of *attingere*.

13-15 **per huiusce regiae deos, qui te melioribus ominibus accipiant quam Syphacem hinc miserunt** "through the gods of this
palace so that they may receive you with better omens than
those by which they sent Syphax from here"; *qui . . . accipiant* is a rel. clause of purpose; *quam* introduces a comparison with *melioribus*, compar. form of *bonus*; understand *illis
ominibus quibus* as following *quam*. Note the three successive
appearances of the prep. *per*, each taking as its object a noun
expanded by a rel. clause: *maiestatem . . . in qua . . . fuimus*;
nomen, quod . . . fuit; *deos qui . . . accipiant*.

15 **hanc veniam supplici des** "that you may grant this favor to a
suppliant," indirect command with *precor quaesoque*, with *ut*
omitted

15-18 **ut ipse . . . statuas . . . sinas** substantive clauses of result with
des, "that you yourself may decide about your captive whatever your mind proposes and you may not allow me to come
into the arrogant and cruel control of any Roman"

18-21 **si . . . fuissem . . . mallem** a mixed condition. The protasis, or
"if-clause," is a past contrary to fact condition; the apodosis,
or main clause, a pres. contrary to fact condition: "if I were to
have been . . . I would prefer to test the honor . . ."

18 **nihil aliud quam Syphacis** "nothing other than the wife of
Syphax." *Nihil* is a predicate nom.

19-20 **in eadem mecum Africa geniti** gen. with *fidem*: "of someone
born with me in the same land of Africa"

20 **quam alienigenae et externi** "than a foreigner and outsider,"
the adj. *externus* is used as a substantive, in a construction
parallel to that of *geniti*.

21-22 **quid Carthaginiensi ab Romano, quid filiae Hasdrubalis
timendum sit vides** "You see what must be feared by a Carthaginian from a Roman, what must be feared by the daughter
of Hasdrubal." *Quid . . . timendum sit* is an impers. pass. periphrastic construction in an indirect question; *Carthaginiensi*
and *filiae* are datives of agent; *ab* here means "from."

23   **nulla re alia potes** "if you are powerful in no other regard"
     ut vindices indirect command governed by *oroque obtestor*

23–24   **morte me ut vindices ab Romanorum arbitrio** "that you
        may liberate me by means of death from the control of the
        Romans." *Morte* is abl. of means.

25–26   **modo genua modo dextram amplectens** "embracing now his
        knees now his right hand"; *modo . . . modo* implies motion
        back and forth between these two parts of his body.

25–27   **cum . . . in id . . . fidem exposceret** "since she was demanding
        a pledge to this effect"; *cum* causal clause

26–27   **ne cui Romano traderetur** negative clause of purpose ampli-
        fying *in id*, "that she not be handed over to any Roman"

27–28   **propiusque blanditias iam oratio esset quam preces** con-
        tinuation of causal clause governed by *cum*: "since her speech
        now was closer to sweet words than to prayers"

28–29   **non . . . modo . . . sed** "not only . . . but"

30   **in venerem praeceps** "impetuous where passion is concerned"
     amore captivae objective gen., "love for the captive." Note the
     close juxtaposition of *captivae* and *captus*, separated only by
     victor. Captus = captus est.

Livy, *Ab Urbe Condita* 30.15.1–8

1–2   **Masinissae audienti** dat. of reference with *rubor* and *lacri-
      mae*; *suffusus = suffusus est*; *obortae = obortae sunt.* "Not only
      was a blush caused to well up but also tears arose in Masinissa
      as he listened to these things [said by Scipio, about the neces-
      sity to surrender Sophoniba].

2–3   **se quidem in potestate futurum imperatoris** "that he would
      indeed be under the power of the commander [Scipio]"; indi-
      rect statement with *dixisset*

2–4   **cum . . . dixisset orassetque** circumstantial clause, "when he
      had said . . . and had begged"

4–5   **orassetque eum ut . . . fidei suae temere obstrictae consuler-**
et "He had begged him that he consider his good word, which
had been recklessly placed under obligation"; *fidei* is dat. with
consuleret.

4   **quantum res sineret** "to however great the extent that the
situation allowed"; indirect question, used adverbially

5–6   **promisisse . . . traditurum** "[claiming that] he had promised
that he would surrender her into the power of no one," indirect statement governed by an implied verb of speaking; *esse*
should be understood with *traditurum*, a fut. act. infinitive
construction. *Se* is the subject of the indirect statement and
eam (her) the direct object.

7–8   **arbitris remotis** "after eye-witnesses had been removed," abl.
absolute

8–10   **cum . . . consumpsisset** *cum* circumstantial clause, with Masinissa as the subject

8–9   **quod . . . posset** "the sort of thing which was easily able to be
heard by those standing around the tent," rel. clause of characteristic referring to *crebro suspiritu et gemitu*

10   **aliquantum temporis** "a little period of time" partitive gen.

10–11   **ingenti . . . edito gemitu** "and after a loud groan had been
emitted," abl. absolute

       ad postremum "finally"

11   **e servis** "from the number of his slaves"

11–14   **vocat . . . iubet** Note the use of the historic pres. tense for dramatic vividness.

12   **regio more ad incerta fortunae** "in the fashion of kings, to
prepare for the uncertainties of fortune"

13   **mixtum in poculo** modifies *venenum*.

13–14   **ferre . . . nuntiare** infinitives governed by *iubet*

14–15   **Masinissam . . . praestaturum fuisse** "that Masinissa was
gladly about to furnish to her the most valuable word of trust,"
indirect statement governed by *nuntiare*

15–16 **quam vir uxori debuerit** "which a husband has owed to his wife," subordinate clause in indirect statement

16–17 **quoniam . . . adimant** "since the kind of people holding power were taking away his control over her," subordinate clause in indirect statement, and hence the subjunctive mood; *qui possint* rel. clause of characteristic

17 **secundum fidem** "in accordance with his word of trust"

17–18 **praestare . . . veniat** "that he was making the provision that she not come into the power of the Romans alive"; *praestare* is also in the indirect statement construction governed by *nuntiare*; *ne . . . veniat* subjunctive in substantive clause after *praestare*

18–19 **memor patris imperatoris** "mindful of her father the military commander," Hasdrubal, son of Gisco. Greco-Roman authors routinely portray elite Roman daughters, such as Scipio's own daughter Cornelia, as honoring their country by publicly behaving in ways that imitate and bring credit to their fathers and families.

19–20 **duorum regum quibus nupta fuisset** "the two kings of the kind to whom she had been married," subjunctive in rel. clause of characteristic; *quibus* is dat. with *nupta fuisset*, plpf. pass. subjunctive of *nubo*.

20 **sibi ipsa consuleret** "she should give serious thought to herself." Livy uses the subjunctive because he is describing Masinissa's command to Sophoniba as part of an indirect statement construction.

22 **cum . . . venisset** temporal subjunctive

25 **melius . . . fuisse** "that I would have been destined to die in better circumstances," indirect statement governed by the imperative *nuntia*, functioning as the main clause in a past contrary to fact condition

25–26 **si non . . . nupsissem** "If I had not been married in the circumstances of my own death," protasis, or "if-clause," in a past contrary to fact condition

26   **ferocius** compar. adverbial form of *ferox*, with *quam*, "she did
        not speak more fiercely than she actually drank . . ."

ᘛ *4 Aulus Gellius, NOCTES ATTICAE 1.23*
How Papirius got the surname *Praetextatus*

The second-century CE Latin author Aulus Gellius called his learned
observations on a wide range of topics *Noctes Atticae,* "The Attic
Nights," because he composed them in the evenings during a win-
ter that he spent near Athens. Gellius' deep interest in early Roman
authors led him to quote, and hence preserve for posterity, numerous fragments of archaic Latin prose and poetry. The passage below
comes from a speech delivered in the mid-second century BCE, by
Marcus Porcius Cato, "Cato the Elder," whose writings on agriculture we have already encountered. Although the rest of the speech is
lost, its title—*Ad Milites contra Galbam*—indicates that it was given
to an audience of Roman soldiers, against Servius Sulpicius Galba,
who was a military tribune at that time.

Here Cato relates an anecdote that purports to explain how the
Papirian family acquired the cognomen *Praetextatus,* "clad in the toga
of a boy." It offers a rationale for why Roman senators in Cato's day
could not bring their sons who had not yet donned the *toga virilis,*
toga of manhood, into the curia, the Roman senate house. As Gellius'
introduction states, Cato shared this anecdote with this particular audience, a group of men whose families were not themselves of senato-
rial rank, in a humorous spirit. Yet his effort to blame the exclusion of
upper-class boys from the senate on the inquisitive and lustful ways
of their mothers mines a vein of Latin misogyny, viewed in other later
authors such as the satirist Juvenal, that cut across Roman class lines.
Fragments that survive from Cato's other speeches—the first-century
BCE historian Livy's representation of a speech Cato made during the
debate over the repeal of the *Lex Oppia* in 195 BCE, and the second-
century CE biographer Plutarch's depiction of Cato—similarly suggest
that this renowned orator and political opinion-shaper advocated limiting women's opportunities to control property and engage in public
activity, even within their own family circles.

Cato emphasizes that the upper-class boy Papirius is awarded the cognomen *Praetextatus* as a reward for his mature discretion: for knowing when to keep silent and when to speak. But both this name and Cato's narrative also emphasize that he is very young, and has not yet assumed the toga of manhood. Still he manages to avoid his mother's determined efforts to find out what was being discussed in the senate. Papirius' discretion and maturity serve to make the behavior of his mother, and all the Roman matrons in the story, seem outrageously emotional, meddlesome, sexually insatiable, and even childlike. This anecdote points to a deeply engrained bias in Roman thinking about women's inability to conduct themselves sensibly, necessitating their lifelong legal oversight by male relatives.

1   **dicta scriptaque** Supply *est*. Gellius indicates that Cato kept written records of the speeches that he delivered. The date of this speech may be as early as 167 BCE, when Cato was in his mid-sixties, or as late as 149 BCE, soon before his death at age eighty-five, and around the time that he legendarily kept proclaiming that *Carthago delenda est* (Carthage must be destroyed) in the Roman senate.

2   **qua** abl. with *usus est* < *utor* ("made; delivered")

    ad Milites contra Galbam Take in apposition to *oratione*.

3   **quidem** The adv. emphasizes *multa*. *Multa* modifies each of the three feminine nouns used to characterize Cato's speech, linked by the connective *atque*: *venustate*, *luce*, and *munditia*. The word *venustate* implies that this story had a ribald, or at least a sexually sophisticated, message.

    luce here "clarity of expression; brilliance"

4–5 **ea Catonis verba huic prorsus commentario indidissem, si libri copia fuisset** past contrary to fact condition, "I would have incorporated the exact words of Cato into these notes if access to the book had been available to me." Gellius reveals that he dictated his notes on this speech at a time when he did not have Cato's exact words on hand, and relied largely on his memory.

    huic . . . commentario dat. with the compound *indidissem*

5   **prorsus** adv. intensifying *huic* ("this very")

libri copia Latin uses a gen. here where English would use the equivalent of a dat. ("access to the book"). Gellius plans to tell us the story in his own words, which, unlike those of Cato, will lack stylistic charm and elegance.

6   **id temporis** "at that time." *Id* is an idiomatic use of the acc.; *temporis*, a partitive gen. dependent on *id*.

quod "but"

7   **rem ipsam** "the plot itself; what actually went on"

8   **ad hunc modum** "in this manner; as follows; along these lines"

senatoribus dat. of possession ("the senators had a custom")

9   **praetextatis** "clothed with or wearing the *toga praetexta*." Free born boys wore this outer garment, bordered with a wide purple stripe, before assuming the *toga virilis* in their fifteenth or sixteenth year, an indication that they had come of age as an adult.

10   **tum** "at that time"

10–11 **cum . . . consultata (est) eaque . . . prolata est placuitque** a temporal clause with triplet verbs. The long preamble to the main clause of the sentence, filled with technical words having to do with transacting Senate business, contrasts with the rather simpler heart of the sentence: the boy's mother strenuously questioning the boy in non-technical terms about the senate's discussion, underscoring her lack of political acumen and knowledge of the situation.

res maior quaepiam "some rather important issue"

11   **placuit** "it was decided, it was voted"

11–12 **ut . . . ne quis enuntiaret** negative clause of purpose dependent on *placuit*, "it was decided that no one divulge." *Placuit ut*, which governs the subjunctive, is followed by the negative purpose clause (some Latin grammars call this an indirect command), also in the subjunctive.

eam rem super qua tractavissent rel. clause of characteristic ("the sort of matter about which they had been having a discussion")

12   **super** takes the abl. when it means "about, concerning."

quis = *aliquis*: after *si, nisi, num,* and *ne*

12–13   **priusquam decreta esset** "before it had been actually decided," anticipatory subjunctive with *priusquam*

14   **percontata est** The compound verb suggests vigorous questioning!

14–15   **quidnam in senatu patres egissent** "what the senators had discussed in the senate," indirect question

quidnam emphatic ("what, tell me")

patres = *senatores*

egissent < *ago* ("discuss")

15   **tacendum esse** acc. and infinitive in indirect statement dependent on *respondit*; impers. pass. periphrastic construction, of which Cato was extremely fond, expressing obligation, duty, and necessity ("silence must be maintained")

16   **id dici** subject acc. and infinitive with the impers. *licere*, itself dependent on *respondit* ("he replied that it was not permitted for this to be told").

fit < *fio*, pass. of *facio*. Note the change to the pres. from the past tense in this sentence and the following one; this use of the pres. tense, for the sake of vividness, is often called the "historical present."

audiendi gen. of the gerund, dependent on *cupidior*, here in the feminine compar. form, "more desirous of hearing." With the sexually charged adj. *cupidior*, Cato suggests—as does the topic that the boy Papirius claims was discussed in the senate—the sexual insatiability of the boy's mother and the other matrons.

17–18   **ad inquirendum** gerund of purpose with *ad*, "to making inquiries"

18   **everberat** "poetic singular" form with pl. subject, *secretum et silentium*, here means "whips up" to an action. This rare but powerful verb is effective in pointing up the urgency of the mother's request. The three short clauses in this sentence emphasize the inappropriate nature of her behavior. The third sentence makes the point bluntly by ending with the forceful pair of compar. adverbs, *compressius violentiusve*. The compar. here, as in *cupidior*, implies that the mother's behavior was not only emotionally excessive under the circumstances, but intensifying in its frenzy.

19   **matre urgente** "since his mother was putting pressure on him," abl. absolute with pres. act. pple. *Urgente* is a powerful verb, suggesting that the mother was pressing the boy hard to get an answer.

20   **consilium capit** idiomatic; takes the gen. case ("forms the plan of inventing an amusing and witty falsehood"). The idiom suggests the deliberate actions of one much older than a *puer*, contrasting his thoughtful conduct to his mother's emotional behavior.

        actum (esse) acc. and pf. pass. infinitive of an impers. verb, dependent on *dixit* ("that it had been discussed; that there had been discussion"). Note the return to the past tense with *dixit*.

21–23   **utrum videretur utilius . . . unusne ut . . . haberet, an ut una . . . nupta esset** "whether it seemed more practical that one man . . . or that one woman be married"; *-ne . . . an* introduces an alternative question.

        utrum . . . videretur . . . an (videretur) alternative indirect questions, dependent on *actum (esse)* and indicated by the enclitic *-ne* and the words *an ut*.

21   **ex . . . republica** idiomatic ("to the advantage of the republic")

        unusne with *utrum, -ne* is sometimes attached to a significant word in the indirect question. Take *unus* inside the first *ut* clause.

22-23 **ut ... haberet ... ut ... nupta esset** subjunctives in purpose clauses dependent on *videretur*

apud ... nupta esset "be married to"

23 **compavescit** a very rare compound verb that suggests total terror and does not reflect well on Papirius' mother. Her panicky actions are emphasized by the asyndeton (lack of connective) with the three verbs: *compavescit, ... egreditur, ... perfert*, all in the "historical present."

domo "out of her house"

24 **perfert** "conveys (this) news"

25 **venit ... caterva** The inverted word order of this short sentence (verb first, subject last) draws attention to the unusual nature of the women's behavior.

familias archaic f. gen. sing. with *mater* ("of the household"), meaning "wife of a respectable Roman man, *pater familias*"; used here to emphasize that these are respectable women behaving in a way that is inappropriate for their social class and gender. Note the juxtaposition of this noun with *caterva*.

caterva used to describe a wild, unruly crowd or group

26 **una potius** These words are emphasized by placing them outside the subordinate clause to which they grammatically belong (*ut ... fieret*). Note the chiastic arrangement of *una ... duobus ... uni duae*. That the women fell for the boy's story depicts them as very naïve and not at all knowledgeable about the world of politics.

potius Take with *quam*.

26-27 **ut ... fieret** indirect command dependent on *orant*; *fieret* = *esset*

27 **duobus** Supply *viris*; dat. with *nupta fieret*.

uni duae The sentence ends with an antithesis that makes a humorous point but nonetheless shows the women in an unfavorable light. They have been bested by a young boy!

28-29 **quae (esset) ... et quid ... vellet** a double indirect question dependent on *mirabantur*

29 **intemperies** "madness, outrageous conduct." With the choice of this noun Gellius emphasizes the emotional and irrational behavior of the women. Supply *vellet*.

quid . . . vellet Read as *postulatio istaec, quid sibi vellet* ("that demand of theirs, what did it mean for them?"). *Quid . . . vellet* is an indirect question, and an idiomatic expression.

31 **institisset** "had determined"

31–32 **quid . . . institisset, quid . . . dixisset** double indirect questions dependent on *rem denarrat*, which—although it is another form in the "historical present," because it describes action in the past—governs these plpf. subjunctive verbs in secondary sequence.

32 **sicut fuerat** "just as it had happened"

denarrat asyndeton (no connective between the clauses)

34–35 **uti . . . ne introeant** negative clause of purpose (some Latin grammars call this an indirect command) dependent on *consultum facit*, "issued a decree to the effect that"

35 **praeter** adv., "with the exception of"

unus "only"

36 **cognomentum . . . inditum** Supply *recepit*, "received a cognomen added."

honoris gratia "on account of the honor"; *gratia* takes the gen. case.

37 **ob** Take with *prudentiam*.

tacendi loquendique gen. of the gerunds, dependent on *prudentiam*. In English we should translate "discretion in . . ."

37–38 **in aetate praetextae** "in the time of his life when he was still wearing the *praetexta*"

∽ 5 *CORPUS INSCRIPTIONUM LATINARUM I.2.2161 and I.2.1837*

Funerary inscriptions for two young girls

Late second century BCE

Neither of these inscriptions comes from the city of Rome itself. Both, moreover, furnish a glimpse of how female identity was defined, and of how young women were valued, by those outside the urban Roman elite. The first commemorates a female slave named Salvia who died at a very early age. It stresses her efforts in wool working, the "signature" Roman activity for women, regardless of their social status. The second is a dedication by a freedwoman named Posilla Senenia to her deceased only daughter.

CIL I.2.2161

This inscription, from Ivrea in Cisalpine Gaul, probably dates to the late second century BCE. It is written in a verse meter, known as iambic senarii, consisting of six iambic feet, frequently used by the Roman comic playwright Plautus, who wrote in the late third and early second centuries BCE, and his younger contemporary Terence, who wrote in the mid-second century BCE.

1   **C(aii) Paguri C(aii) l(iberti) Gelotis** This gen. phrase identifies the grave space as belonging to Gaius Pagurius Gaii Libertus Gelos, Gaius Pagurius Gelos, freedman of Gaius. *C.* is a common abbreviation for Gaius, *l.* for *libertus,* freedman.

2   **hospes** Roman tombstones frequently address those passing by as "guests," and invite them to stop and read their inscriptions. Along with addresses to these readers in the second person sing., they describe the persons buried therein in the first person sing., as if the occupant of the tomb were speaking to this addressee.

3   **quo** "where"

parvae aetatulae gen. of description, used metaphorically for the person whose bones occupy the tomb

4   **sepulta . . . sita sum** asyndeton for *sum haec sepulta et sita* ("I am buried and laid in my grave")

verna quoius aetatula *Verna* seems to function in two different grammatical roles and semantic senses here, as a sophisticated pun. It may be a noun, meaning "slave born in the master's household" and therefore function as the subject of *sepulta . . . sita sum*, modified by *haec*. But *vernus, -a, -um* is also an adj., signifying "occurring in spring-time, spring-like"; thus *verna* can also modify *aetatula*, and mean "spring-like tender age." *Quoius* = archaic form of *cuius*. Understand *haec verna* as the antecedent of *quoius*, and *erat* as the verb in the rel. clause it introduces, *quoius verna erat aetatula*.

5   **praestitei** archaic form of *praestiti*, "I offered, imparted *gravitatem* (acc. direct object) to my *officio et lanificio*" (dat. objects of compound verb)

6   **cassum** archaic form of *casum*

iniquom archaic form of *iniquum*

grave Note the wordplay with *gravitatem* in the preceding line, calling attention to two different meanings of *gravis*, "dignified, serious" and "heavy, painful." *Grave* suggests yet another wordplay by referring to the heaviness of the earth, weighing on Salvia's body.

7   **si quaeras, exoriatur** pres. subjunctive verbs in fut. less vivid condition, "if you should ask, would arise"

Salviae gen. with *nomen*. Salvia, the name of the dead girl, is also a title of the maiden goddess Proserpina (Greek Persephone), who rises up from the world of the dead each spring; this detail may account not only for the description of her tender age as "spring-like" but also for the use of the verb *exorior* to describe the emergence of her name in conversation.

8   **valebis** another play on words, "you will be well" (if her wish
     is granted and the addressee will be more fortunate than she
     has been) and "I will bid you farewell"

     opto ut seis felicior subjunctive with verb of wishing, "I wish
     that you may be more fortunate (than I)"

     seis archaic form of *sis*

CIL I.2.1837

This inscription is also written in senarii. From Monteleone in the
Sabine territory, it is roughly contemporary with the tomb inscription of Salvia.

1   **Posilla Senenia Quart. f., Quarta Senenia C. l.** This phrase
     identifies the dedicatee as Posilla Senenia "daughter of Quar-
     tus" and Quarta Senenia "freedwoman of Gaius." *F.* is a com-
     mon abbreviation for *filius* or *filia*. Presumably this woman's
     father called her Posilla Senenia, whereas her former master
     referred to her as Quarta Senenia, using the feminine form
     of her father's name to identify her in the same way that an
     elite Roman woman such as Cornelia was identified by the
     feminine form of her father Publius Cornelius Scipio's family
     name.

2   **hospes resiste** the same initial words as the tomb inscription
     of Salvia

     pariter also (read as well as stop)

     perlige alternative form of *perlege*

3   **matrem . . . fruei** acc. subject of an infinitive dependent on
     licitum esse

     non licitum esse indirect statement governed by *scriptum*,
     "that it was not permitted"

     gnata archaic form of *nata*

     fruei archaic form of deponent infinitive *frui*, which takes
     unica gnata as its object in the abl. case

4 **quam . . . nescio qui inveidit deus** "whom (f. acc. sing. of rel. pron., with *gnata* as its antecedent) some god or other (*nescio qui . . . deus*) looked upon with envy (*inveidit*)"

nei esset credo expression of indirect prohibition, introduced by *nei (ne* in classical Latin), with *credo* as parenthetical, "so that she might not exist, I believe"

inveidit archaic form of *invidit*

5 **quoniam haud licitum est** "since it was not permitted," governs indirect statement with *eam* as its subject

veivam archaic form of *vivam*, modifies *eam*

ornarier archaic form of pres. pass. infinitive *ornari*

6 **aequom** archaic form of *aequum*, substantive use of n. adj., "just act," modified by *hoc*

extremo tempore "final period of time" (at her daughter's death), "finally"

7 **deilexserat** archaic form of *dilexerat*, "she had cherished"

❧ 6 *Corpus Inscriptionum Latinarum I.2.1570; I.2.1732; and VI.18324*
Funerary inscriptions for two women

First century BCE

Like the two funerary inscriptions from the late second century BCE, all three of these epitaphs commemorate women born into slavery. Like those inscriptions as well, all three are composed in verse meters; two, moreover, were also found outside the city of Rome. Yet they differ from the two earlier inscriptions, and from one another, in important ways.

Both the first and the second inscription are written in the first person singular, and resemble the earlier inscriptions in that regard as well. But both honor married women, although they attest to two very different notions of the appropriate emotional and power dynamics in a Roman marriage. The first represents the dead woman

Horaea as speaking deferentially of her husband, who had freed her, and as likening their relationship to the interactions that she had as a dutiful and subordinate housekeeper to her former owners. By way of contrast, the second, honoring the freedwoman Helvia Prima, emphasizes the mutual affection, emotional harmony, and intellectual equality she enjoyed with her husband Scrateius Cadmus, probably a freedman too.

The date of the third inscription is uncertain. It describes the house slave Dionysia, who—like Salvia in one of the earlier inscriptions—died when still a child. It uses several words often employed in Roman erotic elegies from the first century BCE. Yet it may have been written considerably later: Dionysia's female owner, who dedicated the inscription, shares a name—Annia Isias—with a woman commemorated in an epitaph dated to the second century CE.

Whatever its exact date, the text warrants our attention for highlighting attributes one would not expect to find emphasized in a girl who was dead before the age of eight: her sexual playfulness (*lascivia*) and her efforts at creating "sweet moments of naughtiness." Perhaps Annia Isias was grooming Dionysia to provide sophisticated sexual companionship to a series of men, as a cultivated *meretrix*. But these references might also allude to playful and naughty love poems that Dionysia performed and composed: the inscription claims that if she had lived longer, "no girl on earth would have been more learned." Hence it is also possible that she was training to be a *lectrix*, reader and performer of Greek and Latin literary works, like Sulpicia Petale, whose epitaph we will encounter later.

CIL I.2.1570

From Liris in Latium, this inscription is written in senarii, and dated to around 45 BCE.

1   **P. Larcius P. L. Neicia** *Publius Larcius Nicia*, freedman of Publius. *P.* is the customary abbreviation for the praenomen *Publius*; *Neicia* is an archaic spelling of *Nicia*.

Saufeia [Gaiae]. l. Thalea Saufeia Thalea, freedwoman of a matron. A reversed *C* in Latin inscriptions signifies *Caiae* = *Gaiae*; the name *Gaia* represents any woman not otherwise identified.

2 **L. Larcius, P. f. Rufus** Lucius Larcius Rufus, son of Publius. *L.* is the customary abbreviation for the praenomen *Lucius*; this man is presumably the son of the first man mentioned.

2–3 **P. Larcius, P. f. Brocchus.** Publius Larcius Brocchus, son of Publius; this man is presumably another son of the first man mentioned as well.

3 **Larcia P. [Gaiae] l. Horaea** Larcia Horaea, freedwoman of Publius and [the matron who is] his wife. This woman, presumably the deceased, evidently belonged to both her master and his wife.

4 **boneis** archaic spelling of *bonis*. Here this adj. is to be understood as a substantive, "good people," with *a* or *ab* also understood, "having been approved (*probata*) by *bonis*." Notice the wordplay in *probata . . . proba*

inveisa archaic spelling of *invisa*, from *invideo*, "envy or hate"

proba here "respectable, morally, upright"

5 **domineis** archaic spelling of *dominis*, dat. with *parens*, pres. act. pple. of *pareo*, "obey"

huic to her husband, the first person named in the inscription; dat. with *obsequens*, "accommodating, deferential"

6 **ita leibertate illei me hic me decoraat stola** *leibertate* is an archaic spelling of *libertate*; *illei* is an archaic spelling of *illi*; *decoraat*, a misspelling of *decorant*. Understand *ut illi* (my former masters) *me decorant libertate, hic me decorat stola.*

stola dress of a married woman, here used metonymically for marriage

7 **a pupula** "since I was a little girl"

annos veiginti archaic for *annos viginti*, acc. of duration of time

optinui archaic form of *obtinui*, here meaning "I managed"

9   **veitae** archaic form of *vitae*

ornatum "splendor"

apstulit archaic form of *abstulit*, "took away"

CIL I.2.1732

From Beneventum in Campania, this inscription is written in the elegiac meter and dated to approximately 45 BCE. It refers to its addressee as a *viator*, "traveler," rather than as a *hospes*, "guest."

1   **secura . . . mente** abl. of description, "with a heart free from care"

spatiarus misspelling for *spatiaris*, second person sing. of *spatior*, "walk about in a slow or leisurely manner." Understand *tu, viator, qui secura mente spatiaris.*

2   **nostri** Understand as a misspelling of *nostris*, modifying *inferieis*

voltus archaic spelling of *vultus*, direct object in the acc. pl. of *derigis*, archaic spelling of *dirigis*, "direct [your] gaze"

inferieis archaic spelling of *inferiis*, "tomb," indirect object in the dat. case

3   **quae sim** indirect question, "if you ask who I am," dependent on *quaeris*

4   **tristeis** archaic spelling of acc. pl. *tristes*, modifying *obitus*

5   **coniuge . . . Cadmo . . . Scrateio** "my husband Cadmus Scrateius," in the abl. case as the object of *fructa sum*

7   **Diti** "to Dis," the god ruling the underworld, in the dat. case as the indirect object of *data sum*

mansura fut. act. pple. of *maneo*, "about to remain [in the lower world]"

8   **deducta** "led down," in the fashion of a bride

fatali igne, aqua Stygia ablatives of means

CIL VI.18324

This inscription, from Rome itself, is also written in the elegiac meter; as noted above, its vocabulary resembles that of first-century BCE love elegies, but its date is uncertain.

1   **d. m.** *dis manibus*, dat. of *di manes*, "to the spirits, shades" (of a dead person, in the gen. case)

    Flaviae Dionysiadis gen. of *Flavia Dionysiae*, the dead girl's name, acknowledging her Greek ancestry with a Greek form of her name. The Greek god Dionysus, for whom Dionysia was named, was associated with both tragic and comic drama; the language of this inscription emphasizes these Dionysian literary connections.

2   **exiguis . . . annis** abl. of description, "of few years"

    flebilis "to be wept for, worthy of tears." The Roman love poets Catullus, Tibullus, and Ovid use this adj. in their elegiac verses and even associate it with Latin elegiac poetry itself. It is associated with tragedy as well.

3   **extremum . . . quae . . . rupit iter** "who forced her way though her final passage"

    tenui . . . pede "with delicate step." Roman love poets also employ the adj. *tenuis* to characterize both physical features of the women they love, and Latin elegiac poetry.

4   **in octava . . . messe** "in whose eighth year." *Messis*, "harvest," here used as a metaphor for *annus*, carries connotations of fertility and growth; its use underscores the "tragic irony" of the girl's death at such an early age.

    lascivia "sexual playfulness," the subject of *coeperat*. It governs both the infinitive *surgere* in this line and *fingere* in the following. The related adj. *lascivus* frequently appears in elegiac love poetry, and is even employed by the first-century CE oratorical authority Quintilian to characterize the love poetry of Ovid.

5 **dulces . . . nequitias** "sweet moments, instances of naughtiness." The sing., *nequitia*, occurs several times in Latin love poetry; the late first-century CE poet Martial employs the term, in the pl., to characterize his own erotic poems.

5-6 **quod si longa . . . mansissent tempora . . . nulla puella foret** mixed contrary to fact condition, with *mansissent*, the verb in the protasis/if-clause, in the plpf. subjunctive ("But if long periods of time . . . had remained") and *foret* (= *futura esset*), the verb in the apodosis/main clause, in the impf., with a fut. act. pple. ("no girl would be [on the verge of becoming] more learned").

tuae . . . vitae Note the use of a second person sing. possessive adj. for Dionysia, who is elsewhere referred to in the third person.

7 **doctior** compar. of *doctus, -a, -um*, another adj. used for both the women celebrated in Latin love elegy and for love elegy itself

8 **m. XI** "for eleven months"

9 **b. m.** *beatae memoriae*, "of blessed memory"

7 Suetonius, DIVUS JULIUS 6

Julius Caesar pays tribute to a noble kinswoman and divorces a wife suspected of improper conduct

In his life of the illustrious Roman military and political leader Julius Caesar (100–44 BCE), the early second century CE biographer Gaius Suetonius Tranquillus, known to us as Suetonius, documents the significant roles played by various women in Caesar's rise to political power. Some of them were his blood relations, others were his wives and lovers. Chapter 6, for example, quotes an excerpt from a eulogy that Caesar delivered in 67 BCE when his father's sister Julia died; it then tersely summarizes the details of why Caesar's second marriage to Pompeia ended in divorce five years later. Suetonius discusses the speech in honor of Caesar's aunt and the reasons for Caesar's divorce of Pompeia, because both the speech and the divorce advanced Caesar's political career.

By calling attention to his family's distinguished ancestors when he eulogized his father's sister, Caesar burnished his own political credentials and strengthened his own claims to leadership. That Caesar promoted himself in this way at the funeral of a female relative and did so by mentioning her mother's as well as her father's forebears, documents the importance of maternal as well as paternal ancestry among Roman nobles and the importance of Roman noblewomen themselves as public representatives of their families. It warrants note that the Julian family to which Caesar and his paternal aunt belonged also included the maternal ancestors of Mark Antony, the man remembered for delivering Caesar's own eulogy. Indeed, the name of Antony's youngest son by Fulvia, Iullus Antonius, who was born in 43 BCE, soon after Julius Caesar's death, celebrated his father's maternal Julian lineage.

The brief portion of Caesar's eulogy quoted by Suetonius does not indicate that Julia was married to a man who wielded great political power in Rome: the general and statesman Gaius Marius (157–86 BCE). Perhaps this was because he did not wish to detract from the very distinguished pedigree of Julia's and his own family, although he did include in the procession symbols of Marius' victories, which had been outlawed by Sulla in 88 BCE. Nor does Suetonius mention Caesar's connection with Marius in the earlier chapters of this biography, although he may well have done so in the beginning portion, which is lost. But the passage is distinctive for its style as well as its sentiments, using a series of carefully balanced phrases to describe Julia's ancestry on both sides as equally illustrious.

The *Life of Julius Caesar* by Suetonius' Greek contemporary Plutarch elaborates on the circumstances surrounding Caesar's divorce from Pompeia in 62 BCE. Like Suetonius, Plutarch relates that Caesar ended the marriage because he suspected Pompeia of adultery with Publius Clodius Pulcher. Plutarch also reports that Clodius gained admission to the all-female rites of the Bona Dea, Good Goddess, by disguising himself in women's clothes; he observes as well that the Roman senate decreed that Clodius' violation of these rites be judicially investigated.

But Plutarch provides a number of additional details: that these rites took place in Caesar's own house; that Clodius sneaked in because he had erotic designs on Pompeia; and that, although Pompeia was never found guilty of any sexual misconduct, Caesar justified his decision to terminate their marriage on the grounds that "Caesar's wife must be above suspicion." Plutarch's lengthier account of this episode, like Suetonius' statement here, and like the passage from Plautus' comic *Casina* presented earlier, testifies to the ease with which Roman husbands could and did divorce their wives for displeasing them. Both Suetonius and Plutarch make it clear that Pompeia was a political liability to Caesar because of her blemished moral reputation.

1   **quaestor** when holding the office of quaestor, supervisor of financial affairs, in 67 BCE

     uxorem Corneliam Caesar's first wife Cornelia, daughter of Lucius Cornelius Cinna, consul from 87 to 84 BCE. She was the mother of his daughter and only child, Julia. Cinna, an ally of Marius, became the leading power in Rome after Marius' death.

2   **defunctas** modifies both *Iuliam amitam* and *uxoremque Corneliam*.

     e more "according to custom." Women had received *laudationes funebres*, publicly presented funeral orations, since 102 BCE when Lutatus Catulus (consul in 78) gave a public oration over his mother.

     pro rostris "from the rostrum," platform for public speakers in the Roman Forum

2-3 **et in amitae quidem laudatione** "indeed, in the funeral oration for his paternal aunt"

3-4 **de . . . utra . . . origine** "about . . . the ancestry on each side, paternal and maternal"

3   **eius ac patris sui** "her (Julia's) and his own father's"

4   **sic refert** "recalled in the following manner." A historical pres. tense imagines past events as happening before our eyes.

4–5   **maternum genus** "the family . . . on her mother's side"

5   **ortum** = *ortum est*, "arose, was descended from"

    regibus From its founding in 753 BCE to the establishment of the republic in 510 BCE, the city of Rome was ruled by a series of seven kings.

    paternum understand *paternum genus*.

    diis = *deis*

6   **coniunctum** carries connotations of being joined in marriage, as in the noun *coniunx*, and linked to the gods.

6–7   **ab Anco Marcio sunt** "are descended from Ancus Marcius," Rome's fourth king, who is said to have ruled from 642 to 617 BCE, proof of the family's royal connections going back to the early history of Rome

7   **Marcii Reges, quo nomine fuit mater** "the Marcii Reges, which was the family name of her mother"

7–8   **a Venere Iulii, cuius gentis familia est nostra** "The Iulii, a group of kin of which our family is a member, are descended from Venus." *Gentis* is attracted into the gen. case by the rel. pron. *cuius*, but should be in the nom., in apposition to the noun *Iulii*. Here Caesar again reminds the audience of his family's exceedingly distinguished origins, claiming a goddess as ancestor.

8   **in genere** "in our lineage"

9–10   **plurimum . . . pollent** "are extremely powerful"

10   **caerimonia** "reverence"

10–11   **quorum . . . in potestate** "in whose power"

12   **in Corneliae . . . locum** "in place of Cornelia," "to replace Cornelia"

    duxit = *in matrimonium duxit*

13 **Quinti Pompei filiam, L. Sullae neptem** Pompeia's father was Quintus Pompeius Rufus, who was murdered in the Roman Forum by supporters of the dictator Gaius Marius in 88 BCE; her grandfather was Marius' foe, the dictator Lucius Sulla. Roman senators usually chose wives with an eye to creating useful political associations. Despite his connections with Marius by marriage, it may seem Caesar also wanted to create connections to the opposing side.

14–16 **adulteratam opinatus a Publio Clodio** "having thought that she had been compromised in adultery by Publius Clodius." *Opinatus*: pf. act. pple. of deponent *opinor*, governing the indirect statement *adulteratam* [*esse*].

quem inter publicas caerimonias penetrasse ad eam . . . fama erat "whom a rumor . . . claimed to have made his way to her during public religious rites." *Quem . . . penetrasse* is an indirect statement governed by *fama erat*, with Clodius, represented by the rel. pron. *quem*, as its subject. *Penetrasse* is a syncopated form of the pf. act. infinitive *penetravisse*, "to have penetrated," a verb with sexual connotations that implies that Clodius was thought to have physically entered Pompeia's body.

16 **muliebri veste** abl. of description

17–18 **tam constans fama erat, ut senatus . . . decreverit** result clause in secondary sequence "triggered" by the adv. *tam*; note the use of the pf. subjunctive to emphasize that the senate actually issued this decree.

18 **de pollutis sacris** literally "about the sacred rites that had been defiled"

∾ 8 Cicero, PRO CAELIO 33–36; AD ATTICUM 12.38a and 42, excerpts

Cicero on Clodia Metelli

Cicero, Pro Caelio 33–36

In 56 BCE Marcus Caelius Rufus, an up-and-coming Roman politician and protégé of Cicero's, found himself charged with *vis*, political violence, in the aftermath of a lawsuit he had unsuccessfully brought against another politician on a charge of bribery. The charges leveled against Caelius related to his alleged involvement in incidents connected to an attempt, by Ptolemy Auletes, king of Egypt, to regain his throne with the help of the Roman Senate. A delegation of Alexandrians had come to Rome to oppose Auletes; the leader of the delegation, Dio, an Academic philosopher, was then murdered there in 57 BCE. There were five different charges against Caelius in this complicated case—the fifth that he had tried to poison the aristocratic Clodia Metelli to hide the fact that he had borrowed money from her when he was trying to kill Dio.

The trial took place on April 3 and 4, 56 BCE. The prosecution presented its case on the first day; on the second day, speakers for the defense—Caelius himself and Crassus—gave a rebuttal. Cicero was the third to speak on Caelius' behalf, confronting the issues in the fourth and fifth charges: that he had made an independent attempt on Dio's life; and that he had poisoned and borrowed money from Clodia. Cicero faced several challenges: first, that April 4 happened to be the first day of the *Ludi Megalenses*, a Roman holiday when the many members of the jury as well as the bystanders would have preferred to be enjoying entertainment that included theatrical performances. Secondly, Caelius may indeed have been guilty of some of the charges or at least connected with those who were.

Cicero's solution was not to make the focus of the case the charges themselves, but to concentrate on Clodia, the individual whom he claims was behind them, and to persuade the jury that her jealous desire for revenge after being abandoned by Caelius was the reason for the lawsuit. Cicero turned his legal defense into a form of entertainment for the crowd, and relied heavily on comic technique to achieve its successful outcome, adapting from comedy and mime stock characters such as the stern father, the wayward son, and the sexually tempting older woman. Caelius was acquitted. Of Cicero's many extant speeches, the *Pro Caelio* was recognized in antiquity and is still recognized today as one of his greatest triumphs.

Clodia Metelli has been identified as one of three daughters of Appius Claudius Pulcher, consul in 79, and thus as belonging to a renowned aristocratic Roman family, with a long history of political influence and visibility. Married to her cousin, Quintus Metellus Celer (consul in 60), she was widowed in 59. A sister of P. Clodius Pulcher, notorious popular leader and arch enemy of Cicero (see **Reading 7**), each chose to spell their family name as Clodius, rather than Claudius. She is also believed to be the "Lesbia" addressed in many of Catullus' poems; three of his poems, 58A, 69, and 77, also mention a Caelius, representing him as another of Lesbia's lovers. Nevertheless, neither Catullus' poetry nor Cicero's *Pro Caelio* provides much reliable evidence about what the actual Clodia Metelli was like. As Marilyn Skinner has observed, however, scattered references to her in Cicero's letters furnish a more balanced portrait, suggesting a woman of wide social contacts and considerable political acumen who was capable of managing her own substantial financial resources ("Clodia Metelli," pp. 283–87).

Chapters 33–34

In this section Cicero uses a rhetorical device known as *prosopopeia*, in which someone imagined or absent is called upon to speak, giving the prosecuting lawyer a wonderful opportunity to perform, as it were, by taking on the voice and gestures of the character he is impersonating. This device also allows the prosecutor to distance himself from the verbal attack, in this case aimed at a noble woman from a very distinguished family. Presented as a series of indignant rhetorical questions directed at Clodia, the persona of Appius Claudius Caecus sets the stage for Cicero's destruction of her character and credibility. As a severely moralistic representative of the Roman past and a former censor, Caecus was a very appropriate choice on Cicero's part to chastise his "modern" descendant, since Cicero alleges that her behavior runs totally counter to that expected of her gender and class. Using a member of her own family to reprimand Clodia is also a clever tactic on Cicero's part, since Romans expected that female misbehavior would be punished by male relatives.

Near the end of this section Caecus compares Clodia to two famous female ancestors, the virtuous Quinta Claudia, renowned for her chaste reputation, and the Vestal Virgin Claudia.

1–2   **ipsa** refers to Clodia.

      prius adv., "first; first of all"

      utrum . . . an introduces a double indirect question with the subjunctive ("whether . . . or"), dependent on *quaeram.*

      me acc. subject of the complementary infinitive *agere* ("deal with"), dependent on *malit*

2–3   **severe et graviter et prisce . . . remisse et leniter et urbane** Note the contrast between the sets of triplet adverbs. The second set, placed in the most emphatic position at the end of the sentence, describe frivolous activity and by implication are associated with Clodia and her social set. Romans of Cicero's day placed a premium on austere values, as they were supposedly practiced in the simpler past.

3–4   **aliquis . . . excitandus est** pass. periphrastic with a dat. of agent, *mihi*

      ex barbatis Take with *aliquis.*

4–5   **non hac barbula** abl. of description or quality, "a little beard." Elegant young men in the late Republic wore carefully trimmed beards, rather than full beards, as in earlier times. This rare diminutive form of the noun has a pejorative sense to it.

5   **qua** abl. of means with *delectatur.* Cicero cannot resist drawing Clodia into the picture in a very unseemly way. The verb is suggestive of inappropriate and unsavory behavior.

ista a pejorative way in which to refer to Clodia. *Iste* is used to refer to one's opponent in court and implies antagonism or contempt.

horrida Supply *barba* ("bushy, shaggy"); take as parallel with *non hac barbula.*

6-7 **qui obiurget . . . et qui . . . loquatur** rel. clauses of purpose ("to . . .")

7-8 **ne. . . suscenseat** subjunctive in a negative clause of purpose

7 **mihi** dat. with the compound verb *suscenseat*

8 **exsistat** jussive subjunctive, "Let . . . rise from the dead"

9 **potissimum** adv., "above all, and especially"

Caecus Appius Claudius Caecus, a very well-known and re-vered ancestor of Clodia, was censor in 312 and consul in 307 and 296 BCE. Caecus' accomplishments, to which Cicero will later allude, included building the Via Appia, and the Aqua Appia, Rome's first aqueduct, and also rejecting Pyrrhus' of-fer of peace in 280 (see end of Chapter 34).

ille "famous, well-known," when *ille* follows the noun it modifies

10 **qui . . . videbit** "since . . . ." As his cognomen, Caecus, sug-gests, he was blind.

qui = *is*: coordinating rel. ("he")

profecto adv., "indeed, in fact"

10-11 **si exstiterit, . . . aget . . . loquetur** fut. more vivid condition

11-12 **quid tibi cum . . .** Supply *est* (literally "what is there to you with . . . ; what do you have to do with . . . ?"). The expression is colloquial, taken from the spoken language.

12 **adulescentulo** diminutive, "very young man; a mere youth." This does not reflect on Caelius' actual age as much as it draws a contrast between him and the "older" woman, Clodia.

13 **alieno** "a stranger" (not a man from her own family). The trip-let prepositional phrases with *cum* make the forceful point that Clodia's association with Caelius is very inappropriate because of his youth and the fact that he is not a male relative.

13-14   **ut ... commodares ... ut timeres** parallel result clauses, preceded by parallel antithetical adj. phrases (*aut tam familiaris ... aut tam inimica*). The implication is that in either case Clodia's association with Caelius is improper.

aurum ... venenum charges that Cicero alleges were brought by Clodia against Caelius: that he had tried to poison her to cover up the fact he had borrowed money from her when trying to kill Dio, head of the embassy from Alexandria

17   **consules** With a series of rhetorical questions, anaphora (repetition of the initial word in a phrase), and asyndeton (lack of connective), Caecus reminds Clodia about the great nobility of her family, whose male members had held the consulship in every generation.

17-18   **te ... tenuisse** acc. and infinitive dependent on *sciebas*. Note Cicero's effective use of triplet verbs: *videras*, *audieras*, and *sciebas* with parallel constructions to suggest that Clodia was well aware of her illustrious family connections but chose to behave in a way that did not accord with expectations for a female of her standing.

17   **modo** adv., "recently"

Q. Metelli After Clodia's husband, Quintus Metellus Celer, also a well-known politician, had died suddenly in 59 BCE, there were rumors that she had poisoned him (*Pro Caelio* 59–60). Cicero throws Metellus' name into high relief by placing it before the noun *matrimonium* on which it depends (hyperbaton), and also juxtaposing it with *te*. Additionally, the two superl. adjectives that describe *viri*, a noun in apposition to *Metelli*, are also placed before that noun.

18-19   **matrimonium tenuisse** takes the gen. ("have been the spouse of ...; have been married to ..."). It can be interpreted as both the subject and the object of the pf. act. infinitive *tenuisse*.

clarissimi ... fortissimi ... amantissimi genitives, modifying *viri*

19   **simul ac** "as soon as"

20   **prope** adv. ("nearly"). Modifies the adj., *omnis*, which modi-
      fies the noun *civis*; both are acc. plurals.

20–21 **virtute, gloria, dignitate** abl. of respect. The lack of connec-
      tives (asyndeton) emphasizes these values, which were of high-
      est importance to male members of Roman noble families.

21–22 **in familiam . . . nupsisses** < *nubo in* + acc., "marry into a
      family"

23   **coniunctus** "closely associated"

      cognatus, adfinis, . . . familiaris "a relative, a relative by mar-
      riage, a friend . . ." The triplet adjectives used as nouns with no
      connectives (asyndeton) imply that Clodia had no legitimate
      reason to be associating with Caelius.

24–25 **temeritas ac libido** "reckless passion," literally "recklessness
      and passion," an instance of hendiadys (two nouns in place of
      an adj. and a noun). These are damning words that emphasize
      the sexual nature of Clodia's relationship with Caelius.

25–30 **nonne . . . passa non est** This long rhetorical question intro-
      duces two female ancestors of Clodia as examples of coura-
      geous and virtuous female behavior. The asyndeton between
      the two halves of the sentence emphasizes the point.

25   **imagines** Roman wax funerary masks of the male ancestors
      who had held office as censor, consul, praetor, or aedile that
      were displayed in the atrium of a Roman house

25–28 **te . . . aemulam . . . esse** acc. subject of the infinitive with
      an indirect statement dependent on *admonebat* ("advise;
      suggest")

26–27 **Q. . . . Claudia** an illustrious ancestor of Clodia, daughter or
      perhaps granddaughter of Caecus, who was renowned for her
      chastity, piety, and courage. At *Fasti* 4.291 ff. the Augustan
      poet Ovid tells how, in 204 BCE, this Claudia was falsely ac-
      cused of immoral behavior, and prayed to the great mother
      goddess Cybele for a sign of her innocence. With the goddess'
      help she was able to free the ship bearing the statue of the god-
      dess to Rome when it got mired in a sandbar at Tiber island.

The Megalensia, Rome's festival in honor of the Magna Mater, was being celebrated during the very days of the trial; it has been suggested that the festivities there would have included a reenactment of Q. Claudia's miraculous moving of the ship.

27–28   **in gloria muliebri** "in the sphere of womanly glory." Noble Roman males and females achieved a high reputation in totally different ways. The moral reputation of a noblewoman was based largely on her display of chaste behavior.

28–29   **Vestalis Claudia** yet another formidable female ancestor of Claudia, a Vestal Virgin, who protected her father, Appius Claudius Pulcher, consul in 143, during his triumph, when an opposing tribune tried to pull him from his chariot. Both females in these moral *exempla* are remarkable for their *pudicitia*, moral chastity, and thus provide a striking contrast to what Cicero would have us believe about Clodia.

29–31   **complexa** < *complector*: pf. act. pple. modifying *Claudia*

triumphantem Take with *patrem,* acc. subject of the infinitive *detrahi.*

detrahi pres. pass. infinitive. Take with *passa non est.*

31–33   **te** direct object of *moverunt*

fraterna vitia "your brother's vices." Cicero is referring to P. Clodius Pulcher, whose lifestyle and behavior, as a maverick politician, were notorious in this period. *Fraterna* is placed in an emphatic position, before the noun that it modifies, in a figure of speech called hyperbaton, and juxtaposed with *te.* Both Clodius and Clodia spelled their family name with an *o* rather than an *au* for reasons that are not entirely clear. Jeffrey Tatum has attributed the spelling to a fad in the fashionable social set to which they belonged (*Publius Clodius Pulcher,* 247–48).

32   **a nobis** "from our time." That is, Caecus' time. Cicero confronts Clodia with a large number of male and female behavioral role models going back to the venerable Caecus.

cum . . . tum "not only . . . but also"

33   **repetita** < *repeto*: pf. pass. pple., modifying *bona*. Translate the whole phrase as "the virtues of your father and ancestors, repeated continuously from our time not only among the men but also especially among the women."

33-37   **ideone . . . celebrares** In this carefully constructed sentence, culminating in a tricolon, Cicero makes the case that each of Appius Caecus' great accomplishments has been put to disreputable and shameful use by Clodia.

     ideone = *ideo* (+ *ne*), "Was it for this . . . ?"

     Pyrrhi king of Epirus and Macedon, one of Rome's most formidable enemies in the third century BCE. His name gave rise to the expression "Pyrrhic victory," because several of his victories were so costly that they might as well have been defeats.

34   **diremi** < *dirimo*: "break up, end"

     amorum gen. with *foedera*. English would use "with," another instance of hyperbaton.

34-35   **foedera ferires** "strike treaties or agreements." Cicero, continuing the political imagery from the earlier part of the sentence, refers to Clodia's arrangements with her many lovers. The alliteration draws attention to the brutal nature of the charge—that the aristocratic Clodia is nothing more than a common prostitute. While Cicero only hints at that characterization here, he will later accuse her outright of selling her sexual favors.

35   **ut** introduces a series of parallel result clauses.

     ea abl. sing. referring back to *aquam*

     inceste "unchastely." Brunn (368) interprets this remark as a reference to the practice in this period of brothels illegally siphoning off water from the city's water supply. Cicero continues to insinuate that Clodia is behaving like a prostitute. *Inceste* may perhaps also cause listeners to think of the gossip to which Cicero alluded earlier about Clodia's "relationship" with her brother Clodius.

uterere = *utereris*: impf. subjunctive, second person sing.; takes the abl. case.

36   **eam** refers back to *viam*.

alienis "belonging to other women"

viris abl. dependent on *comitata*

comitata pf. pple. modifying *tu*. Yet another reference to Clodia behaving a common prostitute plying her trade on the street.

Chapter 35

This section serves as a bridge passage between the first impersonation, that of Appius Claudius Caecus, and the second, that of Clodius Pulcher, Clodia's brother.

Cicero begins by anticipating that the severe Appius Claudius Caecus might rightly attack Caelius' life style, stating that later in the speech he will be able to justify Caelius' life to even the severest critic. He then turns to a vicious assault on Clodia's immoral behavior, implying that she is no better than a prostitute.

38   **quid** "why"

38-39   **personam induxi** These are technical words connected with the theater; *persona*, for example, can refer to an actor in a play; *induxi* = "bring on the stage."

39   **ut verear** subjunctive in a result clause, dependent on *ita . . . induxi*

39-40   **ne . . . convertat et . . . incipiat** subjunctives in a clause dependent on a verb of fearing, *verear* ("that")

40-41   **illa sua gravitate censoria** abl. of means. Cicero will spend some time shortly in the speech (Chapters 39–42) making the case that Caelius' youthful indiscretions were just what one would expect of a young man sowing his wild oats, especially with a woman of Clodia's reputation. Such behavior could be forgiven in the case of a young man.

41   **videro** "I will see to"

42-43   **ut . . . confidam** subjunctive in a result clause dependent on
        ita . . . videro

        vel "even"

        me probaturum esse acc. and infinitive dependent on
        confidam

43   **tu vero, mulier** Cicero now puts aside his role as Appius Cae-
        cus and addresses Clodia brutally and directly, using the fig-
        ure of speech called apostrophe. Note that he does not use her
        name but calls her *mulier*, "woman," which may contrast with
        his hints that she is really a *meretrix*, a woman who sells her
        sexual favors.

44   **nulla . . . introducta** abl. absolute

44-46   **si . . . cogitas** "if you are deciding to . . . ; are intending to . . ."

45   **ea** direct object of *probare*

45-46   **quae . . . arguis** five parallel rel. clauses with asyndeton ("what
        you are doing; your actions" etc.). The use of verbs, rather
        than nouns here, emphasizes Clodius' active involvement in
        the situation.

47-48   **familiaritatis . . . consuetudinis . . . coniunctionis** triplet
        genitives dependent on *rationem*. The force of the message is
        emphasized by asyndeton and the repetition of *tantae* with
        each of the three nouns. Latin uses the gen. here ("the reason
        for such intimacy . . .").

48   **reddas . . . exponas** subjunctives with *necesse est* (*ut* is often
        omitted with this expression)

49-51   **libidines . . . navigia** accusatives, direct objects of *iactant*
        ("keep mentioning, keep bringing up"). The asyndeton em-
        phasizes the dissolute activities associated with the good life
        that Clodia and her friends enjoyed at such places as the fash-
        ionable seaside resort of Baiae on the bay of Naples, which had
        the reputation as a place for unseemly behavior. The list of pl.
        nouns is damning.

51   **idem** nom. pl. m., refers back to *accusatores*

52   **se . . . dicere** acc. and infinitive dependent on *significant*

        te invita abl. absolute ("against your will")

        quae = *ea*, coordinating rel., referring back to the list above
        (*libidines* etc.); acc. subject of the infinitive, *deferri*

52–53   **mente . . . praecipiti** abl. of circumstance

52   **nescio . . . qua** modifies *mente* ("with I don't know what;
        some")

53   **effrenata** pf. pass. pple. modifying *mente*

54   **voluisti** The fifth charge against Caelius was his attempt-
        ed poisoning of Clodia. In his speech Cicero tries to make
        the case that Clodia was mainly responsible for the charges
        against Caelius in revenge for having been abandoned by
        him.

54–56   **diluas . . . doceas . . . fateare** Take with the impersonal *opor-
        tet. Ut* is often omitted with this verb.

54   **falsa esse** Supply *ea*, as the acc. subject, in an acc. and infini-
        tive dependent on *doceas*.

55–56   **nihil . . . credendum esse** acc. and infinitive (pass. periphras-
        tic) dependent on *fateare* (literally "that nothing must be be-
        lieved to be true; that no trust must be placed in")

55   **crimini . . . testimonio** dat. dependent on *credendum esse*

Chapter 36

Cicero now conjures up a second witness against Clodia, her own
brother, P. Clodius Pulcher. Since 61 BCE Cicero and Clodius had
been political rivals and were on very bad terms. The contrast between Appius Claudius Pulcher and Clodius could not be greater—
Caecus as a representative of the severe past reproves Clodia for her
unchaste behavior; the flamboyant Clodius encourages her scandalous behavior, reproving her for making such a big deal over Caelius'
abandonment of her. Clodius' introduction also allows Cicero to hint
at rumors of incest between brother and sister.

COMMENTARY READING 8   93

At *Institutio Oratoria* 11.1.39, the later rhetorical authority Quintilian notes that Cicero would have portrayed Caecus as a cranky old man, Clodius in quite a different way. Since the jurors and audience would have known Clodius' manner of speaking and presenting himself, this must have been quite a theatrical feat on Cicero's part.

57   **urbanius** compar. adv., "in a more sophisticated fashion." This word is repeated as a superl. adj., *urbanissimus*, at the end of its clause to characterize Clodius in a highly pejorative way.

At *Institutio Oratoria* 11.1.39, the later rhetorical authority Quintilian notes that Cicero would have portrayed Caecus as a cranky old man, Clodius in quite a different way. Since the jurors and audience would have known Clodius' manner of speaking and presenting himself, this must have been quite a theatrical feat on Cicero's part.

57   **urbanius** compar. adv., "in a more sophisticated fashion." This word is repeated as a superl. adj., *urbanissimus*, at the end of its clause to characterize Clodius in a highly pejorative way.

      me agere acc. and infinitive dependent on *mavis* ("proceed, pursue a course of action")

      mavis second person sing. pres. indicative of *malo*

59   **agrestem** The point is that Appius Caecus from the remote past lacks the sophistication of the modern set that Clodia and her brother represent.

      ex his "from these (modern young men)"

      sumam fut. tense, first person

      ac potissimum "especially"

60   **qui** = *is*: coordinating rel., referring back to *fratrem*

      in isto genere "in that kind of thing"

61   **amat** a verb chosen to suggest the ugly rumors about Clodius and Clodia to which Cicero has alluded earlier

      nescio quam modifies *timiditatem* ("I don't know what; some").

63   **pusio** a colloquial word; nom. sing. in apposition to *qui* ("a little squirt"). Quintilian (*Instituto Oratia*, 8.3.21) notes how effectively Cicero used this word from ordinary speech to carry off a joke and hence add force to what he was saying about the relationship between Clodius and his older sister.

64   **cubitabat** This verb can be taken at a literal and also a more suggestive level. Here Cicero is alluding to rumors of an incestuous relationship between Clodia and her brother—earlier in the speech he had called him her husband, then apologized for what he said was a slip of the tongue!

eum ... loqui acc. and infinitive dependent on *putato*

putato second person sing. fut. imperative, "consider; imagine." The fut. imperative inflates the rhetoric, as if this were an epic situation that is being played out.

66–67   **quid ... facis** Cicero is quoting a line from some unknown comic poet.

67–73   **vicinum ... alio** This short series of sentences with no connectives (asyndeton) allows Cicero, using Clodius as the narrator, to relate his version of what happened between Clodia and Caelius in a rapid and devastating fashion. The initial verbs are in the second person sing. (underlining Clodia's role in initiating and then trying to maintain the relationship); three verbs then refer to her in the third person sing. (describing how Caelius tries to get away); the last verb is in the imperative, in effect telling Clodia to try her chances elsewhere. The power of the narrative is heightened by its telling in the pres. tense.

67   **aspexisti** < *aspicio*: "catch a glimpse of; catch sight of." Caelius at some point had moved to the Palatine hill, renting some rooms from Clodius (*Pro Caelio* 18). Apparently Clodia's villa with its gardens (*horti*) was next door.

adulescentulum The use of the diminutive is not meant to suggest Caelius' extreme youth but to contrast his age with that of Clodia. He is the innocent young man, pursued by the older, experienced woman.

68   **candor huius te et proceritas** The two nouns enclosing *huius* and *te* mirror the connection made between the pair, Caelius and Clodia, and the reason for the connection!

69   **pepulerunt** < *pello*: "impressed; struck a chord in"

69–70   **non numquam** "sometimes"

70   **vis** < *volo*: second person sing. pres.

nobilis mulier nom. in apposition to the subject of *vis*, "you." The use of the adj. *nobilis* in an emphatic position before its noun reminds us how totally inappropriate Clodia's behavior is for a woman of her social class.

71-72   **filium . . . habere . . . devinctum** "to hold the son . . . bound"

71   **familias** archaic gen. sing. Take with *patre*.

     habere complimentary infinitive with *vis*

72-73   **calcitrat, respuit, repellit, non putat** asyndeton. Caelius' rejection of Lesbia is depicted by three powerful verbs, and by a clause that suggests that money was the major reason for Caelius' initial interest in her; all of these charges are of course devastating to Clodia's image as a respectable Roman matron.

73   **tanti** gen. of price or value

     confer second person sing. imperative

     alio adv., "elsewhere; to a different person"

74   **ac diligenter . . . paratos** The suggestion is that Clodia had deliberately arranged to have gardens where young men could come to bathe ("and in fact . . ."). In short, Clodia will not have any trouble finding other young men with whom to have an illicit relationship.

75   **condiciones** "assignations; love affairs"

76   **legas** subjunctive dependent on *licet. Ut* is often omitted with this verb.

     huic dat. with the adj. *molesta*. Refers to Caelius.

Cicero nows turns to Caelius and begins the task of excusing his behavior, making the case that a certain allowance needs to be made for youthful indiscretions.

Cicero, *Ad Atticum* 12.38a and 42, excerpts

After his daughter Tullia's untimely death at age thirty-one in February 45 BCE, Cicero grieved deeply for her. His letters to Atticus show that as early as March of that year he had conceived of the idea of setting up a shrine (*fanum*) in her honor that would lead to deification (*apotheosis*). His friend Atticus was serving as his broker for this project and references to his plans for securing an appropriate property where he could build the shrine but also live himself are a recurrent theme through June. Among the several property owners whom Cicero deemed as having suitable and perhaps available property was Clodia (there are eight references to her in letters from this period). As the passage from the *Pro Caelio* shows, some eleven years earlier Cicero and Clodia had engaged in a bitter adversarial relationship. In these letters, however, it is interesting to note that Cicero treats her as any other property owner with whom he might engage in negotiations to purchase property. In a subsequent letter Cicero expresses the hope that he might buy from her directly, rather than through auction.

Born in 106 BCE of an equestrian family, Cicero went on to enjoy a highly successful legal career in Rome, as well as a political career that culminated in the consulship in 63. One of the larger-than-life players in the last years of the Republic, Cicero has left us a rich treasure trove of writing: legal speeches, rhetorical works, philosophical works, and a large collection of letters with friends, family, and his life-long friend Atticus. The letters, over nine hundred in all, provide an extraordinary record of the period from 68 to July 43. They also give us an intimate look into Cicero's life, his hopes, fears, and concerns on a personal and political level.

Cicero, *Ad Atticum* 12.38a

Dated 7 May, 45 BCE

1   **sal.** = *salutem*. Supply *dat.*

2   **heredes** nom. subject of *cogitant*

    Scapulae the owner of one of the properties in which Cicero was interested. Scapula had apparently recently died and the property awaited distribution among four heirs. It was this property among all the possibilities that Cicero wanted to acquire.

3   **Othonem** one of Scapula's heirs

    partibus . . . factis abl. absolute

    liceri pres. infinitive of the deponent verb *liceor*, "to make a bid for"

4   **loci** partitive gen. with *nihil*

venibunt < *veneo,* "go to sale, put up for sale"

5   **fieri** pres. pass. infinitive of *facio*

locus Publicianus "piece of property belonging to Publicius"

6   **Treboni et Cusini** dat. of possession. C. Trebonius is a Roman politician and military leader of this period, one of the friends of Julius Caesar who later plotted against him. M. Cusinius, a lesser known politican of this period, was praetor in 44 BCE.

erat . . . adlatus (< *adfero*) "had been offered for sale"

7   **aream esse** acc. and infinitive dependent on *scis*

nullo pacto "by no means"

Clodiae Supply *horti.* Scholars have concluded that this Clodia is indeed Clodia Metelli and not one of her sisters (Shackleton Bailey, 412–13).

8   **venalis** acc. pl. modifying the understood *hortos* or some such word standing for "property"

8–9   **quamvis . . . abhorreas** The concessive particle *quamvis* takes the subjunctive. Apparently Atticus had mentioned in one his letters that he did not care for Drusus' property.

9   **eo** adv., "there." Cicero means that as a last resort this property will do.

10   **quid** "something else"

inveneris fut. pf., expressing time before some other action in the fut.

aedificatio "the act of building, building"

movet "disturb, bother"

10–12 **nihil . . . habuero** "For I will build nothing else except that which I shall build in any case, even if I don't have those gardens."

11   **quod etiam** Supply *aedificabo.*

etiam "in any case"

illos Supply *hortos.* Cicero means that the shrine to Tullia is the one thing he is interested in building.

Cicero, *Ad Atticum* 12.42

Dated 10 May, 45 BCE

2   **scripsi\<sti\>** The brackets indicate an editor's correction to the manuscript. The context suggests that the sentence refers to a statement Atticus made, not Cicero.

tamen Cicero says earlier in this letter that he had just gotten a letter from Atticus with no news in it but that it was still pleasurable to get a letter.

nescio quid "I don't know what; something or other"

3   **ventura** Supply *est*. The fut. pple. with the verb *esse* is an alternative form of the fut. tense (act. periphrastic). Apparently Clodia has been out of Rome.

res "her property"

3–4 **ut . . . nihil magis** "above all"

4–5 **hanc vendituram (esse)** acc. and infinitive dependent on *puto*

5   **delectatur** pres. pass., "takes pleasure in, enjoys"

6   **illud alterum** subject of the verb *sit*. Refers no doubt to the difficulties involved in buying the other properties in which Cicero was interested; several different letters in this period detail the issues.

quam sit difficile subjunctive in an indirect question, subject of the verb *non fugit*

7   **enitamur** hortatory subjunctive

aliquid ad id "some means to accomplish that goal"

quod cupio Cicero is very intent in getting the shrine built for Tullia, which, he says in a later letter, he is determined to get done during the summer. Unfortunately it would seem that Cicero was never able to accomplish this task. Julius Caesar's designs for a massive building project in the Campus Vaticanus, where the Scapula property was situated, put a stop to Cicero's plans, just before the auction on Scapula's property took place (Shackleton Bailey, 411). Subsequently there is only

one more reference in the letters to the shrine, which seems
to indicate that the project was no longer under consideration
(*Ad Atticus* 15.15.3).

∾ 9 Cicero, PHILIPPICS 2.77–78, 5.11, 6.4; CORPUS INSCRIPTIONUM LATINARUM XI.6721.305.14; Martial 11.20

Attacks on the Roman noblewoman Fulvia

The Roman noblewoman Fulvia (ca. 77–40 BCE)—wife in turn of the
demagogue Publius Clodius Pulcher (on whom see **Readings 7 and
8**), Clodius' friend Gaius Scribonius Curio, and the triumvir Marcus
Antonius (whom we call Mark Antony)—resembled her sister-in-law
Clodia in several important respects. Both were wealthy, cultured,
socially independent, and politically influential. But Fulvia was also
involved in military affairs, joining her brother-in-law Lucius Antonius and Antony's agent Manius to wage war at Perusia in 41 BCE
against Antony's fellow triumvir Octavian, who would later become
the emperor Augustus.

A variety of ancient sources from long after Fulvia's lifetime portray her as masculine and emasculating, vindictive and cruel. Over
fifty years after she died, the Roman historian Velleius Paterculus
described her at 2.74 as *nihil muliebre praeter corpus gerens*, "bearing nothing female about her except for her body." In his biography
of Antony, which postdates Fulvia's death by a century and a half, the
Greek writer Plutarch characterized her as a woman "who desired to
govern those who governed and to command a commander-in-chief."
Two hundred years after her death, Cassius Dio claimed, at 47.8.4, that
Fulvia desecrated the severed hands and face of Cicero's corpse after
Antony ordered him killed during the proscriptions of 43 BCE.

These later authors base their negative portrayals of Fulvia on
various sources from Fulvia's own lifetime. Three of these contem-
poraneous sources, all written in the late 40s BCE, all noteworthy
examples of ancient Roman invective—denunciatory and abusive

language—against women, warrant close attention. One is a group
of passages from Cicero's *Philippics*, a series of speeches protesting
Antony's conduct, which derived its name from a group of orations
delivered by the fourth-century BCE Greek orator Demosthenes protesting against the conduct of the Macedonian king Philip. A second
source is a group of inscribed sling bullets, *glandes*, found on the
Perusine battlefield, insulting Fulvia, her brother-in-law, and Octavian in sexually charged language. The third is a poem attributed to
Octavian himself by the late first-century CE epigrammatist Martial.
It jokingly blames the Perusine War on Fulvia's sexually aggressive
behavior towards Octavian, in retaliation for Antony's extramarital
dalliance with Queen Glaphyra of Cappadocia.

Cicero, *Philippics* 2.77–78

To illustrate Antony's *levitas* (the opposite of *gravitas*), Cicero relates
an anecdote about how Antony, in disguise, reconciled with Fulvia
upon returning from Gaul in 45 BCE. Presenting the incident in the
form of a dramatic, comic narrative, he portrays her as easily duped
by Antony's written promise to terminate relations with his illicit
lover, the mime actress Volumnia Cytheris, and insults Antony as a
worthless, effeminate, urban criminal.

1   **videte** second person pl. imperative; Cicero is addressing the
     Roman senators.

     hominis = Mark Antony

1–2 **hora diei decima** abl. of time when; at around five o'clock P.M.

     cum . . . venisset "when he had come," *cum* circumstantial
     clause

2   **Saxa rubra** approximately nine miles from Rome, on the Via
     Flaminia, named after the red volcanic rock there

3   **cauponula** "little drinking place, dive." The diminutive im-
     plies a déclassé, sordid establishment.

4   **ad vesperum** "until nightfall"

     ad urbem "to the city of Rome"

5   **capite involuto** abl. absolute, "with his head covered in a cloak"

ianitor = *ianitor dixit*

quis tu? = *quis es tu?*

5-6   **a Marco tabellarius** = *tabellarius missus a Marco*, "a courier sent by Marcus" (Antony's praenomen). Antony is in disguise as one of his own slaves so that Fulvia does not know it is her husband.

6   **cuius causa** "on whose behalf"; *eam* = Fulvia

7   **ei** = Fulvia

quam = *eam epistulam*, connective rel. pron.

illa = *Fulvia*, who is not named in this passage. Cicero aims to put the full spotlight on Antony and his disreputable behavior.

8   **flens** Fulvia is no doubt weeping because she fears something has happened to her husband, surely justifiable because she had already been widowed twice.

erat enim scripta amatorie "for [the letter] had been written in the style of a love note"

8-9   **caput autem litterarum** Understand *erat*, "for the substance of the letter was," followed by several phrases in indirect statement.

9   **sibi cum illa mima posthac nihil futurum** *Sibi* is a dat. of possession. Understand *esse*, "that there was about to be no relationship from that time onward with that mime actress."

mima = Antony's lover, the mime actress and freed slave Volumnia Cytheris, who also is not named here. Earlier, in Chapter 54, Cicero complains that Antony insisted that she be addressed as Volumnia, by the respectable name of her former Roman owner, rather than by the Greek name that she used on stage, Cytheris.

10   **omnem se amorem abiecisse illim** indirect statement with pf. act. infinitive, "that he himself had cast off all passion from that quarter"

10–11   **atque in hanc transfudisse** indirect statement with pf. act. infinitive, "and had poured it into this woman"

   hanc = Fulvia

11   **mulier** = Fulvia

12   **misericors** used sarcastically and ironically. Cicero, who is likely to have invented this episode, implies that Antony is merely acting tenderheartedly because he fraternizes with stage performers.

12–13   **ferre non potuit, caput aperuit, in collum invasit** Note the lack of connectives, or asyndeton, to suggest rapid action.

   in collum invasit "threw his arms around her neck"

13   **O hominem nequam** acc. of exclamation

   quid enim aliud dicam deliberative subjunctive, "what else am I to call him?"

14   **magis proprie** "more appropriately"

14–16   **ut te catamitum . . . aspiceret** purpose clause in secondary sequence, "so that the woman [Fulvia] might catch sight of an unmanly man like you." Roman views of masculinity were based on the male taking the active sexual role. *Catamitum* here implies taking the passive role in the sex act, that is, being penetrated in anal intercourse, hence a term of derision.

15   **nec opinato cum te ostendisses** "when you had shown your-self unexpectedly"

16–18   **idcirco . . . perturbasti** "for this reason you confused"; *perturbasti = perturbavisti*

16   **urbem** = *Romam*

16–17   **terrore . . . metu** ablatives of means. Perhaps an exaggeration, but no doubt the city inferred that Antony's return marked the end of the Civil War and the beginning of a period of re-prisals against those on the wrong side.

17   **multorum dierum** "for many days"

18   **causam amoris** "your love as an excuse"

19   **turpiorem** "a more disgraceful excuse"

19–20   **ne L. Plancus praedes tuos venderet** negative clause of purpose, "that Lucius Plancus not sell your collateral properties." Plancus was one of several praefects that Caesar put in charge of the city when he left for Spain. Cicero here claims that concern about his collateral properties was the reason for Antony's return to the city.

Cicero, *Philippics* 5.11

While charging Antony with financial profligacy and governmental corruption, Cicero claims that Fulvia played a leading role in the selling of political favors. In a gratuitous slur, he also insinuates that she was somehow implicated in the violent deaths of her two previous husbands.

1   **calebant** "were heating up"

in interiore aedium parte "in the inner part of the house," Fulvia's private quarters and bedroom

2   **nundinae** "traffic" in (gen.) is here used as a pejorative term for financial transactions involving items that should not be the objects of trade. Literally the ninth day, the market day.

mulier = Fulvia. Again Cicero does not identify her by name.

sibi felicior quam viris "more fortunate in her own life than in her husbands"; Cicero alludes to the violent deaths of Clodius and Curio, to whom Fulvia was married before Antony.

4   **quasi lege sine lege** "as if under law without law"

quae = *ea quae* "things (= corrupt practices) which"

5–6   **ingressi ... sumus** "we have entered into"

rei publicae recuperandae gen. gerundive, "[the hope of] recovering the Roman republic [from the abuses of power committed by Antony]"

Cicero, *Philippics* 6.4

In the context of claiming Antony's serious moral failings as both a private individual and a public figure, Cicero here characterizes Antony's sexual activities privately within his own home, which at the time he shared with Fulvia, as shameful. He also represents Antony as confusing private marital ties with political responsibilities by being more quick to obey his extremely greedy wife than the Senate and Roman people.

1-2   **semper eo tractus est, quo . . .** "he was always dragged in that direction where . . ."

3-4   **duo dissimilia genera . . . , lenonum et latronum** "two different kinds [of people], sexual procurers and highway robbers." Note the alliteration of these two nouns, which connect them closely even as Cicero presents them as describing different types of men.

4-5   **domesticis stupris, forensibus parricidiis** Note the asyndeton (absence of connective word), linking the phrases for "sexually disgraceful acts in his home" more closely with "murders of close associates in the Forum."

4-6   **ita . . . delectatur, ut . . . paruerit** result clause in primary sequence, "he is so delighted . . . that he has obeyed"

CIL XI.6721.305.14

Sling bullets were almond-shaped projectiles made of lead, stone, or clay, generally about one and three-eighths inches long and three-quarters of an inch wide. They were launched by a military catapult (*ballista*). Some of the bullets contain an inscription with the goal of intimidating the enemy. The sling bullets featuring the first and fifth of these inscriptions were apparently aimed by Octavian's forces at those of Fulvia and Lucius Antonius; those bearing the second, third, and fourth by the armies led by Fulvia and Lucius Antonius at those led by Octavian.

Note how these messages target the leaders of the opposing armies rather than the soldiers who did the actual fighting, and how they aim to wound the reputations of their targets by accusing them—much as Cicero does when assailing Antony in the *Philippics*—of being sexually deformed or deviant.

1   **landicam peto** "I aim at the clitoris." Insulting remarks about women with prominent clitorises by sources such as Martial (for example, 1.90.8) suggest that they were viewed as physically built, and behaving, in a masculine fashion. The first person sing. verb form, *peto*, here and in the next inscription, personifies and accords agency to the sling bullet.

2   **Octaviai** = *Octaviae*, f. gen. sing. In addition to aiming at Octavian's anus, as if to penetrate and thereby disgrace him as an adult male pathic, a male who submits to anal or oral penetration by other men, the inscription calls him by the feminine form of his family name, as if he were a woman.

    Various words inscribed on these bullets—*landica, culum, felas*—are primary obscenities, the equivalent of English "four letter words," which are not acceptable in polite Latin discourse.

3   **felas** = *fellans*. This inscription addresses Octavian by the correct masculine vocative form of his family name, and—with the sing. imperative form *salve*—in the fashion of a "face-to-face" Roman greeting. But at the same time it insults his face by imputing his mouth with performing oral sex, and again disgracing him as an adult male pathic.

4   **Octavi laxe** Also in the vocative case, this inscription calls Octavius "loose, stretched out," referring to the physical condition of his anus as a result of frequent penetration. Here, too, Octavian is ascribed with disgraceful passive sexual conduct.

5   **L. Antoni calve et Fulvia, culum pandite** Addressing both Antony's brother Lucius Antonius, the consul of that year, and Fulvia, as co-commanders with equal military authority,

this inscription insults Antonius by calling attention to his lack of hair, perhaps implying that he has been shaved smooth in the fashion of certain male pathics. By ordering both to open their anuses for penetration, it also threatens Lucius with sexual disgrace and—like the attack aimed at Fulvia's clitoris—represents Fulvia as like a man, in this case an anally penetrated, sexually disgraced man.

Martial 11.20

The first-century CE poet Marcus Valerius Martialis, known to readers in English as "Martial," quotes these six verses by Augustus to justify his own frequent use of primary obscenities in his epigrams. Both Augustus' poem and the four lines of Martial's poem that frame it are in the elegiac couplet, a meter frequently used by Catullus and other Latin poets for the purposes of invective. Certain features of Augustus' language—among them the trisyllabic words ending lines 4 and 6, the form *uti* for *ut* in line 4—render it plausible that he wrote these verses around 41–40 BCE, at the time of the Perusine War.

In these verses Octavian blames Fulvia for this military conflict by claiming that—in retaliation for Antony's affair with a foreign queen—she had sexually propositioned Octavian, insisting that he either gratify her sexual demands or meet him on the battlefield. There is no evidence for this claim. Indeed, Octavian had wed Claudia, Fulvia's barely adolescent daughter by Clodius, immediately before the war, but after a disagreement with Fulvia, he returned his bride to her mother without consummating their union. Octavian explained his decision to fight her on the grounds that his erotic tastes were too discerning, and that his male organ was dearer to him than his life. This poem also attributes deviant, unfeminine conduct to Fulvia in its portrayal of her as taking the sexual initiative, and in likening the act of vaginally penetrating her to that of anally penetrating Antony's agent Manius.

1   **Caesaris Augusti** = Augustus Caesar, the name by which
     Gaius Octavius, called Gaius Julius Caesar Octavianus after
     being adopted by his great-uncle Julius Caesar in Caesar's
     will, was known after 27 BCE

     livide a second declension masculine adj. functioning as a
     substantive, here in the vocative case. Martial is addressing
     an unnamed and ill-tempered male reader critical of his salty
     language.

2   **qui tristis verba Latina legis** rel. clause providing more in-
     formation about his addressee; *tristis*, "you, ill-tempered one,
     who read Latin words," referring to the addressee in the nom.
     case; by *verba Latina* here, and *Romana simplicitate* later,
     Martial means Latin primary obscenities such as *futuo, pedi-
     co*, and *mentula*, which appear in the following six lines.

3   **quod futuit Glaphyran Antonius** "because Antony is fucking
     or has fucked Glaphyra." The form *futuit* can be both pres.
     and pf. tense. *Glaphyran* is a Greek acc. At *Bella Civilia* 5.7 the
     later historian Appian states that Antony placed Glaphyra's
     son Archelaus on the throne of Cappadocia because of his
     physical attraction to her.

4   **Fulvia constituit, se quoque ut futuam** This phrase expands
     the idea expressed in line 3 by *hanc mihi poenam*, "this pun-
     ishment for me," through an indirect command in primary
     sequence, with the pres. subjunctive verb *futuam*.

5   **Fulviam ego ut futuam?** "that I myself fuck Fulvia?" This
     phrase both echoes *ut futuam* in line 4 and functions as a de-
     liberative subjunctive. Note that Augustus—unlike Cicero,
     who often does not identify Fulvia by name—repeats Fulvia's
     name from the preceding line.

     quid si me Manius oret "what if Manius should beg me?"
     Fut. less vivid condition with pres. subjunctive, expressed as a
     question with *faciam*.

6   **pedicem** = *ut pedicem* indirect command with *oret*, "that I
     fuck him in the asshole." Manius was Antony's agent.

faciam? "Should I do it?"

non puto, si sapiam mixed condition. "I do not think so, if I should have any taste."

7   **'aut futue, aut pugnemus,' ait** "'Either fuck me, or let us fight,' she said." *Pugnemus* is a hortatory subjunctive.

quid quod "what about the fact that?; why deny that?"

mihi dat. of possession, which should be taken with both *vita* in this line and *mentula* in the next

vita Modified by *ipsa* in line 8, this is in the abl. case, an abl. of comparison with *carior mentula*.

8   **signa canent** jussive subjunctive, "let the war trumpets sound"

9   **absolvis** "exonerate, justify"

libellos Martial's "little books" of poetry

10   **Romana simplicitate** "with Roman frankness," abl. of means

∾ 10 Horace, *SATIRES* 1.2.37–40, 77–82, 116–19, 127–34

The perils of adulterous affairs with elite Roman women

Written in the early 30s BCE, *Satires* 1.2 criticizes those who engage in behavioral excesses. It focuses in particular on adultery—sexual relations by men with other men's wives—as an example of excessive, inappropriate and indeed dangerous conduct. Horace makes his argument against adulterous liaisons through a series of illustrative anecdotes about actual individuals, some of them, such as the elder Cato, identified by their own names. In his effort to point up various difficulties that adulterers encounter, Horace testifies to the sexually transgressive behavior of some elite Roman women, whom he faults as risky lovers in comparison to commercial sex workers. We should note that in the lines here excerpted from this poem Horace takes issue with one "Cerinthus" for praising adultery with well-born women; Cerinthus is also the pseudonym later employed by the aristocratic female elegiac poet Sulpicia for her younger male lover.

Meter: dactylic hexameter

37   **est operae pretium** (+ infinitive) "it is worth your while to"

procedere recte complementary infinitive with *non voltis,* "you who do not wish for things to go smoothly" [for *moechis*]

38   **ut omni parte laborent** indirect question governed by *audire,* "to hear how they struggle in every part [of their adulterous escapade]." As Porphyrius, a later commentator on this text, notes, these lines recall a passage at the beginning of Ennius' *Annales: audire est operae pretium procedere recte/qui rem Romanam Latiumque augescere vultis,* "it is worth your while to hear, you who wish for the Roman state to go smoothly and Latium to increase."

39   **utque . . . voluptas** = *utque voluptas sit,* the first part of a second indirect question

illis dat. of possession, referring to *moechis*

40   **atque haec . . . cadat** the second part of the second indirect question

haec refers to *voluptas.*

rara Translate as an adv., "infrequently."

pericla = *pericula*

77   **ne paeniteat te** negative clause of purpose, "so it may not cause you regret"

78   **sectarier** = *sectari;* archaic form of first conjugation pres. deponent infinitive

78–79 **unde laboris/plus haurire mali est quam ex re decerpere fructus** "from which there is a greater amount of difficult struggle to drink up than enjoyment to pluck up from the act itself"

laboris plus . . . mali partitive gen.; *fructus* is acc. pl. object of the infinitive *decerpere.* Note the metaphor of wine consumption: *haurire* describes drinking the wine itself, *decerpere fructus,* plucking the grape from which wine is made.

ex re "in reality"

80-81   **nec magis** modifies *tenerum*, and describes *femur*; the phrase is parallel to *rectius,* which describes *crus,* "nor is a woman's thigh more delicate or her lower limb more shapely"

80   **huic** = *mulieri,* dat. of possession

interque niveos viridisque lapillos "amid white and green little stones" (pearls and emeralds). At 3.8.19–20 the Augustan female love elegist Sulpicia may evoke this passage by referring to herself, an aristocratic woman engaged in an illicit romance, as adorned with expensive jewels; as noted above, she uses the name of Horace's addressee here, Cerinthus, as a pseudonym for that of her lover.

81   **sit licet hoc . . . tuum** = *quamvis hoc sit opinio tua,* "although this (that jewels make a woman's limbs appear more delicate and shapely) may be your opinion"

Cerinthe vocative of second declension masculine noun

82   **melius persaepe togatae est** "and very frequently the body of a paid sex worker is better"; *togatae* is a dat. of reference. Roman women who sold their sexual favors often advertised their availability by dressing in a toga.

116   **tument tibi cum inguina** "when your manly parts swell up"; *tibi* is dat. of possession.

num is to be taken with *impetus in quem continuo fiat, malis tentigine rumpi,* "you don't prefer, do you, to be exploded by your swelling erection?"

116-18 **si ancilla aut verna est praesto puer, impetus in quem continuo fiat** "if there is a female slave or a household boy on hand (and if) an attack could be made immediately on whomever"

117   **verna** can be a household slave of either sex or any age; *puer* specifically refers to a boy slave who has not yet grown a beard.

quem = *aliquem,* after *si*

127-31 **nec vereor ne ... recurrat ... frangatur ... latret ... resonet
... desiliat ... clamet ... metuat** "positive" fear clause in primary sequence: "I do not fear that ... her husband may hurry
back from the country ...."

129 **lecto** "from the bed"

130 **miseram se ... clamet** = *miseram se esse clamet,* indirect
statement, "[that] the slave woman conspiring with her may
shout that she is wretched"

conscia here a guilty accomplice, referring to the woman's female slave who has aided and abetted her

131 **cruribus haec metuat** "she (= the female slave) may fear for
her limbs" (which would be beaten)

deprensa = his female partner, caught *in flagrante delicto; doti
deprensa*: understand *doti metuat deprensa,* "my female partner may fear for her dowry" (which would be reduced if her
husband were to catch her in adultery and divorce her).

egomet mi = *egomet metuam mihi,* "I may fear for myself."
Note how this triple fear clause is itself contained within a
longer fear clause.

132 **discincta tunica** "with my tunic unbelted"; *et pede nudo,* "and
barefoot," since he would need to run away speedily, with no
time to put on all his clothes and footwear

fugiendum est pass. periphrastic in impersonal neuter construction : "fleeing must take place, I must flee"

133 **ne nummi pereant ...** negative clause of purpose in primary
sequence: "so that my financial resources or my [tight] buttocks or finally my reputation may not vanish" (since adulterers would be fined for sexual misconduct, anally penetrated
with pain-inflicting objects, and morally discredited)

134 **deprendi miserum est** "it is a wretched thing to be caught in
the act." *Deprendi* is a pres. pass. infinitive; the verb, which
Horace also uses to describe the woman caught in adultery
by her husband, often appeared in Roman comic stage mimes
about illicit lovers discovered by the woman's spouse.

∾ 11   Tibullus 3.9, 3.13, 3.14, 3.16; L'Année Epigraphique 1928.73; Cicero Ad Familiares 4.5

Writings by and about the Augustan elegist Sulpicia

In the third book of poetry that is said to be the work of the Augustan elegist Tibullus, elegies eight through eighteen feature a female
poet-speaker, twice referred to by the name Sulpicia. These elegies
represent her as associated with the affluent, privileged, and cultured household of Tibullus' own literary patron, Marcus Valerius
Messalla Corvinus, consul in 31 BCE. A statement by the fourth-
century CE Christian author Jerome helps to explain this woman's
relationship with Messalla. For he reports at *Adversus Iovinanum*
1.46 that Messalla's sister Valeria refused to remarry after the death
of her husband, the distinguished legal authority Servius Sulpicius
Rufus, in 43 BCE. Under these circumstances, this Valeria would
have then become her brother's legal ward.

What is more, in elegy 3.12, the female poet-speaker mentions
keeping erotic secrets from her mother; in 3.16 she prides herself on
being "Servius' daughter Sulpicia." Scholars have therefore identified
this Sulpicia as Valeria's daughter and Messalla's niece, living under
his legal guardianship when she composed her poetry: presumably
because she was husbandless as well as fatherless at the time. That
time seems to have been around 19 BCE, when Tibullus is known to
have died.

The eleven Sulpicia elegies chronicle her passionate love affair
with a young man whom she calls by the pseudonym Cerinthus. His
name evokes that of a hot-blooded male whom we have encountered
Horace reprimanding in *Satires* 1.2, for favoring illicit liaisons with
well-born, expensively adorned women; Sulpicia calls to mind the
females that Horace's Cerinthus prefers by detailing her own jewels
and costly attire, and by confessing that *peccasse iuvat*, "it's pleasurable to have misbehaved" with her lover. But the name Cerinthus also
puns on the Greek and Latin words for "wax," and thereby makes an
erudite allusion to the wax tablets on which she wrote her poetry.

The four elegies selected for inclusion—3.9, 3.13, 3.14, and 3.16—illustrate the learning and literary skill that Sulpicia's elegies display, features of her poetry that have led many scholars to doubt that she, or any Roman woman, could have authored these elegies, particularly the first five, which are longer and more complex than the second six. Her frankness about the illicit erotic joys that her poetry celebrates has troubled scholars as well, especially those who assume, without any justification, that she must be a never-married girl in her early teens. Such scholars claim that a young woman of Sulpicia's background would not have dared to publicize her involvement in impermissible sexual conduct, nor have acquired the literary education and skills to produce poetry of high quality.

If, however, our poet-speaker is the daughter of the Servius Sulpicius who died in 43 BCE, and if her poems date to around 19 BCE, at the time Sulpicia wrote these elegies she would have been in her mid-twenties and likely to have been married at least once—and subsequently widowed or divorced—already. She would have interacted with the poets fostered by her uncle as a contemporary and equal. Indeed, she would have been about the same age as another one of Messalla's protégés, the poet Ovid, born in 43 BCE himself, who began to write his early love elegies, the *Amores*, at the time of Tibullus' death as well. So, too, the last six of Sulpicia's elegies are just as complex and learned as the first five. Both 3.9 and 3.13, for example, echo the language and revisit the themes of Dido's love affair with Aeneas in Vergil's *Aeneid*; 3.13 alludes to Homer's portrayal of Helen in the *Iliad* as well.

The recent rediscovery by Jane Stevenson and Janet Fairweather of *AE* 1928.73, an epitaph in the elegiac couplet from the city of Rome, datable to around 20 BCE, has done much to quell suspicions about Sulpicia's authorship of the eleven Sulpicia-elegies. Commemorating a Greek slave *lectrix*, a woman who read and performed literature aloud, named Sulpicia Petale, this inscription shares striking stylistic similarities with the eleven elegies, and is thus attributed to Sulpicia herself. Like the eleven Sulpicia-elegies, the Petale-inscription is noteworthy for its clever wordplay: we find, for example, an allusion to both the dead woman and the author of

the epitaph in the opening word, *Sulpiciae*. The presence in Sulpicia's household of a female slave who recited Greek and Latin literary texts does, of course, much to account for the learned allusions
to earlier poetic works in Sulpicia's elegies.

Finally, although such ancient authors as Horace, Ovid, and the
younger Pliny claim that both Sulpicia's father Servius Sulpicius Rufus and uncle Messalla wrote erotic poetry themselves, a letter from
her father to his friend Cicero suggests that, had he lived to read Sulpicia's poems, he might not have approved of their content. Written to console Cicero on the death of his own daughter Tullia, and
describing what Sulpicius believed a young woman of their social
background should hope to achieve in life, it propounds an entirely
different set of values and priorities than those celebrated by Sulpicia's elegies and epitaph for Petale.

 Tibullus (Sulpicia) 3.9

In this, the second of the eleven Sulpicia-elegies and the first to feature her lover Cerinthus, the poet-speaker voices a series of complex
emotional reactions to the prospect of his participating in a hunting
expedition. She first addresses the wild boar he proposes to hunt,
begging him to spare her lover; after blaming the goddess of hunting,
Diana, for luring Cerinthus away, she proceeds to denounce hunting
as a form of madness. But in line 10, now addressing Cerinthus, she
expresses her wish to accompany him on the hunt, and her hopes
that she will be found making love with him in front of the hunting
nets, thereby enabling the wild boar to depart unharmed.

In the final six lines of the poem she addresses Cerinthus again,
insisting that there be no loving on the hunt without her, and indeed
threatening any woman who stealthily usurps her place of love with
being torn to pieces by wild beasts. She then concludes by ordering
Cerinthus to leave hunting to his father, and return to her embrace.
Although this twenty-four–line elegy is written in the first person, its
narrative complexity has led scholars to view this elegy, along with
the other, learned and relatively long elegies 8–12, as by a more liter-
arily accomplished male friend of Sulpicia's. Its allusions to the hunt in

Book Four of Vergil's *Aeneid*, in which Aeneas, Dido, and Aeneas' son Ascanius take part, mark it as particularly clever and witty: one can read Sulpicia's enjoinder to leave hunting to your father as an effort to identify Cerinthus, described as a *puer* in line 20, with Ascanius, and a veiled critique of epic and its values. Yet, as we will see, 3.13, though only ten lines long, features an equally complicated narrative structure and allusions to the Dido and Aeneas episode as well.

Meter: elegiac couplet

1   **meo iuveni** = Cerinthus, who is not named until line 11

      seu quis = *seu aliquis*. This indef. adj. modifies the sing. subject of the second person sing. verb form *colis* and eventually the vocative noun *aper* in the next line; it is best translated "whoever you may be." But until the poem's readers encounter the noun *aper* in line 2, they do not realize that Sulpicia, using the figure of speech known as *para prosdokian*, "unexpected or surprise effect," is addressing the boar Cerinthus will hunt rather than a deity such as Amor or Diana, who are mentioned in the subsequent two couplets. Both *pascua* and *devia* are direct objects of *colis*.

2   Sulpicia's choice of *colis,* a verb often describing agricultural cultivation, to describe the habitation of a wild boar, is witty and ironic.

3   **neu tibi sit** jussive subjunctive, "let it not be your lot"

      in proelia "for the purposes of struggles"

4   **custos . . . Amor** "love as his guardian god"

      servet jussive subjunctive, "let . . . protect"

5   **venandi . . . cura** "owing to a passion for hunting." *Cura* is abl. of means governing the gen. gerund *venandi*; as the word *cura* itself often describes erotic desire, Sulpicia represents hunting as a rival for her lover's affections.

      Delia, a learned epithet referring to the goddess Diana, born on the island of Delos, is also the name of Tibullus' female lover in Book 1 of his elegies. In this instance of learned wordplay, Sulpicia may seek to allude to his work, as well as to give the initial impression that Tibullus' beloved, and not the goddess of hunting, has lured Cerinthus away.

6   **pereant . . . deficiantque** optative subjunctives, "if only [the woods] would perish [and the hunting dogs] disappear"

7-8   **furor** a word frequently used for the frenzied madness of Dido in *Aeneid* 4; *mens*, "state of mind." Both nouns govern the indirect statement *velle laedere*, "to wish to wound," with *claudentem*, referring to Cerinthus, as the subject of the indirect statement, "What madness is it, what state of mind is it for him, closing the thickly packed hills with a hunting net, to wish to wound his tender hands?"

    indagine *Indago*, hunting net, is a rare word also used by Vergil at *Aeneid* 4.121, when the goddess Juno tells Aeneas' mother Venus about the hunt she has planned. In addition to featuring this rare noun *indago* and the noun *venus* twice, this elegy makes heavy use of vocabulary from *Aeneid* 4.115–60: the verb and the nouns *retia, plagae, canis, cervus, campus,* and *mons.* Sulpicia's reference to Diana appears to recall Vergil's simile likening Aeneas to Apollo at 143–50 (which makes reference to Delos). Vergil also portrays Aeneas' son Ascanius at 159 as hoping to hunt an *aper*, wild boar. The prominent role Sulpicia assigns to an *aper* in the poem's scenario and her final command that Cerinthus leave hunting to his father evidently alludes to Vergil's characterization of Ascanius as well.

11   **ut tecum liceat . . . vagari** purpose clause in primary sequence, "so that it may be permitted to wander with you"

13-14   **quaeram . . . demam** "I will follow . . . and remove"
         celeri cani dat. of possession, "of the swift hound"

15-17   **tunc . . . tunc** an example of anaphora, repetition of the initial word in successive phrases

15-16   **placeant . . . si . . . arguar** fut. less vivid condition, "If I should be proven to have bedded down with you before the very hunting nets, then the woods would please me."

17–18   **tunc** continues the anaphora.

veniat licet "although [the boar] may come"

ne veneris cupidae gaudia turbet negative clause of purpose in primary sequence, "so that he may not disturb the pleasures of desiring passion." Note the juxtaposition of *veneris* and its adj. *cupidae*, placing the name of the goddess Venus, here employed for passion itself, next to a word from the same root as the name of her son Cupid, referred to in line 4 as Amor.

19–20   **nunc**, following the anaphora of *tunc*, marks the transition from Sulpicia's imagined sharing of hunting with Cerinthus back to her reality of being left behind.

sit nulla venus jussive subjunctive, "let there be no passion"

lege Dianae abl. of means, "by the law of Diana"

In another memorable play on words, Sulpicia repeats the noun *venus* from the previous line, in a contrast between the passion that she imagines and the passion that she prohibits; here, however, it is also used as the name of the love goddess herself, and contrasted with the *lege Dianae* that Cerinthus is to follow.

casta . . . manu abl., "with a chaste hand." Note the repetition of *caste . . . casta*.

21   **quaecumque meo furtim subrepit amori** "whatever woman stealthily creeps up on my beloved"; *meo amori*, dat. with *subrepit*. Note the repetition of the word *Amor* from line 4, there as the god Cupid and here as Sulpicia's lover.

22   **incidat** jussive subjunctive, "let her fall," *in saevas . . . feras,* "among fierce beasts"

diripienda fut. pass. pple. used to express, simultaneously, both necessity and purpose, characterizing her rival as "deserving to be torn into pieces" and wishing that she would fall among wild beasts "in order to be torn into pieces"

23   **venandi** gen. gerund with *studium,* "enthusiasm for hunting," direct object of *concede*

parenti "father," dat. indirect object with *concede,* "yield"

Tibullus (Sulpicia) 3.13

Like the five elegies that follow, 3.13 is much shorter than the five elegies that precede it. Many regard 3.13 as the first of the elegies that Sulpicia actually wrote. But it is no less complex and learned than the five that it follows. Like them, it abounds in witty wordplay and allusions to earlier literary works: in this case the portrayal of Helen in Homer's epic *Iliad* and of Dido in Vergil's epic *Aeneid*.

Whereas in 3.9 Sulpicia merely imagines the physical joys she would like to experience with Cerinthus, in 3. 13 she proudly announces the physical consummation of her passion. Venus, whose name represents that passion in 3.9, here appears as a goddess, referred to initially by the learned epithet *Cytherea*, "from the island of Cythera," and characterized as susceptible to as well as celebrated in love poetry: Sulpicia credits the Roman Muses, *Camenae,* who inspire her poetry, with winning over the goddess and causing her to bring Sulpicia and her lover together.

Meter: elegiac couplet

1–2   Understand *tandem venit talis amor qualis fama me texisse alicui* [*eum amorem*] *sit magis pudori mihi quam fama me nuda(vi)sse* [*eum amorem*], "Love has finally come to me, of such sort that the rumor (or reputation) that I have hidden it would be more of a source of shame to me than the rumor (or reputation) that I have laid it bare for anyone." An implied *me* functions as the subject of *texisse* and *nudasse*.

   The grammar of this sentence is extremely complicated. *Texisse* and *nuda(vi)sse* are pf. act. infinitives in indirect statement governed by *fama; sit* is pres. subjunctive in a rel. clause of characteristic introduced by *qualem; qualem* is attracted into the acc. by *eum amorem* understood, the direct object of the two infinitives; *alicui* is the dat. indirect object of *nudasse*; the noun and pron. *pudori mihi* comprise a double dat., the first a dat. of purpose and the second a dat. of reference.

Sulpicia here challenges the definition of *fama*, which means both rumor and reputation, that destroys Dido in *Aeneid* 4, by claiming that public reports of her illicit love affair are better for her reputation than keeping this liaison secret.

3   **meis . . . Camenis** "my Roman Muses, my poetry in Latin," abl. of means with *exorata*; *illum* = *Cerinthus*. The epithet Cytherea is also used for Venus at *Aeneid* 4.128. There Vergil describes a conversation between Juno and Venus in which they plan a hunting expedition that will conclude with the physical consummation of Dido's and Aeneas' love.

4   The reference to Venus' dropping Sulpicia's lover into her embrace evokes Homer's description in *Iliad* 3, of Aphrodite, Venus' Greek counterpart, rescuing Helen's lover Paris from a duel on the battlefield with Helen's husband Menelaus and dropping him in Helen's bedchamber, where they make love.

5–6 **mea gaudia narret / dicetur si quis non habuisse sua** "If anyone will be said not to have had joys of their own, let him or her tell of my joys." The construction here is a mixed condition, consisting of a fut. more vivid condition in the if-clause, and a jussive subjunctive in the main clause. *Quis* = *aliquis*, after *si*.

7–8 The main verb is *non . . . velim*, "I would not wish," potential subjunctive.

     signatis quicquam mandare tabellis "to entrust anything to sealed tablets"

     ne legat id nemo quam meus ante "so that no one may read it before my lover"; the double negative (*ne . . . nemo*) also allows the reading "so that someone may read it before my lover," namely Sulpicia's reader. Negative purpose clause with pres. subjunctive in primary sequence.

     quam . . . ante = *antequam*, with its component parts separated in the figure of speech called tmesis, although with the second part of the conj. *antequam* preceding the first

9–10   **sed peccasse iuvat** (*pecasse = peccavisse*) "but it is pleasurable to have misbehaved"

vultus componere famae/ taedet "it is tiresome to wear a false expression for the sake of rumor (or my reputation)"

ferar either fut. indicative ("I will be said") or pres. subjunctive ("may I be said").

Note the repetition of *fama* from line 2, again in the sense of both rumor and reputation, and also evoking Vergil's portrayal of Dido. Note, too, the juxtaposition of *digno*, a "worthy man," with *digna*, "a worthy woman."

Tibullus (Sulpicia) 3.14

Sulpicia addresses this poem to Messalla, whom she calls her kinsman, *propinquus*, to complain that she is being forced to spend her birthday in the country rather than in the city with her lover Cerinthus. Her disparaging remarks about the country contrast with Tibullus' repeated efforts to extol and idealize rural settings.

Meter: elegiac couplet

1–2   **qui . . . agendus erit** rel. clause; *tristis* modifies *natalis (dies)*, the subject of the clause.

agendus erit "will have to be spent," fut. pass. pple. in pass. periphrastic construction

3   **dulcius** modifies *quid*; *urbe* is an abl. of comparison, "what is sweeter than the city (of Rome)?"

an villa sit apta "or would a country house be suitable?"; *puellae*, dat. with *apta*

4   **Arretino . . . agro** = *in Arretino agro*. Note how the word order reinforces the message, with the phrase for "chilly river" actually inside the phrase for "the field in Arretium."

5   **nimium . . . mei studiose** "excessively attentive to me"; *studiose* governs the gen. case, here an unusual objective gen. form of the first person sing. pron., *mei*. Both *studiose* and

propinque are in the vocative case, in apposition to Messalla. Sulpicia also applies the adj. *studiosus* to her mother, Messalla's sister, at 3.12.15.

quiescas "may you calm down," pres. subjunctive command in second person sing.

6   **tempestivae . . . viae** Understand *sunt* with both.

7   **abducta** recalls *abducit* in 3.9 (line 5).

8   **arbitrio . . . meo** "in control of myself," framing the line, is a technical legal term, as is *vis*, "force," "authority," perhaps in homage to her actual father, a celebrated legal expert

     quam acc. rel. pron. referring to Sulpicia

Tibullus (Sulpicia) 3.16

Here Sulpicia confronts her lover, in sarcastic and indignant tones, about his attentions to a female rival. She refers to this woman as a *scortum*, one who takes money for her sexual favors, as dressed in the toga that marked Roman women as prostitutes, and as passing herself off as respectable by carrying a wool-basket; she contrasts this woman of low birth to herself, Sulpicia daughter of Servius. In the final couplet, Sulpicia reminds her lover that she has male kin concerned about her, in sorrow at the prospect of her yielding her place to a bed-partner of unknown origin.

Meter: elegiac couplet

1–2   The subject of *gratum est* is the *quod* clause, to be understood as *quod securus de me tibi permittis multum*, "that you, free from any care about me now, are so indulgent to yourself."

       ne male inepta cadam a negative purpose clause in primary sequence, "in order that I, clumsy as I am, may not suddenly fall badly"

3–4   Understand *sint tibi cura togae potior et scortum pressum quasillo potius quam Servi filia Sulpicia*. Although the pres. jussive subjunctive verb *sit* has both *cura* and *scortum* as its subject, it is in the sing.; similarly, *potior* only agrees with the

f. sing. *cura* and must be understood as modifying *scortum* as well. *Tibi* is dat. of possession. Translate, "Let your concern for a woman in a prostitute's toga and a partner-for-hire loaded with a wool-basket be stronger than Sulpicia, daughter of Servius."

As scholars have noted, the phrase *Servi filia* not only describes Sulpicia, whose aristocratic father, Servius Sulpicius Rufus, had a *praenomen* (first name) apparently meaning "slave," but also her rival, who was presumably the daughter of a slave. This clever play on words, acknowledging that— because elite Roman men had sexual access to women of all social classes—Sulpicia and her rival are similar as well as different, is characteristic of Sulpicia's witty, punning style.

5–6 **pro nobis** literally *pro me*, but the pl. implies that these nameless men are anxious about her lover as well. *Doloris* is an objective gen. with *maxima causa*. Understand the rel. clause describing the *solliciti* as *quibus illa maxima causa doloris est, ne cedam ignoto toro*, "to whom it is the greatest cause of sorrow that I may yield my position in your bed to a total nobody." *Quibus* is dat. of possession; the negative purpose clause *ne cedam* echoes that in line 2, *ne cadam. Ignoto toro* is dat. with *cedam*.

L'Année Epigraphique 1928.73

Epitaph of Petale Sulpicia. Rome, ca. 20 BCE.

Meter: elegiac couplet

This inscription, also in the elegiac meter, found in the center of modern-day Rome during the urban excavations of the 1920s, commemorates a *lectrix*, "female slave who read aloud," in the household of the noble Sulpicii. Various linguistic features allow us to date the text to around 25–20 BCE. They include the forms *quoi* and *longinquom* (for *cui* and *longinquum*), which retain archaic spellings that go out of use soon after that time. After that date, moreover, it became customary to conclude pentameter lines with words of two syllables; three of the pentameter lines here end with three- and four-syllable words.

The dead woman is identified as a slave by the statement in line 2 that the Greek name, Petale, "had been given as her *servile nomen*." However, the feminine form of the Roman family name Sulpicia, employed in apposition with her occupational title in the genitive case, suggests that she was freed and accorded the name of her former owners upon her death.

It is likely, too, that the genitive *Sulpiciae* simultaneously refers to the name of the woman who owned her: that Petale was a female reader "belonging to Sulpicia." Jerome Carcopino [1929] and Jane Stevenson have therefore proposed that her owner was the author of this epitaph: the elegiac poet Sulpicia. A number of stylistic details here strengthen this attribution, as they recall Sulpicia's own learned and carefully crafted poetry. One has already been mentioned, the wordplay involved in the very first word of the poem, since "*Sulpiciae*" appears to be the name of the dead *lectrix* as well as that of her living, surviving owner. Another is the emphasis on art (5 *arte*), beauty (6 *forma*), and cleverness, presumably in the form of literary talent (6 *ingenio*).

1   **Sulpiciae** gen. sing. of the female name Sulpicia, modifying *lectricis,* or referring to the dead woman's owner, or both

     cineres indicates that the epitaph marks a funerary urn, of the woman's cremated remains.

     lectricis "[of a female slave who reads aloud," presumably works of literature as well as correspondence, to household members

     cerne viator "observe, traveler," a standard phrase on Roman funerary inscriptions, seeking the attention of those who pass by

2   **quoi** archaic form of *cui.* The Greek name Petale is also used, as the name of an aged female slave, by the Augustan elegist Propertius at 4.7.43, a poem dated to ca. 16 BCE. It is a poetic

variant of *petalon*, "leaf"; words for flowers and leaves are often used to describe collections of poetry in Greco-Roman literature, such as "anthology," which literally means "a gathering of flowers."

3   **ter denos numero quattuor plus . . . annos** acc. of duration of time = "for 34 years"; *numero* is abl. of specification, "in number."

4   **in terris** = "on earth," i.e., "while alive"

   Aglaon Greek acc. form of masculine noun, in apposition with *natum*. The name means "splendid, gleaming."

   ediderat As the verb *edo, edere*, "to produce, give birth to," can also mean "to create out of words, to publish," Aglaon is characterized as both Petale's child and her brilliant artistic creation.

5   **omnia naturae bona viderat** "she had seen all good things of nature." Note the use of *natum* and *naturae*, which come from the same Latin root, in close proximity, the stylistic device known as an "etymological figure."

5–6   **viderat . . . vigebat/ splendebat . . . creverat** This couplet, which celebrates Petale's art and cleverness in the form of literary talent (*arte, ingenio*) is itself artfully and cleverly crafted. Note the series of four verbs without connective words (asyndeton); the chiastic order of verb tenses (plpf., impf., impf., plpf.), with the two verbs in the impf. tense next to one another, beginning and ending their respective lines; and the series of nouns in the abl. case immediately preceding (in the case of *arte*) or following (in the case of *forma* and *ingenio*).

   arte . . . forma . . . ingenio ablatives of cause, "because of, owing to"

6   **splendebat** perhaps a bilingual Greek-Latin pun on the name of Petale's son Aglaon, "gleaming"

   creverat = "she had grown, increased"

7-8   **invida fors** Of particular stylistic note in this couplet are the two personified nouns serving as subjects of the two verbs *noluit* and *defuit*, placed toward the beginning and at the very end: *fors*, fate, and *colus*, distaff. The latter is a spinning implement associated in Greek and Roman lore with the mythic goddesses called the Fates in Latin, and their ability to prolong or shorten the "thread of a human life." This reference to spinning, which was specifically linked by the Hellenistic Greek female poet Erinna with poetry written by women, may be a gesture of homage to Erinna and her work.

No less noteworthy in terms of style are the asyndetic arrangement of the two verbs *noluit* and *defuit*, the postponement of the first main verb *noluit* and the pron. *hanc* (subject of the indirect statement construction *hanc degere [longinquom] tempus*) until the second line of the couplet, and the ingenious construction of line 7. The first segment of the hexameter line begins with *invida*, an adj., followed by *fors*, the noun it modifies and then the abl. of time *vita*, "in life." Then, following the caesura, "break," the second segment begins with *longinquom*, an adj., separated by *degere,* an infinitive, from *tempus*, the noun it modifies. Thus the word *longinquom*, itself meaning "long," heads the longer of these two noun-adj. phrases, and segments of the hexameter line. *Vita,* moreover, can be taken with both phrases: envious fate "in life" was unwilling for her to spend a long time "in life." *Longinquom = longinquuum*, modifying *tempus*.

8   **fatis defuit ipse colus** "the distaff itself failed the Fates," i.e., the three goddesses called "the Fates" could not prolong Petale's life, and oppose the dictates of "fate" as a singular abstract entity. In modifying *colus,* usually a feminine noun, with *ipse*, and thereby assigning it masculine gender, the epitaph seems to evoke the earlier portrayal of the spinning Fates at Catullus 64.311: they also hold a *colus* of masculine gender: *colum molli lana . . . amictum*, "distaff cloaked in soft wool."

Echoing Catullus, and perhaps this inscription as well, Propertius also treats *colus* as masculine at 4.9.28 (*Lydo . . . colo*),
a poem written around 16 BCE: Here *colus* figures in a speech
delivered by the mythic "he-man" Hercules to describe how
he, clad in female garb, once worked wool himself.

Cicero, *Ad Familiares* 4.5

This letter was written by the distinguished jurist Servius Sulpicius
Rufus, whom many scholars identify as Sulpicia's father, to Cicero
on the death of Cicero's daughter Tullia in 45 BCE, who was in her
early thirties at the time. In it Sulpicius indicates what is regarded as
important in the life of an elite Roman woman: marriage to a prom-
ising young man, to whom she would bear male children capable of
holding on to their inheritance, seeking high public office, and using their connections and resources for the political benefit of male
friends. These values stand in sharp contrast to those expressed by
his own daughter in both the eleven elegies and the inscription commemorating the *lectrix* Petale. What matters most to Sulpicia are the
pleasurable pursuit of love apart from marriage, the cultivation of
artistic talent, and the creation of poetry. (On Cicero's plans to commemorate the loss of his beloved daughter, see **Reading 8**).

1-2   **quid . . . fuit quod . . . posset** rel. clause of characteristic. *Illam*
      refers to Tullia. "What sort of thing was there which was able
      to encourage her . . . ?

      ad vivendum gerund of purpose with *ad,* "toward living, to
      go on living"

2-3   **quae res . . . solacium** Understand the verb *est* with each of
      these three nouns. *Animi solacium,* "solace for her spirit," is
      an objective gen.

3-4   **ut . . . gereret** indirect command with *res, spes,* and *solacium*
      understood: the experience/hope/solace "that she might be
      able to spend . . ."

      coniuncta modifies Tullia (understood).

5   **pro tua dignitate** "at a level with your own worthiness, up to your own standards"

5–6   **ex hac iuventute** "from today's youth"

6–7   **cuius . . . putares** is a rel. clause of characteristic, describing a potential son-in-law; *te* is the subject of the indirect statement governed by *putares*, "the sort of young man to whose reliability you would think that you were entrusting your children safely."

7–8   **ut . . . pareret** is also governed by *res, spes,* and *solacium,* "that she might be able to bear children fathered by him." *Sese* refers to the prospective son-in-law.

       quos . . . laetaretur rel. clause of characteristic, "the kind of children in whom she might rejoice"

       cum florentis videret *cum* circumstantial clause, "whenever she saw them thriving"

8–10 **qui . . . possent . . . petituri essent** rel. clause of characteristic within another rel. clause of characteristic; *rem* "estate"; *honores,* "high political offices"; *usuri libertate* fut. act. pple. modifying the prospective male grandchildren; the abl. *libertate* is governed by *usuri*: "The kind of male children who would be able to hold on by themselves to an estate bequeathed by a parent, who would in the future seek high political offices following the traditional order in our state, about to employ their freedom in the services of their friends."

✍ 12 *Propertius 4.8.51–88*

Love and war: Erotic violence

In this elegy, dated to around 16 BCE, Propertius offers a vivid dramatic account of a quarrel—and subsequent reconciliation—that he purports to have had with his lover Cynthia. He portrays Cynthia as having abandoned him to attend a festival in another town with another man, and himself as having sought consolation elsewhere, with two women named Phyllis and Teia. But he reports that he found himself unable to perform sexually in this threesome because he could not stop thinking about Cynthia. What is more, in the midst of this failed erotic encounter, Cynthia suddenly returned, and proceeded to take harsh emotional and physical revenge on Propertius' two partners, Propertius' male slave Lygdamus, and Propertius himself before he and Cynthia made up by making passionate, gratifying love.

In his use of military language to characterize Cynthia's conduct in this poem (see below, *in exuviis victrix*, line 63, for example), Propertius draws on a long tradition in Latin poetry of using vocabulary from the realm of war to describe the challenges of love (Cahoon, among others). But in 4.8 he varies this literary convention as well, by emphasizing the extensive physical violence that Cynthia inflicts on him and others as well as the erotic pleasure that he takes in suffering the pain she causes.

51   **nec mora** = *nec mora est*. Propertius uses the historic pres. tense in much of the narration that follows.

       totas resupinat . . . valvas "flings the doors completely on their backs." The action represented by the verb *resupinat* describes a physical sexual assault by a conquering military male on human female victims. Propertius uses this verb to striking dramatic effect in depicting Cynthia's treatment of mere physical objects.

52   **non operosa comis** *comis* is abl. of respect, "not having taken pains in respect to arranging her hair," "with hair disheveled"

       sed furibunda decens "attractive but full of rage"

53   **mi** = *mihi*, dat. of possession; *mi digitos inter remissos*, "among my fingers, which had lost their grip"

54   **ipso labra soluta mero** "my lips, loosened by the wine itself"

55   **fulminat** "hurls thunderbolts"

       quantum femina saevit "as much as only a woman expresses rage." Propertius assumes that his audience agrees with him that women are more emotional, and more prone to violent anger, than men.

56   **spectaclum . . . nec minus . . . fuit** "the spectacle was no less"

capta . . . urbe "than a city that has been taken capture," abl. of comparison. Propertius casts Cynthia in the role of a general here and hyperbolically likens her assault on him and his social event to the military siege of an urban stronghold such as the mythic Troy.

57   **Phyllidos . . . in vultum** "in Phyllis' face"

58   **vicinas . . . clamat aquas** "shouts for water from the neighbors," as if a fire had broken out

59   **lumina . . . elata** "the torches that had been brandished by the women"

      Quirites "local citizenry," an elevated term for the humble residents of this neighborhood

60   **semita** = *via*, an ironic word for an urban alley, usually applied to a rural path

      insana . . . nocte "in the wild and crazy night"

61–62 Understand *prima taberna obscurae viae excipit illas* (the two women) *direptisque comis tunicisque solutis. Direptisque comis tunicisque solutis*, abl. of description, "with torn locks of hair and clothes hanging loose."

63   **exuviis . . . victrix** military terms, which add to the characterization of Cynthia as a conquering warrior

64   **mea . . . ora** is acc., "my face."

      perversa . . . manu is abl. of means, "with her hand turned back" (to enable slashing him, as she did his two female partners, with her nails).

66   **meruere** = *meruerunt*. Propertius claims that his eyes deserved to be struck because he "looked at" other women.

67   **nostris . . . plagis** "by blows on me," "by hitting my body"

68   **Lygdamus ad plutei fulcra sinistra latens** "Lygdamus, crouching under the raised left end of the couch." Lygdamus is Propertius' slave, in charge of the drinks at this gathering and also the subject of Cynthia's rage because of his participation in the party.

69   **genium . . . meum protractus adorat** "dragged out, appealed to my divine spirit for mercy"

70   **nil potui** "I was helpless."

     captus eram Propertius returns to the figurative language of a captured city to describe Cynthia's behavior and its effects.

71   **supplicibus palmis** "with the palms of my hands in suppliant position"

     ad foedera literally "to treaties," a euphemism for military surrender

72   **cum vix tangendos praebuit illa pedes** "when she barely offered her feet to be touched in supplication." *Tangendos* is a fut. pass. pple., here to be translated literally.

73   **admissae si vis me ignoscere culpae** "if you want me to forgive the wrong you have committed"

74   **nostrae formula legis** Cynthia now employs legal language when indicating the terms of surrender that she will accept.

75   **neque . . . spatiabere cultus** "you will not stroll, dressed up and groomed." Note the fut. tense and indicative mood of *spatiabere* (= *spatiaberis*).

     Pompeia . . . in umbra "in the portico of Pompey," a locale celebrated as an ideal place for men and women to pick up prospective sexual conquests.

76   **nec cum lascivum sternet harena Forum** "nor when the sand will sprinkle the sexually playful Forum." Here Propertius refers to the use of the Forum for gladiatorial games, another occasion when "pick-ups" commonly occurred.

77   **colla cave inflectas ad summum obliqua theatrum** "be on your guard that you do not bend your neck at an angle (to look) at the the top of the theater," where the women sat. *Inflectas* and *det* in the following line are both pres. subjunctive verbs governed by *cave*, with *ne* understood.

78   **aut lectica tuae se det aperta morae** "or that an open litter offer an occasion (literally "provide itself") for your delay."

79 **omnis mihi causa querelae** "the entire reason for my complaint." Cynthia unfairly blames Propertius' slave and accomplice rather than Propertius himself for his attempted dalliances.

80 **veneat** "let him be sold at auction," jussive subjunctive

81 Note the two appearances of *lex* (*legem* and *legibus*) as well as Propertius' use of the fut. tense, responding to Cynthia's *spatiabere,* with *utar. Legibus* is the abl. object of *utar.*

82 **imperio facta superba dato** "made arrogant by the military power which I had given her." The adj. *superbus,* associated with Rome's last king, Tarquinius Superbus, likens Cynthia to a tyrannical monarch.

83-84 Understand *suffiit quemcumque locum externae puellae tetigere. Tetigere* = *tetigerunt.* The *externae puellae,* "girls from outside," are Phyllis and Teia. In spite of Propertius' sexual failure with these two women, he and Cynthia purify the premises as if he had actually committed a disgraceful deed.

87 **ita mutato per singula pallia lecto** "after every covering of the bed had been changed"

88 **respondi** is repeated from line 81, but here refers to his ability to perform sexually again.

solvimus arma = "we made peace." As *arma,* however, is also a figurative term for the male sexual equipment, this phrase at the same time alludes here and elsewhere in Propertius to sexual activity.

❧ 13 Ovid, *Tristia* 3.7.1-4, 21-30
Ovid encourages Perilla to keep writing poetry

The Roman poet Ovid spent the years 8 through 17 or 18 CE in exile in Tomis on the Black Sea (modern Constanța in Romania) after incurring the enmity of the emperor, Augustus. In *Tristia* 2.207 Ovid writes that two crimes caused his ruin: *carmen et error* (a poem and a mistake) but the reason for his exile has never been entirely clear. It is surmised that behind the official accusations against the immorality of his poetry Ovid may have had knowledge of a conspiracy against the emperor in which Julia, Augustus' granddaughter, was involved.

Ovid was miserable in exile, far from his audience and the city he loved. Among his works written lamenting his fate is the *Tristia*, from which this selection has been taken. In 3.7 Ovid asks the letter he has just written to go quickly to Rome and address Perilla (perhaps a pseudonym for his stepdaughter), encouraging her to continue with her poetry even though he is not there to serve as her guide and mentor, as he once did. The poem makes a strong case for the delights of writing poetry and the power of poetry as a means to ensure immortality; it also suggests that Romans believed that women had talent and interest in the pleasures of the mind (Ovid refers to Perilla as *doctissima* in the poem, suggesting her talent as a poet, as well as indicating that only Sappho would surpass the quality of her work).

Ovid's *Tristia* 4.10 provides a great deal of information about his life, describing himself as *tenorum lusor amorum* (a playful poet of tender love). Born in 43 BCE, Publius Ovidius Naso's literary career is remarkable for the variety and quantity of his poetry written in an elegant style. His works include elegiac poetry (*Amores, Heroides*); didactic poetry in elegiac meter (*Ars Amatoria, Remedia Amoris*); an epic, the *Metamorphoses*; a poetic calendar in the elegiac couplet (the *Fasti*); and elegaic poems written in exile (*Tristia, Epistulae ex Ponto*). Additionally, he was the author of a tragedy, *Medea*, now lost. He died in Tomis about 17 or 18 CE, never having been allowed to return home to Rome.

1   **vade** imperative of *vado* ("go quickly"), addressed to the letter he has just written, as if it were the messenger himself. The poem maintains the fiction that the messenger/letter is talking to Perilla.

      salutatum acc. of the supine, used after a verb of motion to express purpose

      subito adv., "hastily"

      perarata vocative of the pf. pass. pple., modifying *littera*

Perillam usually identified as Ovid's stepdaughter Perilla. Other scholars suggest that it is a pseudonym, such as elegiac poets use to hide the name of their beloved. This poem should be read with *Tristia* 3.3, addressed to his wife, since they both treat the same theme of poetry as a means of attaining immortality. Hence we are inclined to take Ovid at his word here.

2   **sermonis . . . mei** Note the chiastic word order (ABBA). The letter is personified as a "*fida ministra.*" In the opening poem of the *Tristia*, Ovid similarly addresses his first book of poems and tells it to go swiftly (*vade*) to Rome, where he cannot go, and visit the places he loves there.

3-4   **aut . . . suas** a charming picture of the favorite pursuits of the young woman

     Pieridas an epithet for the Muses, so named from the Pierian district of Mount Olympus. It is not until later in the poem that we learn that she actually is an accomplished poet herself.

     suas This reflex. adj. suggests that literature and the arts are very important to Perilla.

21   **mea . . . fortuna** Ovid is referring to his own banishment and the effect it may have had on Perilla's studies and writing.

22   **postque** = *post* + *que*

     sit subjunctive dependent on *vereor.* Supply *ne.*

     tibi dat. of possession

     pectus "mind"

23   **tua . . . mihi, tibi nostra** The chiasmus underlines the mutual nature of their interaction.

     legebam The repeated impf. tenses in this sentence, five in all, suggest that the poet and Perilla's inaction was a commonplace activity in the past.

23-24   **saepe . . . saepe** anaphora. Ovid chooses a different word-order strategy in this line to make the point that he served both as critic and teacher to his stepdaughter in her efforts to write poetry.

25 **factis . . . versibus** abl. absolute

modo adv. ("recently")

26 **ubi** "whenever." This construction, like a past general condition, takes the impf. subjunctive in the subordinate clause, the impf. indicative in the main verb.

27 **exemplo** abl. of cause. The poet in fact sets himself up as an example for Perilla: despite the difficulties poetry has created for himself, his devotion to poetry is still a model worth imitating. In the poem he establishes a series of parallels between himself and the young woman to prove this (Nagle, 150–51).

laesere = *laeserunt* < *laedo*. This is a verb that Ovid uses repeatedly of the damage done to himself by his poetry.

28 **poenae . . . meae** chiasmus (ABBA)

secunda "a copy of, a duplicate of" + dat. (*poenae*). Ovid believes that Perilla fears that her poetry too might result in the same punishment as her stepfather's.

30 **neve** "and let not"; used with the subjunctive in a negative prohibition

amare a reference to Ovid's *Ars Amatoria*, apparently one of the two causes of his exile. To avoid getting into the same trouble Ovid's poetry has caused him, Perilla is urged to avoid writing elegiac poetry.

✆ 14 Petronius, SATYRICON 111–12, excerpts
The *matrona* of Ephesus

This simple and elegant tale in which every word counts is a story within a story from Petronius' *Satyricon*. Eumolpus tells the tale to maintain good spirits among the motley group with him (Encolpius, Giton, Lichas, Tryphaena) who have just engaged in a mock battle on board ship and come to a truce. As a lead-up to the story, Eumolpus makes fun of the fickleness of women (*levitatem*), how easily they conceive a sexual passion and their willingness to abandon children for lovers. He insists that no woman was so chaste that she could not be seduced by a stranger, and then goes on to tell the story as proof (*Eumolpus . . . in muliebrem levitatem coepit iactare, quam facile adamarent, quam cito etiam filiorum obliviscerentur, nullam feminam esse tam pudicam quae non peregrina libidine usque ad furorem averteretur*, 110).

The reaction of the listeners is as varied as the meanings of the tale: the sailors laugh heartily; Tryphaena, the only woman in the group, blushes and tried to hide her head in embarrassment against Giton's shoulder. Lichas is not amused, claiming angrily that the governor should have had the husband returned to the tomb and the wife put up on the cross!

The bibliography on this artfully told little tale is surely as immense as the number of subsequent pieces of literature that owe their inspiration to it. The themes in the story are universal: she who protests too much will ultimately succumb; the weakness of women when it comes to sexual temptation; abstinence from food and sex equals death; eating, drinking, and sex equate to a return to life; the tomb is no place for the living. Parody of the lover as soldier from elegiac poetry and of Vergil's epic Dido and Aeneas story adds another dimension to the text.

As scholars have noted, there is something very repugnant about the end of the story: a wife willing to profane her husband's corpse by having it substitute for the stolen body of a thief on the cross. On the other hand, one cannot help but applaud the resourceful solution that the *matrona* proposes to the soldier, now that she is fully prepared to embrace life. In the final analysis, this is a tale told by a man, warning about the fickleness and dangerous potential of women.

Titus Petronius Niger, author of the *Satyricon*, is believed to have been a member of Nero's court, known for his elegant and sophisticated approach to life. Almost all the information we have about his life (27–66 CE) can be found in Tacitus *Annals*, 16.18–19, which describes the elegant manner of his forced suicide, after he ran afoul of Nero. The *Satyricon*, which Tacitus does not mention in connection with Petronius, has variously been described as Menippean satire or an ancient novel.

1-2   **matrona** By not giving her a name and simply calling her
matrona quaedam Petronius focuses our attention on the status and expectations for a woman in such a position and that
she is indeed a wife and married woman. The noun *pudicitiae* confirms the expectation that a wife will remain faithful
to her husband and a widow not remarry. In reality Roman
women finding themselves widowed at an early age frequently
did remarry. Still the highest approbation was reserved for the
woman who remained a widow (*univira*, as described in Propertius 4.11).

Ephesi Ephesus was the capital city in the Roman province of
Asia; after Rome it was the largest city in the Roman Empire.

tam adv., modifying the adj. *notae*. This adj. has a positive connotation on the surface but like the word "notorious" in English
can also have a negative undertone. (Cf. Cicero *Pro Caelio*, 31:
cum Clodia, muliere non solum nobili, sed etiam nota.)

notae . . . pudicitiae gen. of description. *Notae* is emphasized
here by its position before the noun it modifies (hyperbaton).
Pudicitia is the preeminent female virtue among the Romans.
One wonders how such a degree of chastity as the *matrona*
was known for is visible to others!

3   **sui** reflex. pron., objective gen., "of herself"

haec subject of *prosecuta est* and *coepit*. By opening the sentence with *haec*, the author puts us on notice that the focus
will be on the *matrona*. In one remarkable and lengthy sentence Petronius gives all the details of the exaggerated manner in which she mourned her husband. A short *cum* clause
at the beginning of the sentence disposes of the fact that her
husband had died.

4   **extulisset** < *effero*, "carry out of the house for burial, bury"

vulgari more abl. of manner

4-5   **passis . . . crinibus** abl. absolute

5-6   **prosequi . . . aut . . . plangere** infinitives dependent on
contentus

7 **Graeco more** that is, laying out the body in an underground tomb, rather than burning it, as the Romans did

8 **custodire** As the story develops, we will discover that, like the *matrona,* the soldier has a similar task, that is, guarding the bodies of the crucified thieves (see *custodiam,* 62) and, like the *matrona,* will neglect his duties for love.

 totis . . . diebusque abl. of time within which

In the several lines omitted here Petronius tells us that no one (not parents, not even the magistrates) was able to convince the *matrona* to leave the tomb or eat—she had not eaten for five days and there were fears she would starve herself to death.

9 **aegrae** dat. with the compound verb, *assidebat.* Supply *matronae.* Vergil also uses this adj. to describe Dido's state of mind after the death of her husband (*Aeneid* 4.35).

10 **et . . . et** "both . . . and"

 lugenti pres. act. pple., "to the mourning [woman]"

12 **renovabat** Supply *id* (referring to the *lumen*).

 una Take with *fabula.* Note the emphatic position at the beginning of the sentence, removed from the noun it modifies, *fabula* ("one, and only one").

13 **solum illud affulsisse** (< *affulgeo*) acc. and infinitive dependent on *confitebantur. Affulsisse* is an interesting choice of word, since it recalls the *lumen* the *matrona* has with her in the tomb that will eventually attract the attention of the soldier (*lumen . . . clarius . . . fulgens*).

13–14 **verum . . . exemplum** acc. in a predicate completion with *affulsisse* ("had shined forth, had appeared as a true example")

 omnis ordinis gen. of description with *homines.* One gets the impression, even if the author does not say so, that public opinion and recognition were among the motivating factors

in the *matrona*'s behavior. The opening passage of the anecdote certainly gives that impression with the words *spectaculum* and *in conspectu frequentiae*. Scholars have noted the
theatrical nature of the *matrona*'s behavior.

15–16   **cum . . . iussit** an example of the *cum inversum* construction
where the principal action is put into a *cum* temporal clause
and the definition of time is put in the main clause. Emphasis
is thereby placed on the information in the *cum* clause.

crucibus dat. with the compound infinitive, *affigi*

17   **casulam** a diminutive, "a small or humble cottage," here a
tomb. In the inverted world of the *matrona*, she is using the
tomb as a virtual home.

recens cadaver n. acc., object of *deflebat*

cadaver matrona a telling juxtaposition of words

18   **proxima . . . nocte** abl. of time

19   **ne . . . detraheret** subjunctive in a negative purpose clause

ad + acc., "for the purpose of burial." Those who were crucified were denied the right of burial, as a further mark of dis-
honor. Additionally the ancients believed that those who were
not buried could not get admitted to the lower world.

notasset = *notavisset*, plpf. subjunctive in a *cum* temporal
clause

sibi dat. of indirect object ("for himself")

20   **fulgens** n. sing. acc. of the pres. pple., modifying *lumen*

vitio abl. of cause, "because of a fault of human nature." Curi-
osity got the best of the soldier.

22   **concupiit** This compound and iterative verb suggests that the
soldier's interest in the *matrona* will be more than an interest
in simply knowing what she was doing there (he has not yet
seen her but has heard her voice mourning).

23   **visa . . . muliere** abl. absolute

24   **monstro . . . imaginibus** abl. of means with *turbatus*

25   **iacentis** pres. act. pple., gen. case, "of the one lying dead, of the corpse"

27   **sectam** < *seco*, pf. pass. pple. modifying *faciem*. Even with only her maid as an audience, the *matrona* produces a theatrical scene. Shortly she will also perform for the soldier, as she initially rejects his entreaties to stop mourning and live.

    ratus < *reor*, pf. pple. of a deponent verb, pass. in form but act. in meaning. The pf. pple. of *reor* is sometimes used in the sense of a pres. tense. Translate as "realizing."

28   **extincti** partitive gen. dependent on *desiderium*, "grief for . . ."

    non posse feminam acc. and infinitive dependent on an implied verb of cognition in the phrase *id quod erat*, "namely that, the woman was not able . . ."

30   **ne perseveraret** negative indirect command dependent on *hortari*. Note how the narrator highlights his persuasiveness with a compound verb and a powerful adj., *supervacuo*. Such persuasive language foreshadows the success the soldier will shortly have in persuading the *matrona* to succumb to his charms!

31   **ignota consolatione** abl. of means dependent on *percussa*. *Ignota* suggests that to the *matrona* the soldier's attempts at consolation are not welcome because they aimed at undermining her image as a lofty example of *pudicitia*.

    percussa < *percutio*, pf. pass. pple. ("deeply affected"), modifying *illa*

32–33   **ruptos . . . crines . . . imposuit** literally "she placed . . . her hair, having been torn out; she tore out her hair and placed it . . ." Rather than use two main verbs, Latin prefers to compress one of these into a pple.

33   **non recessit** the first use of military vocabulary in this passage. The soldier is not beaten yet but continues his siege! The very long sentence that these words introduce ends with the soldier's success with the maid and her subsequent attack on

her mistress, urging an end to her mourning. The Roman elegiac poets were fond of using military imagery to characterize the actions of the lover or beloved (see, e.g., **Reading 12**).

34   **mulierculae** diminutive, "poor little woman"

35   **corrupta** < *corrumpo*, pf. pass. pple., modifying *ancilla*; foreshadows the *matrona*'s imminent downfall

36   **invitantis** pres. act. pple., gen. case, dependent on *humanitatem*, "of the man inviting [her]"

37   **refecta** < *reficio*, pf. pass. pple., modifying *ancilla*

      potione et cibo The reverse order of these two items draws attention to them.

      expugnare military terminology! The soldier will shortly launch a full attack on the *matrona*'s virtue.

38   **pertinaciam** Petronius will use this noun again in lines 44–45 to indicate that she was willing to surrender (*passa est frangi pertinaciam suam*).

39   **id . . . sepultos** This line from Vergil's *Aeneid* 4.34 is from a speech in which Dido's nurse, Anna, tries to persuade the queen to forget her oath to remain faithful to her first husband and to give in to her new love for Aeneas. Vergil's line uses the infinitive *curare* ("care about") rather than the more expressive *sentire* ("feel") that Petronius uses. The use of *sentire* is poignant: do the dead really "feel?" Since Dido does eventually surrender, this reminiscence of Vergil reminds us what the end of this story is likely to be.

      id refers to all the things Dido has given up by remaining faithful to her dead husband (Vergil lists a lost youth spent in mourning, the lack of sweet children and the rewards of love).

      cinerem . . . sentire acc. and infinitive dependent on *credis*

40   **vis** second person sing. pres. of *volo*

      discusso . . . errore abl. absolute. The *error* of the *matrona* is the mistaken idea that a woman needs to remain faithful to her husband even after death!

41   **licuerit** fut. pf. of the impers. verb *licet*

lucis = *vitae*; gen. dependent on *commodis*. "Light" and "dark" (life and death) have been a recurring theme throughout the story.

commodis abl. with the deponent infinitive, *frui*

ipsum Take with *corpus*, subject of *debet*.

te object of *admonere*. Note the emphatic juxtaposition of *te* and *iacentis* in the chiasmus, *ipsum . . . corpus*.

iacentis gen. of the pres. act. pple., "of the one lying dead; of your dead husband"; foreshadows the love-making of the soldier and the *matrona* (*iacuerunt . . . una*, line 56)

42   **ut vivas** indirect command dependent on *admonere*

42–43   **nemo . . . vivere** a sarcastic comment by the narrator, Eumolpus. The idea of "life" is a recurrent theme in this section, hammered home by the repetition of the verb *vivere* or one of its compounds.

44   **aliquot** an indeclinable adj., agrees with *dierum*, dependent on *abstinentia*. The words in this line can be understood as also having a sexual connotation.

abstinentia abl. of cause dependent on *sicca*

46   **prior** Latin uses an adj. here, modifying the subject of the sentence. Translate in English as an adv.

victa est continuation of the military imagery begun above

47   **quid . . . soleat** subjunctive in an indirect question dependent on *scitis* (literally "what is accustomed to tempt the condition of a man being glutted with food"). The suggestion is that a man in such a condition would naturally think of sex.

48–49   **quibus blanditiis . . . , isdem** *Quibus* here is a coordinating rel. = *eis*, placed outside the rel. clause (literally "with the flatteries with which . . . with the same [flatteries]; with the same flatteries with which"). *Blanditiis*, the antecedent noun, has been placed inside the rel. clause.

impetraverat ... ut takes the subjunctive in a clause of result ("succeeded in his request that ... ").

50   **aggressus est** < *aggredior*: military imagery

51   **castae** with the use of this adj. and the noun *pudicitiam* Petronius reminds us of the *matrona*'s claim to fame, now under siege and shortly to surrender! *Castae* also makes a wonderful contrast with the adjectives, *nec deformis aut infacundus*, used to describe the *iuvenis* (*miles*).

51–52   **conciliante ... ancilla ... dicente** abl. absolute with pres. participles ("winning over her favor [toward the soldier]")

53   **placitone ... amori** The line is from Anna's entreaties to Dido to embrace the love for Aeneas she was beginning to feel (*Aeneid* 4.38).

54   **ne ... quidem** "not even"

55   **victor** Take in apposition to *miles*.

utrumque that is, both to eat and to make love

56   **iacuerunt** Petronius has already used this verb several times in the passage to refer to the dead husband (*iacentis*). Here it is used in the sense of "have sex." One is reminded of the haunting lines from Marvell's "To His Coy Mistress," "The grave's a fine and private place, but none, I think, do there embrace." In the inverted world of this tale the tomb is in fact a place for sex.

illa nocte abl. of time when

nuptias Like Dido the *matrona* calls an illicit relationship marriage, thus excusing herself for her behavior.

57   **postero** Supply *die* ("the second day").

57–58   **praeclusis ... foribus** abl. absolute. We are reminded that the doors of the tomb were open while the *matrona* was keeping watch over her husband's body and that is how the soldier entered. The symbolism of open and closed doors will be apparent to readers.

58–59   **ut ... putaret** subjunctive in a purpose clause

quisquis . . . venisset subjunctive used to state a repeated action in past time with the indef. pron. *quisquis*

60   **expirasse** = *expiravisse*; the double meaning of this verb in this context will be obvious to readers.

expirasse . . . uxorem acc. and infinitive dependent on *putaret*. The juxtaposition of nouns in the series *viri pudicissimam uxorem* reminds us that the once very virtuous wife is now in fact not sleeping with her husband but with a stranger in the husband's tomb!

61   **ut** + indicative, "when"

62   **detraxere** = *detraxerunt*

62-63   **supremo . . . officio** "burial"

circumscriptus "circumvented, cheated"

desidet that is, while he was neglecting his duty

65   **veritus** pf. pple. of the deponent verb *vereor* ("fearing"). In a few deponent verbs such as *vereor*, the pf. pple. is used in the sense of a pres.

quid accidisset subjunctive in an indirect question dependent on *exponit*

66-67   **nec se expectaturum (esse) . . . sed . . . (se) dicturum (esse)** acc. and infinitives dependent on an implied verb of cognition ("saying that . . .")

ius dicturum "would administer justice"

ignaviae suae gen. of the charge, "for his neglect of duty." Like Vergil's Dido, the soldier plans to kill himself because he has let love get in the way of duty.

67-69   **commodaret modo . . . et . . . faceret** clauses of proviso with the subjunctive, "provided only that . . ."

68   **perituro** fut. pple. of *pereo* (that is, the soldier)

fatale "deadly." The tomb has indeed been *fatale* for the soldier, since he is about to lose his life on account of his dalliance in it with the *matrona*. The emphatic position of the adj. makes the point strongly.

<commune> "the same; common to all." The angled brackets indicate that this word has been added to the text by a modern editor to make clear that husband and lover would share the same tomb.

70 **nec . . . dii sinant** pres. subjunctive, expressing a wish, "may the gods not allow . . ."

70–72 **ut . . . spectem** subjunctive in a clause dependent on *sinant*

duorum . . . carissimorum . . . duo funera The gen. dependent on *funera* precedes it (hyperbaton), further emphasized by the repetition of *duorum . . . duo*. One can no longer call the *matrona* an *univira*!

mihi dat. with *carissimorum*

72–73 **mortuum . . . vivum** direct objects of the infinitives. Powerful antithesis strengthened by the use of interlocked word order, ABAB (synchesis).

impendere < *impendo*, "expend." A wordplay on the look-alike infinitive, *impendere* < *impendeo*, "hang"

74–75 **tolli atque . . . affigi** pres. pass. infinitives

illi Take with *cruci*, dat. dependent on the compound verb, *affigi*.

ingenio abl., dependent on *usus est*

76–77 **qua ratione . . . isset** subjunctive in an indirect question dependent on *miratus est*

isset < *eo*, plpf. subjunctive

ꙮ 15 Suetonius, NERO 34
Nero decides to kill his mother

This chapter from Suetonius, *Lives of the Caesars*, focuses on the reasons why during the years 55–59 CE the emperor decided to murder his mother, Agrippina; how he accomplished this horrendous crime; and his reaction afterwards. Readers will want to compare Suetonius' brief account to the more famous and sensational version in

Tacitus, *Annales*, 14.1–13, as well as the account in the fragments of Dio Cassius 61.1–16.5. Unlike Tacitus, Suetonius unfolds the event solely from Nero's point of view. Nor does he actually describe the matricide itself.

Fig. 1 Marble bust of Agrippina the Younger, mother of Nero. 54–59 CE. As the sister of an emperor, wife of an emperor and mother of an emperor, Agrippina was a force to reckon with in her own right. Stuttgart, Landesmuseum Württemberg. Wikimedia Commons.

Our Roman sources provide substantial evidence about the influential role mothers played in the lives of their adolescent and adult sons (Dixon, 168–209). We can find numerous examples of the reverence shown by sons to mothers and mother figures, such as the Julius Caesar's eulogy for his aunt Julia (**Reading 7**). Still we can also find evidence of tensions between some famous mother-son pairs, such as Cornelia and Gaius Gracchus (**Reading 3**). In the case of Agrippina and Nero, we see a situation arising "of the mother who had worked diligently to achieve eminence for her son, only to encounter resentment when she made too many subsequent claims on the basis of her earlier efforts" (Dixon, 184–85). In analyzing the narrative it will be useful to remember that Suetonius is writing biography that evaluates his male subjects against a consistent ideal. As has recently been shown, women are valued in *Lives of the Caesars* for being wives and mothers and are used primarily to cast light on the behaviors of men with whom they are associated (Pryzwansky, 71–93). Agrippina, as bad mother, does not reflect well on Nero as ruler. Absent in Suetonius, however, is Agrippina's lust for power, so colorfully depicted in Tacitus' account. Nor does Suetonius move us to sympathy for her (Ginsburg, 50–51).

Suetonius' style has been described as "the businesslike style of the ancient scholar" (Wallace-Hadrill, 19). Background information is laid out in complex sentences using ablative absolutes, subordinate clauses, and present participles; the main verb or verbs in the perfect tense indicates what the emperor did. The occasional short sentence provides variety and focuses attention on imperial behavior of special interest. Still in this chapter that deals with such an emotional and lurid subject there is considerable evidence of Suetonius' effort to create an impact on the reader.

Gaius Suetonius Tranquillus (ca. 70 to after 130 CE) was a member of the equestrian class who enjoyed the patronage of such influential individuals as Pliny the Younger. As a member of the emperor's court, he served Trajan as director of public libraries and Hadrian as secretary in charge of the emperor's correspondence. Suetonius is best known for his biographies, *Lives of the Caesars*, which extend from Julius Caesar to Domitian. Each biography follows the same general formula, with various aspects of the emperor's public and private behavior arranged under headings, rather than a chronological telling of events. Emperors are then measured by their virtues and vices against the ideal emperor—with Augustus coming closest to the ideal.

1–10   **matrem . . . inquietarent** This long introductory sentence paves the way for the second sentence where we learn that Nero has made the momentous decision to kill his mother: here we discover why Nero arrived at this decision and the steps he took leading up to the decision. The sentence revolves around four main verbs enhanced by a series of participial phrases and abl. absolutes: *gravabatur* (the impf. tense is important here), *privavit*, *expulit*, and (*neque . . . pensi*) *habuit*. Nero is the understood subject of each of these verbs. Translating will require breaking down such an elaborate periodic sentence into several shorter sentences.

1–2   **exquirentem . . . et corrigentem** pres. act. participles modifying *matrem*. In this chapter we see Agrippina depicted as the "bad mother" (see below, for example, *minis eius ac violentia*). Unlike Tacitus, Suetonius does not mention Poppaea Sabina, Nero's mistress and eventually his wife, as the motivation for Nero's desire to get rid of his mother.

     hactenus "to this extent." Introduces the result clause that follows, *ut . . . oneraret,* but also sheds light on *primo.*

     primo contrasts with *mox.*

     invidia abl. with the verb *oneraret*, "so that he might burden her with unpopularity"

3   **oneraret** Supply Nero as the subject and *eam* as object.

     cessurus fut. pple. of *cedo*

     imperio abl. of separation with *cessurus*

4 **Rhodumque ... abiturus** There is no confirmation from ancient sources that Nero actually made this threat. Suetonius perhaps intended to remind the reader of another famous mother-son pair, Tiberius and Livia, and that emperor's withdrawal from civic life to Rhodes in 6 CE (Warmington, 91).

5 **privavit** Supply *eam*. Takes the abl. of separation. Understand *expulit* similarly.

5–6 **abducta ... statione** abl. absolute

militum et Germanorum Tacitus 13.18 tells us that as empress and then as mother of the emperor Agrippina had been given a bodyguard of praetorians that had recently been strengthened with the addition of German soldiers. Since the time of Augustus, elite German soldiers had served as a bodyguard to the emperor.

7 **neque ... quicquam pensi habuit** idiomatic, "nor did he care anything about," "nor did he have any scruples about." *Pensi* is gen. of value. Suetonius means to say that it did not at all bother Nero to cause his mother to be publicly harassed whether she was in the city or at rest at the seashore.

divexanda a rare verb ("harass"); here a gerundive in the abl. with *in*. Supply *ea* referring to Agrippina.

8 **summissis** Supply *eis* as antecedent to *qui* in an abl. absolute.

8–10 **qui ... inquietarent** rel. clause of purpose. Supply *eam* as the object, modified by *morantem* and *quiescentem*.

praetervehentes pres. act. pple. modifying *qui*

11 **verum** emphatic, indicating a statement in opposition to what precedes. Nero has now decided to take his harassment of his mother to the next level: murder.

13 **[eam esse] praemunitam** acc. and infinitive dependent on *sentiret*. Tacitus 14.3 also tells us that Agrippina had taken precautions against attempts on her life by poison.

lacunaria n. pl., "ceiling panels." The participial phrase, *laxata* (nom.) *machina* (abl.), explains how these were to cause her death. Somehow given Nero's interest in theater and staging theater, it is perhaps not surprising that his plans for Agrippina's destruction took such a turn.

13–14   **quae . . . deciderent** a rel. clause of purpose ("to . . . fall")

   dormientem Supply *eam.*

14–24   **hoc . . . exosculatus** another periodic sentence that describes Nero's elaborate plans to have his mother drowned in a collapsible boat. The sentence is built around the main verbs *commentus est, evocavit, protraxit,* and *optulit,* and ends with participles describing the repulsive details of his farewell to her as she gets set to depart.

14–15   **hoc consilio . . . celato** abl. absolute

   parum adv., "not, not sufficiently." Take with *celato.*

16   **vel naufragio vel . . . ruina** abl. of means. Understand *camarae* (gen. dependent on *ruina*) here as the deck (over her ship's cabin).

17   **commentus est** < *comminiscor,* "devise"

   reconciliatione simulata abl. absolute

18   **Baias** Baiae was a fashionable seaside resort on the north end of the Bay of Naples; Nero had a villa there.

   evocavit Supply *eam.*

18–19   **ad sollemnia . . . celebranda** gerundive expressing purpose

   Quinquatruum celebrations in honor of Minerva, 19–23 of March

   dato . . . negotio abl. absolute

20–21   **qui . . . confringerent** rel. clause of purpose

22   **repetenti** Supply *ei* (Agrippina).

   Baulos Bauli was the site of an imperial villa where Agrippina was apparently to stay the night, also on the Bay of Naples, not far from Baiae.

   corrupti pf. pass. pple.; refers to Agrippina's boat that had been deliberately damaged so it was not seaworthy

23   **machinosum** a word found only here, used to describe the substitute boat fitted up to collapse. Take with *illud*.

   optulit = *obtulit* < *offero*

23–24   **hilare . . . exosculatus** Note how skillfully Suetonius saves for the emphatic end of the sentence the revolting details about Nero's farewell to his mother; they make a striking contrast with his behavior in the next sentence (*cum magna trepidatione*).

   prosecutus atque . . . exosculatus Translate these pf. participles of deponent verbs as act. ("having . . .").

   atque "and even"

   exosculatus The force of this compound verb adds to the revulsion of this detail of Nero's good-bye to his mother.

24   **temporis** = *noctis*

26–27   **ut . . . comperit** a temporal clause with the indicative, "when he learned . . ."

   diversa (esse) omnia; **evasisse eam** acc. and infinitives, dependent on *comperit*

28   **consilii** gen., dependent on the adj. *inops* ("without, destitute of")

   L. Agermum Take as acc. subject of the infinitives *arripi* and *constringi*, dependent on *iussit*. In this highly subordinate sentence, *Agermum* is modified by the participial phrase introduced by *nuntiantem*.

28–29   **salvam et incolumem (esse eam)** acc. and infinitive dependent on *nuntiantem*

29–30   **abiecto . . . pugione** abl. absolute

30   **ut percussorem** Take in apposition to *L. Agermum* ("as an assassin").

   sibi reflex. pron., referring back to the subject "he" (Nero); dat. of disadvantage with *subornatum*

31   **matrem occidi** the third infinitive dependent on *iussit*. The lack of connectives, asyndeton, the change of acc. subject, and the juxtaposition of *matrem* with *occidi* make a powerful stylistic impact. Nero has made the unthinkable decision to have his own mother killed.

31-32 **quasi . . . vitasset** In this conditional clause the plpf. subjunctive expresses a contrary to fact action. This elaborately constructed sentence begins with the news of Agrippina's delivery from the plot involving the collapsible boat and ends with the order for her murder on the false charge that she had plotted against her son and committed suicide when the truth was uncovered.

       vitasset = *vitavisset*

33   **nec incertis auctoribus** abl.; the negative introduction to this phrase emphasizes that Suetonius has the revolting information that follows on good authority. Tacitus 14.9 is not quite so certain that these details are accurate. Dio 61.14.2 has Nero exclaim that he didn't know he had so beautiful a mother!

34-36 **accurrisse (eum) . . . contrectasse . . . vituperasse . . . laudasse . . . bibisse** acc. and infinitives dependent on an implied verb of saying in *adduntur . . . nec incertis autoribus*

       siti . . . oborta abl. absolute

37   **et militum . . . populique** genitives dependent on *gratulationibus*

40   **exagitari se** acc. and infinitive dependent on *confessus*

       Furiarum recalls Orestes of Greek myth, who, after murdering his mother, Clytemnestra, was pursued by Furies. Nero, after his mother's death, began performing on the stage in public; one of his favorite arias was Orestes the matricide (Suet. 21)!

41   **quin et** "and furthermore"

       Magos Magi, Zoroastrian priests. Nero was introduced to the religion of the Magi as a result of the visit of Tiridates, king of Parthia, to Rome.

Eleusinis sacris dat. with *interesse*. In 67 CE Nero travelled
to Greece to participate in the Olympic games as a charioteer
and also to perform as an actor and singer—he returned with
over 1,800 first prizes! During his nearly year-long trip he
visited Eleusis, site of the famous Eleusinian mysteries, but
according to Suetonius did not get initiated into the mysteries
because of a guilty conscience over the murder of his mother.

❧ 16 *CORPUS INSCRIPTIONUM LATINARUM* X.810 and 813

Eumachia's building

On the east side of the Forum in Pompeii the largest building in the
complex bears an inscription on the architrave over the entrance on
the Via dell' Abbondanza; the inscription identifies Eumachia as the
benefactor of the structure. (For pictures of the building see the University of Virginia Pompeii Forum Project at http://pompeii.virgin-
ia.edu/images/b-w/levin/small/levin.html; for a helpful plan of the
building see Cooley and Cooley, 99). As the inscription indicates,
Eumachia, a public priestess, paid for the building and dedicated it
to Concordia Augusta and Pietas in her own name and in the name
of her son. (For a picture of this inscription see **Fig. 2**). The exact
function of this magnificent building is unknown but it has been
conjectured to be a hall for various functions of a cloth workers guild
(headquarters, meeting place, even a center for the wool auction)
or perhaps a slave market. It more likely served as a multi-purpose
building for the conducting of business and recreation for different
groups. Another inscription from Pompeii records Eumachia's dedication of a statue but the location and nature of the statue are not
known (Cooley and Cooley, 101).

Having inherited a large fortune from her father, a member of one
of the leading families of the town, Eumachia married into another
prominent family. Her husband, M. Numistrius Fronto, was duumvir
(one of two chief magistrates in the city) in CE 2/3. (Some scholars
believe that it was her son who was duumvir in that year and that the

erection of the building was intended to assist his political career). Scholars have also noted that the building took inspiration from the Porticus Liviae dedicated to Concordia Augusta by the empress in conjunction with her son Tiberius in BCE 7. The scale and visibility of the building, as well as its connection to the imperial model, suggest what a powerful public statement Eumachia is making as one of the most prominent women of Pompeii. Her tomb outside the city is also remarkable for its size, although the inscription is modest ("Eumachia, daughter of Lucius, for herself and her family").

Public patronage was extremely important to Roman society, since recognition of unusual support for one's municipality confirmed the high social status of the donor. As the recipient of one of the most prestigious priesthoods in Pompeii, it is likely that Eumachia was expected to make a donation to the city, befitting her wealth and status.

Fig. 2 Dedicatory inscription over one of the entrances to the grandiose building of Eumachia. The scale and visibility of the building speak to Eumachia's prominence as a wealthy benefactor to the city. Early first century CE. Via dell'Abbondanza, Pompeii. Mentnafunangann/Wikimedia Commons.

CIL X.810

1   **L F** *L(uci) F(ilia)*

     SACERD PVBL *sacerd(os) publ(ica)*. She was priestess of Venus, an office held by the members of the highest municipal aristocracy. Venus was the patron deity of Pompeii.

2   **M** *M(arcus)*

     M NVMISTRI FRONTONIS FILI Supply *nomine*.

2–3   **CHALCIDICVM CRYPTAM PORTICVS** the several parts of the building ("the porch, covered passage, and colonnades")

3–4   **CONCORDIAE AUGUSTAE PIETATI** Take these datives with *dedicavit*. Eumachia dedicated the building to Concordia Augusta, a deity favored by the imperial family, and Pietas.

4   **PEQVNIA** = *pecunia*

5   **EADEMQVE** = *eadem* + *que*; acc. pl. n., referring to the three parts of the building mentioned in the inscription

CIL X.813

This inscription is on the base of a statue dedicated to Eumachia by the fullers of Pompeii as their patron. The statue, in which she is depicted veiled as a priestess, was found inside the building described above, in an alcove at the rear of the building. (For a photograph of a copy of the statue and inscription see http://www2.cnr.edu/home/sas/araia/Eumachia.html. The original is in the Naples Archaeological Museum.)

1   **EVMACHIAE** dat.; supply *dedicaverunt* as the verb for this sentence.

     LF *L(uci) F(ilia)*

2   **SACERD PVBL** *Sacerdot(i) publ(icae)*, dat. in apposition to *Eumachiae*

3   **FVLLONES** "fullers, drycleaners"; nom., subject of an understood *dedicaverunt*. During the production of wool, fullers finished the woven fabric to make it softer and thicker.

∾ *17 Pliny, LETTERS 4.19 and 8.10, excerpts*
Calpurnia: The model wife

Pliny the Younger, Gaius Plinius Caecilius Secundus, born in 61 or 62 CE, enjoyed a long and successful legal and political career in Rome, culminating in a consulship and serving as a legate in Bithynia. His extant writings consist of ten books of Letters, *Epistulae*, of which the first nine books are letters to friends and relatives from between 97 and 108 and which he published himself.

Apparently from the outset Pliny intended his letters for publication and hence they are a different kind of witness to life and culture of his times than those of a Cicero. Still since Pliny knew the emperor Trajan and many important political figures and writers of his time, his letters are a significant source of information on the ruling class of his day and contemporary events. Among the most well known are the two letters to his friend, Tacitus (6.16 and 20), describing the eruption of Mount Vesuvius in 79 CE and the subsequent death of his uncle, Pliny the Elder.

Letter 4.19 is addressed to Calpurnia Hispulla, aunt to Pliny's wife, Calpurnia Fabata. (It is not clear from his letters whether she was his second or third wife.) Some scholars argue that they married in 103/104; others as early as 97 or 98. Pliny will have been in his late thirties or early forties, his wife much, much younger, probably in her mid-teens.

In the opening sentence of the letter (omitted here) Pliny mentions that Calpurnia Hispulla loved his wife as a daughter and this was especially important since she had lost both her father (Hispulla's brother) and her mother.

Pliny, *Letter* 4.19, excerpt

2   **maximo . . . fore** literally "it will be of the greatest joy to you; you will be overjoyed"

tibi gaudio double dat. construction

fore fut. infinitive of *esse* in an acc. and infinitive construction dependent on *dubito*

3   **dignam** modifies the understood acc. subject, *eam* (refers to Calpurnia, Pliny's wife), as a predicate adj. with *evadere* ("turn out as").

4   **evadere** Supply *eam* as the acc. subject of *evadere* in an acc. and infinitive, dependent on *cognoveris*.

    summum . . . summa Anaphora (repetition of the opening words of each clause) and asyndeton (no connectives) emphasize the compliment Pliny pays his young wife. Supply *ei*.

5   **castitatis** The Romans put great store in female chastity in women—in fact it is the preeminent virtue of a good woman. For married women this is defined as fidelity to one's husband.

6   **accedit** literally "is added to" + dat.

    his that is, all her good qualities Pliny has just mentioned in the last several sentences

    studium litterarum "love of literature"

    mei partitive gen., "for me"

7–8   **habet, lectitat, ediscat** triplet verbs, asyndeton (no connectives between the verbs)

7   **lectitat** frequentative, "often reads, eagerly reads"

8   **illa** nom., subject of *adficitur*; refers to Calpurnia

    videor "I am seen; I am"

9   **acturus** fut. pple. of *ago*, "speak in court"

    egi < *ago* pf. act. indicative

10   **qui** Supply *eos* as the antecedent.

    qui nuntient subjunctive in a rel. clause of purpose ("to report . . .")

    quem adsensum Supply *excitarim* in an indirect question dependent on *nuntient*. Note that this is the first of three parallel indirect questions that Pliny uses to point up Calpurnia's eagerness to know the kind of applause, shouts of approval, and verdict Pliny had received. It is this kind of stylistic evidence that indicates how Pliny's letters are written with an eye to publication.

11   **excitarim** = *excitaverim*

12   **eadem** refers to Calpurnia ("she also").

        recito Reciting literary works in front of an audience was one
        of the means of publication in the period and also a form of
        entertainment.

        in proximo "close at hand, nearby"

13   **discreta** pf. pass. pple. of *discerno*, modifying *eadem*. By sit-
        ting discretely behind a curtain, Calpurnia could hear with-
        out being seen!

14   **quidem** "and what is more"

15   **format** "sets to music"

        cithara abl.

16   **artifice . . . docente** abl. absolute

19   **nobis** dat. of possession

        in dies "day by day"

19-20   **futuram esse concordiam** acc. and infinitive dependent on
        adducor.

        concordiam In this period "harmony" in a married relation-
        ship has become a very important ideal for Romans. Compare
        what Juvenal 6 has to say about wives who are chiefly respon-
        sible for disharmony in marriage.

Pliny, *Letter* 8.10, excerpt

This letter is addressed to Calpurnia's maternal grandfather, Cal-
purnius Fabatus, on the subject of his granddaughter's miscarriage.
The date of the letter is uncertain, perhaps several years earlier than
107. Roman marriages might take place before girls were twelve but
were not legally recognized until that age. Roman medical sources
from the period suggest fifteen to eighteen as the earliest age to have
children (Sherwin-White, 459). (The next letter in the collection is
addressed to Calpurnia Hispulla on the same subject).

2   **quo . . . hoc** abl. of degree of difference used correlatively with comparatives (*magis, tristior*) to express "the more . . . the more sadly. . ."

3   **tristior** Latin uses an adj. here, modifying the subject, rather than an adv. as in English.

         neptem . . . fecisse acc. and infinitive dependent on *audies*

3-4   **se . . . esse** acc. and infinitive dependent on *nescit*

4   **puellariter** "with a young girl's lack of experience"

5   **custodienda** the gerundive, used here as an adj., modifying *quaedam* and expressing necessity ("which . . . ought to have been careful about . . .; which pregnant women ought to have been careful about")

         praegnantibus dat. of agent with *custodienda*, used to denote on whom the necessity rests

6   **omittenda** same construction as *custodienda* above. Supply *quaedam*. It is not clear from Pliny's circumspect description what Calpurnia had done or not done to inadvertently cause the miscarriage.

         quem = *eum* connecting rel. modifying *errorem* ("this")

         magnis documentis "harsh warning"

7   **adducta** pf. pass. pple. modifying "she," the understood subject of *expiavit*. Apparently Calpurnia nearly lost her life as a result of the miscarriage.

8   **accipias** *Necesse est* often takes the subjunctive after it, without *ut*.

8-9   **quasi paratis** Pliny means that Calpurnia's pregnancy gave them every good reason to expect grandchildren eventually.

9   **destitutam** pf. pass. pple. modifying *senectutem*. Takes the abl. ("robbed of, deprived of").

         dis dat. pl. of *deus*

         agere . . . gratias + dat.: "give thanks to"

10-11   **ut . . . servarent** clause of result

11   **illos** refers to *pronepotes*.

reddituri fut. pple. expressing purpose, modifying an understood *di*, subject of *servarent* ("in order to")

12 **haec ipsa** Take with *fecunditas*.

   parum prospere "not happily"

13 **explorata** "ascertained, confirmed"

∾ 18 Sulpicia; Martial 10.35 and 10.38
Sulpicia's poetry and Martial's praise for her poetry

Almost no poetry by Roman women is still extant. Interestingly the two Roman female poets whose poetry we do have are both named Sulpicia. From the Augustan period there are eleven poems by the elegiac poet, Sulpicia, four of which are included in **Reading 11**, although, as is noted there, scholars have made the claim that some, and perhaps all, of these cannot have been written by a female author because no Roman woman could have written such suggestive and learned verses. The second Sulpicia, from the time of the emperor Domitian (81–96 CE), also wrote erotic verse.

The allusive two lines that we have of the second Sulpicia's poetry had the good fortune to survive because they were preserved by an Italian Renaissance scholar in his edition of Juvenal's *Satires*. In seeking to explain the rare and prosaic word *cadurcum* in the Juvenal text at 6.537, he mentions that the fourth century commentator, Probus, used an example from Sulpicia to explain the word. Sulpicia can be identified as the female poet mentioned in Martial 10.35, where her poetry is praised for its sexual playfulness that is directed specifically at her husband. Martial 10.38 identifies Sulpicia's fortunate husband, Calenus, as one of his friends. At least on the surface this poem appears to have been written as a consolation on Sulpicia's death.

Sulpicia

These two lines are all we have of Sulpicia herself, although later sources suggest she was very productive and well known. But was she simply a writer of erotic verse, remarkable for its female outspokenness? Richlin makes a provocative and persuasive case that she may have been a satirist, writing in a genre very hostile to women in the Roman world ("Sulpicia the Satirist").

Meter: iambic trimeter

1   **cadurci** gen. with *fasciis*, "a bed-frame"; by metonomy, "the marriage bed." This is the kind of noun more likely to be found in satire than elegy.

    restitutis fasciis abl. absolute, "after the bindings of my marriage bed have been put back in place." This image suggests some kind of break in the relationship, perhaps a quarrel.

2   **nudam** Take with *me*. See Hallett ("The Fragment of Martial's Sulpicia") for a discussion of how this reference and these lines evoke Propertius 2.15, a poem that celebrates a night the poet and his beloved spent in bed making love.

    Caleno dat. with the compound verb, *concubantem*. As the Martial poems below confirm, Calenus is her husband.

    concubantem Take this pple. with *me*. This verb, not otherwise found in Latin literature, provides a vivid image of the lovers together—Sulpicia does not mince words when describing erotic situations. As Hallett has shown, this pple. recalls both Propertius 2.15 and the other Sulpicia 3.9 (contemporary of the Roman elegiac poets, such as Tibullus).

    proferat Because of the fragmentary state of this sentence, it is not clear what the subject of *proferat* is ("it [?] would reveal"). Hallett suggests Venus, based on a reference in the other Sulpicia's poetry at 3.13. For a female writer, this line appears to be startlingly frank in its erotic suggestiveness.

Martial 10.35

In this poem Martial praises Sulpicia as a writer of erotic, yet chaste verse, suggesting that she might have served as a teacher or fellow student of Sappho. Echoes of Sappho, the other Sulpicia, and Roman male writers of erotic verse, such as Catullus and Propertius, permeate the poem, as a male poet makes the case for a female poet who even here does not speak for herself.

An intriguing question for scholars in putting this poem and the next into their literary context is how much information can we derive about Sulpicia's place as a poet. Is she, as Richlin (134) suggests, writing "consciously as a woman for a female audience?" Can we conclude with Hallett ("Martial's Sulpicia and Propertius' Cynthia," 120–23) that her appropriation of Propertius' language and erotic scenarios that have to do with extramarital love is a challenge to acceptable social norms for women?

Martial (Marcus Valerius Martialis), a native of Spain, is best known for his twelve books of epigrams published from 86 to 101 or 102 CE. Ranging from a single verse to thirty or forty lines in length, these little poems in a variety of meters are remarkable for their wit and elegant and polished style, as well as their commentary on the foibles of everyday life. Among his friends he counted other writers of the period, such as Juvenal and Pliny the Younger. A letter of Pliny's, announcing Martial's death (*Ep.* 3.21), predicts that his epigrams will not be immortal!

Meter: hendecasyllabic (said to have been invented by Sappho), frequently used by Catullus, among others

1–4   **omnes . . . nuptae** By repeating whole phrases in the exact same place in the line, Martial places emphasis on the words that are not expected: *mariti* and *placere nuptae*. *Nuptae* is further thrown into relief by the reversal of the phrase *viro placere* into *placere nuptae*, which places *nuptae* into the emphatic position at the end of the line and the end of the sentence. Romans expected their wives to be faithful; wives did not have the same expectation for their husbands!

1   **legant** jussive subjunctive, "let . . . read"

      puellae here "young women, young wives"

2   **uni** Take with *viro*. Placing the adj. at the beginning of the sentence and ahead of its noun gives it prominence (hyperbaton).

      placere takes the dat.

5   **non** introduces what Sulpicia does not write about: three great epic themes; but (*sed*) she does teach *amores, lusus, delicias,* and *facetias*. A commonplace theme of Roman poetry, this device is called a *recusatio*.

      haec refers to Sulpicia ("she").

      adserit "claim as her own, claim as her subject (of poetry)"

5–7   **non . . . credit** The poet alludes to four mythological stories (grouped as a triplet: *non . . . nec . . . nec*) that Sulpicia chooses not to treat in her poetry: all involve some aspect of immoral love and consequently immoral actions. Hallett notes that in all four cases the Greek mythic characters treated their blood relations in a heinous fashion.

      Colchidos Greek gen. of *Colchis*, "a Colchian woman." The poet uses this epithet to stand for Medea, a native of Colchis.

6   **diri** Take with *Thyestae* (gen.): According to the myth, Thyestes was tricked by his brother into eating his own sons at a banquet.

7   **Scyllam, Byblida** (< *Byblis*) **. . . fuisse** accusatives and infinitive dependent on *credit*. Scylla betrays her father for the love of his enemy, Minos; Byblis feels an incestuous love for her brother that ultimately causes her death. Note the asyndeton (lack of connectives) between the two nouns.

8   **castos . . . et probos** The position of these adjectives before their noun, *amores,* (hyperbaton) draws attention to the unexpected nature of what they are saying—elegaic poetry cannot be said to deal with *castos . . . et probos amores*. Again these four nouns are arranged in a group of three (*amores, lusus, delicias facetiasque*) by the lack of connectives between the first two, contrasted with the tight connective *-que* between the second pair.

8–9   **amores, lusus, delicias, facetias** These nouns remind one of the vocabulary of earlier erotic male poets, such as Catullus and Propertius, but they are celebrating passion between extramarital partners, not husband and wife.

10   **cuius** connecting rel. ("of whom, of her"), dependent on *carmina*

    (is) qui ... aestimarit Take this rel. clause as subject of *dixerit*.

    bene "fairly"

    aestimarit = *aetimaverit*

11   **dixerit** like *aestimaret*, fut. pf. This sentence follows the syntax of a more vivid fut. condition. Translate: "if any one judges, he will say. . ."

    nequiorem < *nequam*, "more licentious, naughtier." The similar structure of lines 11 and 12 underlines the contrast made at the end of the line: no woman is naughtier in her verses than Sulpicia; no woman is more pure! Is this because Sulpicia writes sensual verses but they relate to her husband, to whom she is faithful? Martial here develops the contrast that he hinted at in *castos . . . et probos amores* juxtaposed with *lusus, delicias, facetias.*

13   **Egeriae** in Roman mythology the nymph wife to Numa Pompilius, legendary second king of Rome. Numa is said to have met her in her sacred grove, where she taught him to be a wise and just king. Egeria and Numa are evoked as a persuasive model of marriage from Rome's mythic past to validate Sulpicia's naughty yet acceptable erotic verses.

14   **udo** Take with *antro*. Presumably the cave is "damp" because of a spring within: hyperbaton.

    crediderim pf. subjunctive, "I might have believed"

15–16   **hac ... Sappho** In this direct address to the poet Sappho, Martial claims that Sappho might have learned wisdom and been sexually pure had she had Sulpicia as her teacher!

17   **visam** pf. pass. pple. of *video*; take with *Sulpiciam.*

18   **durus** "hard-hearted"; take with *Phaon* (Greek nom.). Tradition claimed that Sappho fell in love with the beautiful ferryman Phaon and when he rejected her she threw herself off a cliff and drowned.

Sulpiciam The position of her name between *durus* and *Phaon* underlines the point that Phaon would have fallen for her, even if he did not succumb to Sappho's charms.

amaret In this implied contrary to fact condition we would expect *amasset* ("he would have loved"). The impf. can refer to past time, when a repeated or continued action is intended.

19   **frustra** Supply *amaret*.

namque a stronger form of *nam* ("for indeed")

Tonantis epithet for Juppiter. *Uxor Tonantis* = Juno. In Catullus 72 the poet has Lesbia say that she would prefer no one but him, even if Juppiter himself should come seeking her.

20   **puella** Take with *Bacchi* and *Apollinis*, that is, Ariadne and Daphne, predicate nouns. Translate *puella* here "as the love." Sulpicia is a remarkable example of the Roman *univira* who, should she lose her husband, would not even consider being the wife or beloved of a god.

21   **erepto . . . Caleno** abl. absolute. The poem fittingly places Calenus' name as the last word and the link to poem 38.

sibi reflex. pron. referring back to Sulpicia: here dat. of separation with *erepto*

Martial 10.38

This poem, addressed to Calenus, Sulpicia's husband, opens with three exclamations, extolling the pleasures of their marriage. Hallett has shown how these lines recall in structure and vocabulary Propertius 2.15, an elegy commemorating a night that the poet and his beloved spent in bed making love. Scholars have also noted that 10.35 and 10.38 should be taken together as a pair (the poems seem to owe a great deal to the mutual pledge of love made by the lovers,

Acme and Septimius, in Catullus 45, for example). Although the poem is generally understood as a consolation on Sulpicia's death, Richlin ("Sulpicia the Satirist," 128) raises other interesting possibilities that may have given rise to the poem—perhaps on the occasion of their divorce.

Meter: hendecasyllabic

1–3   **molles** Take with *quindecim . . . iugales . . . annos* (antecedent of *quos*).

      tibi Take with *molles.*

5   **caris . . . lapillis** abl. of means with *notata est.* The image is that of an hour glass filled with tiny precious stones from India.

6   **proelia . . . pugnas** The love-as-war metaphor also recalls Propertius 2.15, as do the affectionate diminutives, *lectulus* and *lucerna.* It has been suggested that these lines are a direct allusion to Sulpicia's own poetry (Parker 1992, 92).

8   **ebria** Take with *lucerna.*

      nimbis . . . Nicerotianis "clouds of Nicerotian scent." Niceros was the name of a fashionable maker of perfume, Nicerotian the adj., meaning perfume made by Niceros.

9   **tribus . . . lustris** "during three five-year periods; during fifteen years." Abl. of time within which to express the period in which the event lasted, implying that it only lasted during that period.

10–11   **aetas . . . mariti** The poet means that Calenus considered his years as husband the only years of his life.

10   **tibi** dat. of reference or dat. of agent

      tota Take as predicate adj. with *aetas.*

11   **mariti** a limiting gen., used instead of a noun in apposition ("days as husband")

12–14   **si . . . redderet . . . malles** contrary to fact condition in the pres.

13   **lucem** "day of life"

     Atropos one of the three Fates; it is she who ended an individual's life by cutting with her shears the thread that had been spun at birth. Calenus would prefer to have back even one day of his married life than four times the age of the long-lived Nestor.

14   **quam . . . senectam** Construe as *quam* (refers to *lucem*) *malles quam senectam Pyliam*.

     Pyliam "from Pylos, Pylian." Refers to Nestor, aged hero in the *Odyssey*.

✎ *19 TABULA VINDOLANDA 2.291 and 2.292*

A Roman woman writing on the frontiers of Empire: The letters of Claudia Severa from Vindolanda

Until the 1980s, the list of women's writings in Latin still surviving from Roman antiquity terminated with the two-line fragment by the poet we have called "Martial's Sulpicia." Our roster of Roman female writers at that point consisted solely of women residing in the capital city and belonging to Rome's most distinguished households and leading literary circles. But excavations at a Roman fort in northern England known as Vindolanda have recently yielded some other Latin texts by women from the classical era, all of them dated to approximately 100 CE. Two such texts have been shared with a wider audience: letters written to Sulpicia Lepidina, wife of the military prefect Flavius Cerealis, by Claudia Severa, who was married to another officer named C. Aelius Brocchus. Both husbands were members of Rome's second highest class, the equestrian order, and corresponded with one another on a regular basis.

These letters are significant for the study of both Roman social and Latin literary history. First and foremost, they testify that the wives and children of Roman military officers resided with them in far-flung posts during the imperial period. A speech written around the same time as these letters by the Roman historian Tacitus, at *Annales* 3.33, implies that their presence was a relatively recent development:

its speaker claims that even wives of provincial governors and generals did not accompany their husbands on tours of duty until the reign of Tiberius, approximately seventy-five years earlier.

Two different scribes appear to have written Claudia Severa's letters. Yet one of these letters ends with three lines in her own hand. In noting the elegance of the Latin style found in both letters, scholars call attention to these three lines as evidence that Severa herself deserves credit for their high literary quality.

Like the other extant writings in Latin by women, these two letters evoke earlier Latin as well as Greek literature; emphasize family relationships; and portray women as involved in ritual celebrations, in this case Severa's birthday. But whereas the texts by the two Sulpiciae and Cornelia are not written expressly for a female audience, these letters have a female addressee; what is more, Sulpicia Lepidina is addressed in affectionate, at times erotically flavored language. Most obviously, Severa calls her "sister" three times in the first letter and twice in the second, although their different family names make it clear that they are not blood relations. She also refers to her as "most precious soul" (*anima . . . karissima*) and "most precious and adored soul" (*karissima et anima desideratissima*) in the second.

By bidding Lepidina "farewell . . . and hail" (*vale . . . et have*) in the first letter, Severa may well allude to the emotionally charged phrase "hail and farewell" (*ave atque vale*) that concludes Catullus' celebrated elegy 101. It laments the death of Catullus' beloved brother far from home, in the eastern Mediterranean. Another literary model for this letter appears to be the fourth book of Vergil's *Aeneid,* in which Queen Dido and her sister Anna, who have fled their native Tyre for the shores of Carthage, converse about Aeneas and his plight as a Trojan exile. At *Aeneid* 4.8 Vergil refers to Anna as Dido's *unanimam sororem*, "sister sharing a soul"; at 4.31 he has Anna describe Dido as "cherished more than life by her sister" (*luce magis dilecta sorori*).

We know nothing about the educational background of these two women, and should not automatically assume that they would have been familiar with these earlier Latin texts. Nevertheless, another letter in the Vindolanda archive, written by a man who addresses another man as dearest brother (*karissime frater*), directly quotes a line from the ninth book of the *Aeneid*. Here Vergil describes how a Trojan woman in Aeneas' entourage learns that her son Euryalus and his male beloved Nisus have fallen in battle on Italian soil. These allusions suggest that the residents of this Roman military outpost in far-off Britain found comfort and inspiration in Latin poetry—especially poetry about family ties, and the losses of family members, in distant locales.

Tab. Vindol. 2.291, Claudia Severa to Sulpicia Lepidina

The letters enclosed in brackets are conjectures.

1–2   **[sa]l[u]tem** = *salutem dicit*, "sends greetings." *Lepidinae* [*suae*], dat. indirect object with *salutem* [*dicit*]. Note that Claudia Severa refers to both herself and Sulpicia Lepidina in the third person, the latter with the reflex. third-person possessive adj. *suae* in the greeting; she then switches to the first person for herself and the second for her addressee.

3–4   **iii Idus Septembr[e]s** = *ante diem* III *Idus Septembres*, "on the third day before the Ides (13th) of September"; acc., time construction

   ad diem sollemnem natalem meum = *ad diem sollemnem natalem meum celebrandum*, "for the purpose of celebrating my birthday in accordance with ritual practice"

   soror is vocative, an affectionate address to Sulpicia Lepidina, who was not a blood relation of Severa, as "sister."

4–8   **rogo/ libenter facias ut venias/ ad nos iucundiorem mihi/ [diem] interventu tuo factura si / s** = *rogo libenter ut facias ut venias ad nos factura tuo interventu* [*hunc*] *diem iucundiorem mihi, si* [*venie*]*s*. "I warmly invite you so that you make sure that you come to us, in order to make the day more pleasant for me if [you will come].

   rogo [ut] facias is an indirect command; *facias ut venias* is a substantive clause of result; both *facias* and *venias* are pres. subjunctives in primary sequence. **iucundiorem** modifies *diem* in the following line; they are the object of the fut. act. pple. *factura*, to be understood as conveying a sense of purpose.

7   **interventu tuo** "by your arrival." Note the repetition of the root *ven-*, previously seen in *venias*; the juxtaposing of two words derived from the same root but representing different parts of speech is known as a *figura etymologica*, "etymological figure." It is possible that the *s* in the next line is the final letter of the verb form *venies*, "you will come," and that Severa has in fact placed three words with the root *ven-* in close proximity.

factura is the fut. act. pple. of *facio*, and literally means "about to make"; it, too, shares a sentence with another form of the same verb—*facias*—and creates an etymological figure too.

9–10   **Cerial[em t]uum saluta** = *Cerialem tuum maritum saluta*. "Send greetings to your husband Cerialis." *Saluta* is a sing. imperative.

Aelius meus/et filiolus salutant = *Aelius maritus meus et filiolus meus te salutant*.

11   **sperabo te soror** = *sperabo te videre, soror*.

12–14 **vale soror anima/ mea ita valeam /karissima et have** = *vale, soror, anima mea, ita valeam, carissima, et ave. ita valeam*, "thus may I be well." These are the lines evidently written in the hand of Claudia Severa.

15–17 **Sulpiciae Lepidinae Cerealis** "to Sulpicia Lepidina, wife of Cerealis"

Tab. Vindol. 2.292, Claudia Severa to Sulpicia Lepidina

1   **salutem** = *salutem dico*

2–3   **ego soror sicut tecum locuta fueram** = *sicut ego, soror, tecum locuta eram*. Roman authors sometimes use "plus-pluperfect" verb forms, with the plpf. rather than the impf. of the verb *sum*, when describing actions that occurred at different times in the past, to emphasize that the earliest action was completed well before the other action or actions.

2-3 **promiseram/ut peterem a Broccho et venirem at te** = [*sicut*] *promiseram ut peterem a Broccho et ut venirem ad te*. *Promiseram* introduces an indirect command, which contains the verbs *peterem* and *venirem*: "I had promised that I would seek (permission) from Brocchus and that I would come to visit you," in secondary sequence with verbs in the impf. subjunctive. *At = ad.*

peti = *petivi*, beginning a new sentence

4 **et res[po]ndit mihi <i>ta corde semp[er li]citum una** = *et respondit mihi una semper esse licitum et esse ita cordi*, "and he replied that it was at the same time always permitted to me and so pleasing." Indirect statement governed by *respondit*; the verbs to be understood in the indirect statement are *licitum esse*, "it was permitted," and *corde esse*, "it was pleasing," united by *una*, "at the same time as"; the adv. *ita* triggers the result clause in the following line.

5-6 **quomodocumque possim/ at te pervenire** = *ut possim ad te pervenire quomodocumque*, "that I be able to visit you in whatever way." One would expect the impf. subjunctive *possem* rather than the pres. *possim*, since the main verbs are in the past tense.

6 **sunt** begins a new sentence.

7 **necessaria quaedam qua[e]** The clause introduced by the n. pl. rel. pron. *quae*, which has *necessaria quaedam*, "certain necessary matters," as its antecedent, is missing.

8 **rem meum** The grammatical relationship between the f. acc. sing. noun *rem* and the m. or n. acc. sing. adj. is unclear. A new sentence begins with the acc. pl. noun and adj. *epistulas meas*, the direct object of *accipies* in the following line.

9-10 **quibus scies quid/ sim actura** *quibus*, abl. of means, with *epistulas meas* as the antecedent. *Quid actura sim* is an indirect question in pres. subjunctive, "what I am about to do." The grammatical relationship of *haec nobis*, "these things to us," with the previous sentence is unclear, and these words probably belong to a separate sentence that is mostly lost.

11   It is also unclear what word the letters *ra* end, but it may be a
        fut. act. pple. like *mansura*.

        eram et Brigae mansura = *eram et mansura sum Brigae. Bri-*
        ga is the name of a town, in the locative case.

12   **Cerialem tuum a me saluta** These words form a new sen-
        tence, contained within the line. *A me saluta,* "send greetings
        . . . from me."

13–15   It is unclear what the *m* in line 13 signifies, perhaps an abbre-
        viation of *mea;* the *ma* in line 15 is similarly obscure.

16–18   **Sulpiciae Lepidi/nae Ceria[li]s/ a Severa Brocchi** *Sulpiciae*
        Lepidinae is in the dat.; *Cerialis* is gen. sing., "[wife of] Cerea-
        lis"; *Brocchi* similarly means "wife of Brocchus."

∾ 20 *Juvenal,* SATIRES 6. 161–71
Why wives are insufferable

Although scholars cannot agree on the theme or structure or intent
of Juvenal's sixth satire, it is clear that it would be hard to find a
more virulent attack on women as wives and rejection of marriage
than the 650 lines this poem provides. In anecdote after anecdote,
the poet rants about wives' capacity to humiliate and even harm and
kill husbands who seem defenseless against their attacks: infidelity
is one of the major indignities suffered by husbands. In our passage
Juvenal makes the case that the perfect wife is equally unbearable.
Even such a paragon as Cornelia, mother of the Gracchi, is likely to
display arrogance and so is not acceptable.

As the satirist depicts them, wives are adulterous, extravagant,
domineering, cruel, indifferent, and murderous. In this early imperial period (this satire is usually dated about 116 CE) Romans, we
know, idealized a close and harmonious partnership (*concordia*) in
the married relationship. Tacitus' description of his parents-in-law's
marriage provides a wonderful example of that ideal: *vixeruntque*
mira concordia, per mutuam caritatem et in vicem se anteponendo,
nisi quod in bona uxore tanto maior laus, quanto in mala plus culpae
est (*Agricola* 6.1). *Mira concordia* here also means mutual affection

and concern for the other. Imperial marriages since the time of Augustus and Livia were especially seen as models of harmony for others. From roughly the same period as Juvenal, Pliny's *Panegyric to Trajan* describes the imperial marriage as a model of harmony because of Plotina's efforts that it be so. She is praised for a range of behaviors including devotion to her husband, obedience, modesty, moderation, an unassuming demeanor, and respect for her husband. The same passage makes the case that wives, although subordinate, hold significant power because their behavior reflects on their husband's reputation.

One of the messages of Juvenal's sixth satire would seem to be that disruptive and non-compliant wives make impossible the Roman ideal of *concordia* in marriage. Perhaps Juvenal is also lashing out at changing mores of the period during which, scholars have argued, emerged a new concept of marriage that focused on a conjugal partnership in which a man views his wife as a friend and a life's companion.

We have little specific information about the life of the satirist Juvenal (Decimus Iunius Iuvenalis); he is conjectured to have lived roughly between 50 and 127 BCE, and the poet Martial is known to have been a contemporary and friend of his. His poetic work consists of sixteen satires of varying length. The hallmark of Juvenal's *Satires* is the indignation and rancor with which he attacks what he sees as the vices and moral and political decline of the time in which he lived. Women are selected for especially abusive treatment at his hands.

161   **nullane** Juvenal leads off this part of the poem with a rhetorical question that appears to expect an answer of either "yes" or "no," but it is soon clear that the answer is "no."

162   **sit** a main verb ("jussive") subjunctive, "she may be, let her be." Similarly *disponat*.

         formonsa . . . fecunda Commentators have noted that the list of adjectives describing the "good woman" reads like a Roman epitaph. Attention is drawn to these adjectives by alliteration and chiastic word order (ABBA). Asyndeton (no connectives) is also a prominent feature of this sentence.

vetustos Take with *avos*. Emphatic because it is pulled far forward of its noun.

163 **porticibus** Supply *in*. Roman noble families displayed death masks of their famous male ancestors in the atrium of the house to advertise their glorious past. Here the poet suggests a similar display—perhaps of statues in the porticoes of the house.

omni Take with *Sabina*.

164 **crinibus effusis** abl. absolute. Unfastened hair in antiquity was a sign of mourning.

dirimente pres. act. pple. modifying *Sabina*. *Bellum* is the direct object of the pple.

Sabina Early Roman legend had it that after neighboring Sabine women had been forcefully taken by the Romans for wives they intervened to prevent war between husbands and brothers and fathers (Livy 1.9; 11.1–4). Sabine women had a reputation as being chaste.

166 **constant omnia** imagery from accounting ("all [sums] are in balance, are correct"). Here the poet means that such a wife is perfect in every way.

166–67 **malo, malo** The figure of speech where the same word ends one line and begins the next is called *anadiplosis,* allowing the poet forcefully to make the point about where his preference lies when it comes to a wife.

167 **Venustinam** The name, related to the name of the goddess Venus, suggests an ordinary woman, perhaps even a prostitute—certainly a woman without a fancy pedigree. Note the contrast with the noble Cornelia that follows and the shock value of the attack on such a well-known example of the model wife and mother.

Cornelia On this renowned Roman mother of Tiberius and Gaius Gracchus, see notes on **Reading 3**. Her illustrious family included her father, Publius Cornelius Scipio Africanus, who defeated both Hannibal's ally, the Numidian leader

Syphax in 203 BCE, and Hannibal himself in 202 BCE, thus putting an end to the Second Punic War.

169 **supercilium** "arrogance, haughtiness." The implication is Cornelia has the strong potential to be arrogant because of her family name and the very famous accomplishments of her male relatives.

triumphos all the military triumphs earned by her male relatives, especially her famous father

170–71 **tolle . . . migra** The two imperatives in emphatic positions at the beginning and end of the sentence are addressed to Cornelia (cf. *tuum*), as the poet rather rudely dismisses her. Here *tolle* is best translated as "remove, take away."

Syphacem in castris The reference refers to the fact that Scipio surprised Syphax in his own camp before defeating his forces.

cum tota Carthagine Translate *tota* in the emphatic position in this phrase as "with your Carthage, lock, stock, and barrel."

migra "off you go, be off!"

✸ 21 Aulus Gellius, *Noctes Atticae* 1.12, excerpts

"Taking" a Vestal Virgin

Between the age of six to ten, girls were chosen as Vestal Virgins and served for thirty years, some for their entire lifetime. During their time of service the six Vestals lived in the house of the Vestals in the Roman Forum, adjacent to the temple of Vesta (*aedes Vestae*); their main responsibility was to tend the sacred fire in the temple and keep it going as a guarantee of Rome's safety. They also performed other religious tasks and duties, such as fetching water from a special spring to purify the temple and preparing the *mola salsa* ("ground spelt") used in every Roman sacrifice. As Vestals they enjoyed special privileges that set them apart from other women. At the same time punishment for being unchaste (*crimen incesti*) was burial alive in an underground chamber.

Recent scholarship has shown Vestal Virgins to be "the embodiment of the city and citizenry of Rome" (Parker 2004, 567). Since the Vestals did not participate legally in the Roman family structure, they were able to represent Rome as a whole in the religious sphere (Wildfang, 64–75). The virginity of the Vestal Virgins was central to the institution—they had to be pure in every way since "they were both the symbol of the inviolability of Rome but also its guarantee" (Parker 2004, 568).

For information on Aulus Gellius, see **Reading 4**.

Fig. 3 View of the courtyard of the House of the Vestals. This reconstruction of the building dates to the early third century CE. Part of a complex of related buildings, the House of the Vestals served as the residence for the six Vestals during their years of service. Carole Raddato/Wikimedia Commons.

1   **qui** = *ei qui*. The rel. clause, *qui . . . scripserunt*, is subject of the
     verb *negaverunt*.

     de virgine capienda "about taking a Vestal Virgin; about
     choosing a Vestal Virgin," the technical terminology the Ro-
     mans use to describe the ritual of choosing and admitting a
     Vestal Virgin into the college of Vestals by the Pontifex Maxi-
     mus. The long opening sentence detailing qualifications for
     selection indicates the young girl had to be perfect in every
     way, as defined socially and legally in Rome; admission to
     this Roman priesthood broke all ties with her family. Her new
     unique legal status set her apart from all other Romans, male
     and female (Staples, 143–44). This allowed her to symbolize
     Rome as a whole.

     capienda gerundive modifying *virgine*

2   **Labeo Antistius** Marcus Antistius Labeo, a prominent Ro-
     man jurist of the time of Augustus

2–3 **minorem . . . maiorem** compar. adjectives modifying *natam*
     (here a noun, not a pple.)

3   **natam** acc. subject of the pres. pass. infinitive, *capi*

3–4 **natam, negaverunt capi fas esse** "(they) have stated that it is
     not lawful for a girl to be taken . . ." This clause is also to
     be understood before each of the rel. clauses of characteristic
     that follow.

4   **quae** Supply *natam* as the antecedent.

     item "besides"

5   **lingua debili** abl. of description, "with a crippled tongue, with
     a speech defect"

     sensuve = *sensu* + *ve*; *sensu* is abl. dependent on *diminuta*.

6   **deminuta (sit)** takes the abl., "may be deprived of . . ."

     aliave qua Take with *labe. Aliave* = *alia* + *ve*.

7   **quae ipsa** Supply *emancipata sit*.

     emancipatus sit "has been released from the power of the *pa-
     ter familias*." Note that *emancipatus* get its gender from *pater*,

the closest noun, not from *quae ipsa*. Roman women their whole lives were either under the power of a father, guardian, or husband.

8   **vivo patre** abl. absolute. If a man were emancipated after the birth of children, the children remained under the control of the grandfather (Gaius, *Institutes of Roman Law*, I.133).

9   **servitudinem servierunt** "may have been in slavery." In this construction, the intransitive verb, *servierunt*, takes *servitudinem*, a noun of similar meaning, as a cognate acc.

10   **sordidis** "low, degrading." Upper-class Romans viewed paid labor and especially manual labor as unsuitable professions.

versantur "may be engaged in." The text that is omitted goes on to detail other exemptions that involve girls whose relatives hold various priesthoods or whose sister is a Vestal.

11   **simul** "as soon as"

11–12   **atrium Vestae** the building in which the Vestals lived in the Roman Forum, near the temple of Vesta

12   **deducta** Supply *est*.

pontificibus The college of *pontifices* consisted of the highest ranking officials of Roman state religion: the *Pontifex Maximus*, six Vestal Virgins, *Rex Sacrorum*, and fifteen *flamines*.

13   **sine emancipatione** that is, without the ceremony of emancipation that released her from the power of her father. The legal status of a Vestal gave her an unusual position in Roman society. Exempted from the power of her father (*patria postestas*), she did not pass into the ownership of any other family. Since legally she had no family (the state was now her family), she could no longer inherit property nor did she leave property to her family. If she died without a will, her property reverted to the state.

sine capitis minutione "without the loss of civil rights"; *capitis* < *caput*

14   **faciundi** gen. of the gerundive agreeing with *testamenti*, "of making a will"

17–18   **quae . . . est** Supply *eam* as the antecedent.

18   **Numa (Pompilius)** legendary second king of Rome. He is credited with a number of Roman religious institutions, among them, the establishment of the Vestals in Rome and the founding of the Temple of Vesta.

         (eam) esse captam acc. and infinitive dependent on an implied verb of cognition in *litterae non extant*. The text that is omitted goes on to describe the *Lex Papia* of unknown date providing that twenty girls be selected by the Pontifex Maximus and of these one chosen by lot for selection as a Vestal Virgin. Aulus Gellius notes that in his time that method was not necessary, undoubtedly because it was hard to find twenty candidates willing to participate in the lottery.

19–20   **si . . . adeat . . . atque offerat** pres. subjunctives in a less vivid fut. condition

19   **honesto loco** "of respectable position, respectable birth"

21   **cuius** Take with *ratio*, "candidacy."

         salvis . . . observationibus abl. absolute, "without violation of the requirements"

22   **gratia . . . fit** + gen., "exemption from . . . is granted"

24   **prensa** pf. pass. pple. of *prendo*

25   **veluti bello capta** Scholars have noted similarities between *captio* and the Roman wedding ceremony; in the Roman wedding ceremony the bride is "forcibly abducted" like a captive in war (Beard, 13–14).

26   **Fabii Pictoris** one of the earliest Roman historians, writing at the end of the third century BCE.

         quae Take *verba* as the antecedent, which has been placed inside the rel. clause.

         verba . . . Take in apposition to the main clause, "this has been written, the words which . . ."

26–27   **pontificem . . . dicere** acc. subject of the infinitive, dependent on *oporteat*

27   **oporteat** subjunctive in a rel. clause of characteristic

28   **Sacerdotem Vestalem** acc. in apposition to *te*

28-29 **quae . . . faciat** subjunctive in a rel. clause of purpose ("to perform . . .")

29   **quae ius . . . facere** "which the law allows for a Vestal Virgin to do . . ."

      siet archaic Latin for *sit*

30   **Quiritibus** ("Quirites"), in apposition to *populo Romano*. A name given to the citizens of Rome collectively in their civilian status.

      uti quae . . . fuit "on the same terms as she who was a Vestal on the best terms (*optima lege*)." This part of the legal formula is much disputed. It is now believed to mean that whoever is appointed is required to have all the original rights and privileges of the position as the original holder of the position, regardless of limitations placed by subsequent laws (Wildfang). One might also understand the phrase as follows: "as one who has been found to be in accordance with the most valid legal right; as one who has fulfilled all the legal requirements."

31   **Amata** Gellius' explanation for this name that follows at the end of the text is but one of several possible explanations.

32   **virginem . . . debere** acc. and infinitive dependent on *putant*

      dici pres. pass. used as a complementary infinitive with *debere*, "ought to be said to be taken (*capi*)"

33-34 **flamines . . . Diales, pontifices, augures** three different Roman priesthoods, which apparently also used the verb *capi* to describe the selection process

35   **inter** Take with the acc. of the gerund, "while being taken."

36   **quae** Supply *ei* as the antecedent, "for the one who . . ."

36-37 **hoc . . . nomen** acc. and infinitive dependent on *traditum est*

Timeline

❧ *The Latin Texts*

Reading 1.   Plautus, *Casina*, 185 BCE

Reading 2.   Cato the Elder, *On Agriculture*, exact date unknown, perhaps about 160 BCE (he lived from 234–149 BCE)

Reading 3.   Quotations from a letter of Cornelia, 124 BCE (reported by Cornelius Nepos, probably published about 32 BCE). Narrative about Sophoniba's suicide in BCE 203 (reported by Titus Livy in his *Ab Urbe Condita*, probably written shortly after BCE 19)

Reading 4.   Cato the Elder's speech on Papirius Praetextatus, delivered in the period 167–149 BCE (reported by Aulus Gellius, *Attic Nights*, written shortly before 170 CE)

Reading 5.   Two funerary inscriptions, late second century BCE

Reading 6.   Three funerary inscriptions, first century BCE

Reading 7.   Julius Caesar's tribute to his aunt Julia, 67 BCE (reported by Suetonius who lived from ca.70–130 CE but exact date of his *Lives of the Caesars* is unknown)

Reading 8.   Cicero, *Pro Caelio*, 56 BCE. Cicero, *Letters to Atticus*, 45 BCE

Reading 9.   Cicero, *Philippics*, 44–43 BCE. Sling bullet inscriptions, 41/40 BCE; Martial *Epigrams*, published from 86–101 or 102 CE (writing about the events of 41/40 BCE)

Reading 10.   Horace, *Satires*, ca. 35 BCE

Reading 11.   Tibullus, *Elegies*, ca. 25–19 BCE, featuring the female poet Sulpicia, a contemporary of his. An epitaph belonging to Sulpicia Petale, ca. 20 BCE. Cicero, *Letters to his Friends*, 45 BCE

Reading 12.   Propertius, *Elegies*, 16 BCE

Reading 13.   Ovid, *Tristia*, ca. 9–10 CE

Reading 14.   Petronius, *Satyricon*, exact date unknown (he died in 66 CE)

Reading 15.   Nero's behavior towards his mother from 55–59 CE, as reported by Suetonius who lived from ca. 70–130 CE; exact date of his *Lives of the Caesars* unknown

Reading 16.   Two dedicatory inscriptions (Eumachia), ca. 2/3 CE

Reading 17.   Pliny, *Letters*, ca. 97–104 CE

Reading 18.   Juvenal, *Satires*, ca. 100–127 CE, quoting two lines by the second Roman female poet named Sulpicia, from the period 81–96 CE. Martial, *Epigrams*, published from 86–101 or 102 CE

Reading 19.   *Tabula Vindolanda*, the letters of Claudia Severa, ca. 100 CE

Reading 20.   Juvenal, *Satires*, ca. 100–127 CE

Reading 21.   Aulus Gellius, *Attic Nights*, written shortly before 170 CE

Note: Conte, *Latin Literature: A History*, is a major source for the information in the timeline. In the situation where the exact date of an author's work is unknown, dates for the author's life have been provided.

Complete Vocabulary

ā, ab, abs, *prep.* + *abl.,* from, by

abavus, -ī, *m.,* great-grandfather

abdūcō, -ere, -duxī, -ductum, to remove, to lead away, take away

abeō, -īre, -iī (-īvī), -itum, to go away

abhorreō, -ēre, -uī, —, to be averse to, not to agree with

abiciō, -ere, -iēcī, -iectum, to throw down

abortus, -ūs, *m.,* miscarriage

absolvō, -ere, -ī, -ūtum, to absolve, exonerate

abstinentia, -ae, *f.,* abstinence from food, fasting

abstineō, -ēre, -uī, -tentum, to hold back

ac. *See* **atque**

accēdō, -ere, -cessī, -cessum, to be added to

accidō, -ere, accidī, —, to happen

accipiō, -ere, -cēpī, -ceptum, to accept, receive, bear; to learn

accurrō, -ere, -cucurrī, -cursum, to hasten to

accūsātor, -ōris, *m.,* accuser

accūsō (1), to accuse

ācer, -cris, -cre, *adj,.* severe, harsh

acta, -ae, *f.,* sea-shore

acūmen, -inis, *n.,* intelligence, shrewdness

acuō, -ere, -uī, -ūtum, to sharpen

ad, *prep.* + *acc.,* to, toward; for; for the purpose of; to (my) house (with a pron. like **te**); by, near to

addecet, -ere, *impers.,* it is fitting

addō, -ere, -didī, -ditum, to add

addūcō, -ere, -duxī, -ductum, to bring, bring a person into a certain condition

adeō, -īre, -iī (-īvī), -itum, to go to, approach

adferō, -ferre, attulī, allātum, to bring to one's notice, report

adficiō, -ere, adfēcī, adfectum, to affect, do something to one

adfīnis, -is, *m.,* relative by marriage

adimō, -ere, -ēmī, -emptum to deprive, take away

adipiscor, -ī, -eptus sum, to acquire, obtain

admittō, -ere, -mīsī, -missum, to acknowledge; to commit (in a legal sense)

admoneō, -ēre, -uī, -itum, to advise, remind, suggest, warn

adōrō (1), to worship, beg

adsensus, -ūs, *m.,* approval, assent

adserō, -ere, -seruī, -sertum, to claim as one's own (subject)

adsum, -esse, -fuī, to be present

adulescens, -entis, *m.,* youth, young man

adulescentulus, -ī, *m., diminutive,* a very young man, mere youth

adulterium, -iī, *n.,* adultery

adulterō (1), to defile by adultery (sexual relations between a married woman and a man not her husband)

advehō, -ere, -xī, -ctum, to convey, transport, bring a person to a place

adversor, -ārī, -ātus sum, + *dat.,* to oppose, stand against

adversus *or* **adversum,** *prep.* + *acc.,* against, opposed to

advolvō, -ere, -vī, -volūtum, to roll towards; **genibus advolvor,** to fall at the knees as a suppliant

advorsor. *See* **adversor**

advorsum. *See* **adversus**

aedēs, -ium, *f. pl.,* house

aedificātiō, -ōnis, *f.,* act of building, building

aedificō (1), to build

aeger, -gra, -grum, *adj.,* sad, suffering, sorrowful

aegrē esse, *idiom,* to be upsetting

aemula, -ae, *f.,* rival

aequus, -a, -um, *adj.,* fair, just

aestimō (1), to value, judge

aetās, -ātis, *f.,* lifetime, age, period of life, time of life; time period

aetatula, -ae, *f., diminutive,* early time of life, youth, tender age

aevum, -ī, *n.,* age, period of time

afferō, -ferre, attulī, allātum, to bring to; to bring a thing to a place

affīgō, -ere, -ixī, -ixum, to fix on, fasten to or on; to attach to

affulgeō, -ēre, -ulsī, to shine forth, appear

Africa, -ae, *f.,* Africa

ager, -grī, *m.,* field

aggredior, -ī, aggressus sum, to attack, assault

agmen, agminis, *n.,* procession, troop, army in formation

agō, -ere, ēgī, actum, to spend; to act; to speak, discuss; to speak in court, plead a case; to give thanks (with **grātiās**); to deal with

agrestis, -e, *adj.,* rustic

ait, *defective verb,* he/she says, said

aliēnigena, -ae, *m.,* stranger, foreigner

aliēnus, -a, -um, *adj.,* not one's own, another's

aliēnus, -ī, *m.,* stranger

aliquantum, *adv.,* a moderate amount

aliquis, aliquid, *indefinite pron.,* someone, anyone, anything; somebody, something or other; any

aliquot, *indecl. adj.,* a few, several

alius, -a, -ud, *adj.,* other, another, any other

alter, -era, -erum, *pron.,* one (of two), the other

amābō, *conversational,* please (literally "I shall like [you], if you do . . .")

amans, -ntis, *pres. act. pple.,* fond of, devoted to

Amāta, -ae, *f.,* Amata (name given to a Vestal Virgin)

amātor, -ōris, *m.,* lover

amātōriē, *adv.,* in a loving fashion

ambō, -bae, -bō, *pl. adj.* and *pron.,* both

ambulātrix, -īcis, *f.,* woman who gads about, walks about in public

amīca, -ae, *f.,* mistress

amīcus, -ī, *m.,* friend

amita, -ae, *f.,* father's sister, paternal aunt

amnis, -is, *m.,* river

amō (1), to love

amor, -ōris, *m.,* love, lover; Cupid (the god of love); passion

amplus, -a, -um, *adj.,* splendid, glorious

an, *conj.,* or

ancilla, -ae, *f.,* maid, handmaid, female slave

ancillula, -ae, *f.,* diminutive, little slave girl

anima, -ae, *f.,* soul, spirit

animus, -ī, *m.,* mind, state of mind; courage; soul; passion, affection; spirit

annus, -ī, *m.,* year

ante, *prep. + acc.,* before

anteā, *adv.,* before, in time past

antehāc, *adv.,* before this time, formerly

antequam, *conj.,* before

antidotum, -ī, *n.,* antidote, counterpoison

antīquus, -a, -um, *adj.,* ancient

antrum, -ī, *n.,* cave, grotto

aper, -prī, *m.,* wild boar

aperiō, -īre, -eruī, -ertum, to open, unveil

Apollo, -ōnis, *m.,* Apollo (Greek god of the sun and of poetry and music among other things)

appellō (1), to address as, call

aptus, -a, -um, *adj. + dat.,* fitting, suitable

apud, *prep. + acc.,* at the home of, in the presence of; to (with **nūbō**)

aqua, -ae, *f.,* water

arbiter, -trī, *m.,* witness

arbitrium, -iī, *n.,* judgment, decision-making; authority

arca, -ae, *f.,* coffin

ardeō, -ēre, -rsī, -rsum, to burn

ārea, -ae, *f.,* a vacant space, bare site

arguō, -ere, -uī, -ūtum, to prove, assert; to allege, accuse

āridus, -a, -um, *adj.,* dried

arma, -ōrum, *n. pl.,* military weapons, arms; *metaphor for male sex organs*

armātus, -a, -um, *pf. pass. pple.,* armed; (as substantive) armed man

Ārrētīnus, -a, -um, *adj.,* in the region of Arretium outside Rome

arripiō, -ere, -ripuī, -reptum, to seize, lay hold of

ars, artis, *f.,* art, skill

artifex, -ficis, *m.,* master, expert

aspiciō, -ere, -spexī, -spectum, to look on or upon; to catch a glimpse of, catch the eye of

asservō (1), to watch, guard

assideō, -ēre, -sēdī, -sessum, + *dat.,* to sit beside, sit by

at, *conj.,* but, yet, however

atavus, -ī, *m.,* great-great-grandfather

atque, *conj.,* and

ātrium, -iī, *n.,* entry, forecourt, house

Ātropos, -ī, *f.,* Atropos (one of the three Fates)

atrox, -ōcis, *adj.,* heinous, gruesome

attingō, -ere, -tigī, -tactum, to touch; to arrive at, achieve

auctiō, -ōnis, *f.,* public sale, auction

auctor, -ōris, *m.,* author, source

auctōritās, -ātis, *f.,* authority, power

audeō, -ēre, ausus sum, to dare

audiō, -īre, -īvī, -ītum, to hear

auferō, -ferre, abstulī, ablātum, to take away

augur, -uris, *m.,* augur (a member of a particular college of priests, who forecast the future from various signs)

auris, auris, *f.,* ear

aurum, -ī, *n.,* gold

auscultō (1), + *dat.,* to listen to

austērus, -a, -um, *adj.,* harsh, stern

aut, *conj.,* or

aut . . . aut, *conj.,* either . . . or

autem, *adv.,* moreover, but; also; however; nevertheless

avārus, -a, -um, *adj.,* greedy

aveō, -ēre, to be eager; **avē,** "hail"

avidē, *adv.,* greedily

avidus, -a, -um, *adj.,* eager

avis, -is, *f.,* bird

avītus, -a, -um, *adj.,* of or pertaining to a grandfather or ancestor

avus, -ī, *m.,* grandfather; ancestor

Bacchus, -ī, *m.,* Bacchus (Greek god of wine and ritual madness, among other things)

Bāiae, -ārum, *f. pl.,* Baiae (a seaside resort on the Bay of Naples that upper class Romans like to visit)

barbātus, -a, -um, *adj.,* bearded (a Roman of the olden time)

barbula, -ae, *f., diminutive,* a little beard (of the type worn by young Romans)

Baulī, -ōrum, *m. pl.,* a place near Baiae

beātus, -a, -um, *adj.,* blessed

bellum, -ī, *n.,* war

bene, *adv.,* well, properly, fairly

bibō, -ere, bibī, —, to drink

bīnī, -ae, -a, *adj.,* in twos

blanditiae, -ae, *f. pl.,* flattery; persuasive, sweet words

bona, -ōrum, *n. pl.,* good qualities, virtues

bonī, -ōrum, *m. pl.,* good people

bonus, -a, -um, *adj.,* good, fine

bracchium, -iī, *n.,* arm

brevis, -e, *adj.,* brief, short

Briga, -ae, *f.,* town in northern England

Byblis, -idis, *f.,* Byblis

cadāver, -eris, *n.,* corpse, dead body

cadō, -ere, cecidī, cāsum, to fall; to occur

cadurcum, -ī, *n.,* bed frame; marriage bed

Caecus, -ī, *m.,* Caecus (the agnomen of Appius Claudius, so known because he was blind)

Caelius, -iī, *m.,* M. Caelius Rufus (Clodia's former lover, now prosecuting her on various charges)

caerimōnia, -ae, *f.,* reverence, religious rite

calcitrō (1), to resist, be stubborn

Calēnus, -ī, *m.,* Calenus (husband of the poet Sulpicia)

caleō, -ēre, caluī, to be warm or hot

calvus, -a, -um, *adj.,* bald, depilated, smooth-skinned

camara, -ae, *f.,* deck (over a ship's cabin)

Camēnae, -ārum, *f. pl.,* Camenae (Italian Muses, goddesses of poetry)

campus, -ī, *m.,* field

candidus, -a, -um, *adj.,* white, bright, shining

candor, -ōris, *m.,* beauty

canis, canis, *m. or f.,* dog

canō, -ere, cecinī, cantum, to sing, sound

cantō (1), to sing

cantus, -ūs, *m.,* concert

capiō, -ere, cēpī, captum, to take; to choose; to seize, capture

captīva, -ae, *f.,* female captive, prisoner of war

caput, capitis, *n.,* head; main point; summary; civil rights (with **minūtiō**)

cāritās, -ātis, *f.,* love, affection

carmen, -inis, *n.,* song, poem

Carthāginiensis, -e, *adj.,* Carthaginian

Carthāgō, -inis, *f.,* Carthage (city in north Africa, in the vicinity of modern Tunis)

cārus, -a, -um, *adj.,* dear, beloved, precious

cassis, -is, *m.,* hunting net

castitās, -ātis, *f.,* chastity, fidelity

castra, -ōrum, *n. pl.,* camp

castus, -a, -um, *adj.,* chaste, modest, pure, sexually virtuous

casula, -ae, *f.,* a small house

cāsus, -ūs, *m.,* misfortune, disaster; outcome

catamītus, -ī, *m.,* pathetic, unmanly man

caterva, -ae, *f.,* crowd; band

caupōnula, -ae, *f.,* a little drinking place

causā, *prep. + gen.,* for the sake of

causa, -ae, *f.,* cause, reason, reason (for)

caveō, -ēre, cāvī, cautum, to beware, watch out for

cēdō, -ere, cessī, cessum, to go away from, withdraw from

celebrō (1), to frequent, go to a place often; to celebrate

celer, -is, -e, *adj.,* swift, fast

celeriter, *adv.,* quickly

cēlō (1), to conceal

cēna, -ae, *f.,* dinner

censeō, -ēre, -uī, censum, to reckon, estimate

censōrius, -a, -um, *adj.,* of or belonging to a censor, censorial

cēnula, -ae, *f., diminutive,* little dinner

cernō, -ere, crēvī, crētum, to observe, look at

certē, *adv.,* certainly, surely

certus, -a, -um, *adj.,* certain

cervus, -ī, *m.,* stag

cessō (1), to be idle

cēterī, -ae, -a, *pl., adj.,* the other, other

cēterum, *adv.,* well, besides

cēterus, -a, -um, *adj.,* the rest of

chalcidicum, -ī, *n.,* porch

cibus, -ī, *m.,* food

cinis, -eris, *m. or f.,* ashes (of a corpse that has been burned); ash

circumscrībō, -ere, -scrīpsī, -scriptum, to cheat

circumstō, -āre, -stetī, to stand around

cisium, -iī, *n.,* two-wheeled carriage

cithara, -ae, *f.,* lyre

citius, *adv.,* more quickly

cīvis, -is, *m.,* citizen

cīvitās, -ātis, *f.,* city; state; government

clam, *adv.,* secretly

clam, *prep. + acc.,* as a secret from, unknown to

clāmō (1), to shout

clāmor, -ōris, *m.,* shout, friendly shout; applause

clārus, -a, -um, *adj.,* distinguished, illustrious, bright

claudō, -ere, -sī, -sum, to close

coepī, -isse, coeptum, *defective verb*, to begin

coeptum, -ī, *n.*, undertaking, work begun

cōgitō (1), to decide, reflect on

cognātus, -ī, *m.*, relative

cognitus, -ūs, *m.*, a becoming acquainted with; a getting to know

cognōmentum, -ī, *n.*, surname

cognōscō, -ere, -gnōvī, gnitum, to learn, know

cōgō, -ere, coēgī, coactum, to compel

Colchis, Colchidis, *f.*, a woman from Colchis, Medea

collis, -is, *m.*, hill

collum, -ī, *n.*, neck

colō, -ere, coluī, cultum, to inhabit; to care for, cultivate; to take care of, groom

colus, -ī, *f.* (rarely *m.*), distaff, spinning equipment

comae, -ārum, *f. pl.*, hair

cōmissātiō, -ōnis, *f.*, Bacchanial revel

comitor, -ārī, -ātus sum, to accompany

commentārium, -iī, *n.*, commentary

comminiscor, -ī, -mentus sum, to contrive, devise something by careful thought

committō, -ere, -mīsī, -missum, to entrust

commodē, *adv.*, suitably, appropriately

commodō (1), to lend, supply; to give, provide for someone's use

commodum, -ī, *n.*, reward, benefit, blessings

commoveō, -ēre, -mōvī, -mōtum, to touch, move

commūnis, -e, the same; shared; in common

compavescō, -ere, —, to be thoroughly terrified

comperiō, -īre, -perī, -pertum, to find out with certainty, ascertain

complector, -ī, -plexus sum, to embrace

compōnō, -ere, -posuī, -postum, to compose, arrange

compressus, -a, -um, *adj.*, urgent

concēdō, -ere, -cessī, -cessum + *dat.*, to yield to; to yield

conceptus, -a, -um, *pf. pass. pple.*, in a solemn or formal utterance, conceived

conciliō (1), to win over

concipiō, -ere, -cēpī, -ceptum, to take or lay hold of

Concordia Augusta, -ae, *f.*, Concordia Augusta (a Roman deity, a special favorite of the imperial family)

concors, -cordis, *adj.*, harmonious, compatible

concubō (1), to lie with

concumbō, -ere, -cubuī, -cubitum, to lie down with

concupīscō, -ere, -cupiī, -ītum, to long much for something, be very desirous of

concursus, -ūs, *m.,* collision, crashing together

condiciō, -ōnis, *f.,* assignation, love affair

condisciplina, -ae, *f.,* fellow student

conditōrium, -iī, *n.,* tomb

condō, -ere, -didī, -ditum, to preserve

conferō, -ferre, contūlī, collātum, to turn; to devote one's self

confestim, *adv.,* immediately, speedily

confīdō, -ere, confīsus sum, to be confident

confirmō (1), to encourage, hearten

confiteor, -ērī, -fessus sum, to acknowledge, admit; to confess

confringō, -ere, -frēgī, -fractum, to break in pieces

confugiō, -ere, -fūgī, fūgitum, to take refuge there, come to

confundō, -ere, -fūdī, -fūsum, to mix together, confuse

cōniciō, -ere, -iēcī, -iectum, to throw together, fling, hurl

coniunctiō, -ōnis, *f.,* close connection, friendship

coniunctus, -a, -um, *pf. pass. pple.,* closely associated

coniungō, -ere, -iunxī, -iunctum, to join, connect; to ally, ally in marriage

coniunx, -iūgis, *m. or f.,* spouse

conputō (1), to sum up, compute, reckon

conscientia, -ae, *f.,* a consciousness of right or wrong

conscius, -a, -um, *adj.,* conscious, complicit, guilty

conscius, -iī, *m.,* accomplice

consīderō (1), to look at closely

consilium capiō + *gen., idiomatic,* to form a plan

consilium, -iī, *n.,* plan

consōlātiō, -ōnis, *f.,* comfort, consolation

conspectus, -ūs, *m.,* sight, view

conspiciō, -ere, -exī, -ectum, to catch sight of, see, glimpse

constans, -ntis, *adj.,* abiding, persistent

constituō, -ere, constituī, constitūtum, to decide

constō (1), to be in balance (of accounting)

constringō, -ere, -strinxī, -strictum, to bind

consuētūdinō, -inis, *f.,* familiarity, companionship

consul, -is, *m.,* consul, one of two highest magistrates in the Roman government

consulō, -ere, -luī, -ītum, to take counsel, consider; to confer with; (+ dat.) to look to, give thought to

consultō (1), to discuss, deliberate

consūmō, -ere, -sumpsī, -sumptum, to take in, consume

contentus, -a, -um, *pf. pass. pple.,* satisfied

contineō, -ēre, -tinuī, -tentum, to contain, hold in

continuō, *adv.,* immediately, at once

contrectō (1), to handle

contubernium, -iī, *n.,* companionship, company

convertō, -ere, -tī, -versum, to turn; to transform, make tidy

convīcium, -iī, *n.,* abuse, insults

convivium, -iī, *n.,* banquet; feast

cōpia, -ae, *f.,* access to (+ gen.), opportunity; supply

cōpiae, -ārum, *f. pl.,* wealth

cōpiōsus, -a, -um, *adj.,* have plenty of money, rich

coquō, -ere, coxī, coctum, to cook

cor, cordis, *m.,* heart; **esse cordī,** to be dear to

corōna, -ae, *f.,* wreath

corpus, corporis, *n.,* body

corrigō, -ere, -rexī, -rectum, to correct

corrumpō, -ere, -rūpī, -ruptum, to spoil, destroy, damage; to seduce, entice

cotīdiē, *adv.,* daily, everyday

crēber, -bra, -brum, *adj.,* thick, frequent

crēdō, -ere, -idī, -itum + *dat.,* to believe, trust in

crescō, -ere, crēvī, crētum, to grow

crīmen, inis, *n.,* charge, accusation; crime

crinis, -is, *m.,* hair

cruciārius, -a, -um, *adj.,* one who is crucified

crūdēlis, -e, *adj.,* cruel, unfeeling

cruentō (1), to stain with blood

crūs, crūris, *n.,* lower leg, shin

crux, crucis, *f.,* cross

crypta, -ae, *f.,* a covered passage

cubitō (1), to go to bed with often

cubō, -āre, -uī, -itum, to lie down, sleep (with **īre**)

culpa, -ae, *f.,* fault, guilt; blame; wrong

cūlus, -ī, *m.,* primary obscenity for anus, "ass-hole"

cum ... tum, *correlative conjs.,* not only ... but also; both ... and

cum, *conj.,* when, since; *prep.* + *abl.,* with

cupidus, -a, -um, *adj.* + *gen.,* desirous, eager

cupiō, -ere, -īvī (-iī), -ītum, to desire

cūr, *conj.,* why

cūra, -ae, *f.,* care, concern, passion for

cūria, -ae, *f.,* building in which the Senate met; senate house

cūrō (1), to see to it, attend to, take care; to look after, care for

currus, -ūs, *m.,* chariot

custōdia, -ae, *f.,* watch, guard; protection

custōdiō, -īre, -iī (-īvī), -itum, to watch over, guard; to be careful about

custos, -ōdis, *m.,* guard, guardian, protector

cȳcnus, -ī, *m.,* swan

Cȳtherēus, -a, -um, *adj.,* of Cythera (epithet for the goddess Venus worshipped on this Greek island)

dē, *prep.* + *abl.,* about, concerning; from among

dēbeō, -ēre, -uī, -itum, ought, ought to, must; to owe, be indebted to

dēbilis, -e, *adj.,* crippled

decem, *numeral,* ten

decens, -ntis, *adj.,* attractive, becoming, seemly, handsomely shaped

decernō, -ere, -crēvī, -crētum, to make a decision (on an issue); to decree

dēcerpō, -ere, -cerpsī, -cerptum, to pluck, pull off

dēcidō, -ere, -cidī, —, to fall, fall down

decimus, -a, -um, *adj.,* tenth

decorō (1), to adorn, decorate; to endow with beauty; to glorify

dēdicō (1), to dedicate

dēdūcō, -ere, -duxī, -ductum, to lead away, lead down; to escort, escort a bride in a marriage ceremony

deferō, -ferre, -tulī, -lātum, to report, carry

dēficiō, -ere, -fēcī, -fectum, to cease, fail, die; to go out

dēfleō, -ēre, -ēvī, -ētum, to weep over, lament

dēformis, -e, *adj.,* unsightly, ugly

dēfungor, -ī, -functus sum + *abl.,* to bring a matter to an end, die

dēgō, -ere, dēgī, to spend time, love

deierō (1), to take an oath, swear

dein *or* **deinde,** *adv.,* then, next; thereafter

dēlectō (1), + *dat.,* to delight, delight in, enjoy; to charm

dēliciae, -ārum, *f. pl.,* pleasure, delights

dēlicuom = dēlicuus, -a, -um, *adj.,* lacking

dēligō, -ere, -lēgī, -lectum, to pick, choose

dēlitescō, -ere, -tuī, to go into hiding, lurk

Dēlius, -a, -um, *adj.,* of Delos (epithet of the goddess Diana, who was born on the island of Delos)

dēmentia, -ae, *f.,* madness

dēminuō, -ere, -uī, -ūtum, to deprive of

dēmō, -ere, -psī, -ptum, to take away

dēmum, *adv.,* finally, at last

dēnarrō (1), to tell or relate in detail

dēni, -ae, -a, *adj.,* by tens

dēnique, *adv.,* finally, lastly

dens, dentis, *m.,* tooth

densus, -a, -um, *adj.,* thick

dēpōnō, -ere, -posuī, -positum, to put down, deport

dēprehendō *or* dēprendō, -ere, -dī, -sum, to catch, catch in the act, catch by surprise; to find out

descendō, -ere, -dī, -sum, to go down

dēserō, -ere, -ruī, -rtum, to desert, abandon

dēsideō, -ēre, -sēdī, —, to be off duty

dēsīderātus, -a, -um, *pf. pass. pple.*, desired, longed for

dēsīderium, -iī, *n.*, grief

dēsiliō, -ere, -uī, -ultum, to leap down

dēsinō, -ere, -īvī, -itum, to cease, stop

dēspicātus, -a, -um, *pf. pass. pple.*, + habēre, to hold in contempt

dēspicor, -ārī, -ātus sum, to despise, distain

dēstitūtus, -a -um, *pf. pass. pple.* of dēstituō, robbed of, deprived of

dēsum, -esse, -fuī, to be lacking, fail

dētrahō, -ere, -traxī, -tractum, to take down, drag down

deus, -ī, *m.*, god; dī, *pl.* of deus

dēvia, -ōrum, *n. pl.*, out of the way places

devinciō, -īre, -nxī, -nctum, to bind fast

dextra, -ae, *f.*, right hand

Dī Mānēs, -ōrum, -ium, *m. pl.*, spirits, shades of the dead

Diālis, -e, *adj.*, of or belonging to Jupiter; (with flāmen) the priest of Jupiter

Diāna, -ae, *f.*, Diana (goddess of the hunt)

dīcō, -ere, dixī, dictum, to say, speak, tell; to administer (with iūs)

dictō (1), to compose, dictate

dīdūcō, -ere, -duxī, -ductum, to break

diēs, dieī, *m. or f.*, day

difficilis, -e, *adj.*, difficult

dignitās, -ātis, *f.*, worth, worthiness, merit; prestige, greatness

dignus, -a, -um, *adj.*, worthy, suitable

dīgressus, -ūs, *m.*, departure

dīligens, -ntis, *pres. act. pple.*, careful, accurate

dīligenter, *adv.*, carefully, diligently

dīligō, -ere, -lexī, -lectum, to cherish, hold dear

dīluō, -ere, -uī, -ūtum, to remove, disprove

dīrigō, -ere, -rexī, -rectum, to direct, guide

dirimō, -ere, -ēmī, -emptum, to break off, interrupt, delay; to break up, destroy

dīripiō, -ere, -uī, -eptum, to tear to pieces

dīrus, -a, -um, *adj.*, accursed, detestable

Dīs, Dītis, *m.*, Dis (god ruling the underworld)

disceptātor, -ōris, *m.*, judge

discernō, -ere, -crēvī, -crētum, to separate

discinctus, -a, -um, *pf. pass. pple.,* wearing loosely wrapped clothes

discō, -ere, didicī, —, to learn

discutiō, -ere, -cussī, -cussum, to shake off, break up

dispōnō, -ere, -posuī, -positum, to display, arrange; to dispatch, post

dissimilis, -e, *adj.,* dissimilar, different

diū, *adv.,* for a long time

diūtius, *compar. adv.,* longer, for a longer time

dīversus, -a, -um, *adj.,* contrary, not the expected outcome

dīves, -itis, *adj.,* rich

dīvexō (1), to harass

dīvīnus, -a, -um, *adj.,* divine, sacred

dīvortium, -iī, *n.,* legal termination of a marriage

dō, dare, dedī, datum, to give, grant

doceō, -ēre, -uī, -ctum, to teach; to show, tell

doctus, -a, -um, *pf. pass. pple.,* learned, erudite

documentum, -ī, *n.,* warning

dōlium, -iī, *n.,* large earthenware storage vessel

dolor, -ōris, *m.,* sorrow, pain; grief, mourning; relief

domesticus, -a, -um, *adj.,* of or belonging to one's family; domestic; of the home, private, personal

domī, *locative,* at home

domina, -ae, *f.,* mistress, she who rules or commands in a household; wife of a slave owner

dominus, -ī, *m.,* master; slave owner

domus, -ūs *and* **-ī,** *f.,* home

dōnec, *conj.,* until

dōnum, -ī, *n.,* gift

dormiō, -īre, -īvī (-iī), -ītum, to sleep

dōs, dōtis, *f.,* dowry

dubitō (1), to doubt

dulcis, -e, *adj.,* sweet

dum, *conj.,* while

dumtaxat, *conj.,* so long as, provided

duo, -ae, -o, *adj.,* two

dūrus, -a, -um, *adj.,* hard, tough; stern, severe; hard-hearted; difficult

ē *or* **ex,** *prep. + abl.,* of, out of; from; according to; because of, on account of; **ex rē pūblicā,** *idiomatic prepositional phrase,* for the good of the state, for the public benefit

ēbrius, -a, -um, *adj.,* drunk

ecquandō, *adv., interrog.,* when

ēdiscō, -ere, -didicī, —, to learn by heart, commit to memory

ēdō, -ere, -didī, -ditum, to produce, publish; to put forth

ēducō (1), to rear, bring up

efferō, -ferre, extulī, ēlātum, to bring, carry out; to raise; to bury

effrēnātus, -a, -um, *pf. pass. pple.,* unrestrained, ungoverned

effundō, -ere, -fūdī, -fūsum, to loosen (of hair); **effūsus, -a, -um,** *pf. pass. pple.,* disheveled

Ēgeria, -ae, *f.,* Egeria (a nymph in Roman mythology)

ego, meī, mihi/mī, mē, mē, *pron.* I, me

egomet, *pron.,* I (intensive form of **ego**)

ēgredior, -ī, -gressus sum, to go out

Eleusīnus, -a, -um, *adj.,* Eleusinian (related to the mysteries celebrated at Eleusis)

ēmancipātiō, -ōnis, *f.,* emancipation (the ceremony that released a Roman son from **patria potestas**)

ēmancipō (1), to release from the power of the **pater familias**

emptor, -ōris, *m.,* buyer

ēn, *interj.,* behold!

enim, *adv.,* indeed

ēnītor, -ārī, -ātus sum, to make an effort, exert one's self

ēnuntiō (1), to disclose, report

eō, *adv.,* there, to that place

eō, īre, iī (īvī), itum, to go

Ephesus, -ī, *f.,* Ephesus (capital city in the Roman province of Asia)

epistula, -ae, *f.,* letter, written communication

ergō, *adv.,* therefore, accordingly; thus, so, in this way

ēripiō, -ere, -uī, -eptum, to take away, snatch away; to snatch away by death, die

error, -ōris, *m.,* mistake; failing, delusion

ēruō, -ere, -uī, -utum, to pluck up, overturn

et . . . et, *conj.,* both . . . and

et, *conj.,* and, even

etiam, *adv.,* even, also; especially

etiamsī, *adv.,* even if

ēvādō, -ere, -sī, -sum, to escape; to turn out as, become

ēventus, -ūs, *m.,* outcome

ēverberō (1), to stir up, stimulate, excite

ēvocō (1), to draw, call forth; to invite

exagitō (1), to harass, torment

exaudiō, -īre, -īvī, -ītum, to listen closely

excelsus, -a, -um, *adj.,* raised, lofty

excerpō, -ere, -psī, -ptum, to pick out, select

excipiō, -ere, -cēpī, -ceptum, to receive, listen to; to welcome

excitō (1), to cause, produce, receive; to call up

excōgitō (1), to contrive, devise

exemplum, -ī, *n.,* example, model

exeō, -īre, -iī, -itum, to leave

exhortātiō, -ōnis, *f.,* encouragement

exiguus, -a, -um, *adj.,* small, small in number, few

exitus, -ūs, *m.,* outcome

exordior, -īrī, -orsus sum, to begin, embark on; to raise

exorior, -īrī, -ortus sum, *irregular verb,* to arise

exōrō (1), to obtain by pleading; to beg for forgiveness; to appease

exosculor, -ārī, -ātus sum, to kiss fondly; to praise greatly

expectō (1), to await, wait for

expellō, -ere, -pūlsī, pulsum, to drive out

experior, -īrī, -ītus sum, to test, try; to endure, experience

expetō, -ere, -iī (-īvī), -ītum, to seek after, desire, long for; to seek eagerly; to demand

expiō (1), to make amends for

expīrō (1), to breathe one's last

explōrō (1), to ascertain, confirm

expōnō, -ere, -posuī, -positum, to set forth, explain

exposcō, -ere, -poposcī, to demand

expugnō (1), to take by storm, storm, capture

exquīrō, -ere, -quisīvī, -quisītum, to investigate, look into aggressively

exsistō, -ere, -stitī, -stitum, to arise, arise from the dead

exsolvō, -ere, -solvī, -solūtum, to set free; to perform

exsul, -is, *m. or f.,* exile

externus, -a, -um, *adj.,* external, foreign, outside; from outside

extinguō, -ere, -nxī, -nctum, to kill, deprive of life

extō, -āre, —, to exist, be extant

extrēmus, -a, -um, *adj.,* final, last, remaining

exuviae, -ārum, *f. pl.,* spoils of battle

Fabius Pictor, Fabiī Pictōris, *m.,* Fabius Pictor (one of the earliest Roman historians from the end of third century BCE)

fabula, -ae, *f.,* story, opinion

facētiae, -ārum, *f. pl.,* witty remarks, amusements

faciēs, -ēī, *f.,* face

facilis, -e, *adj.,* easy, achievable

faciō, -ere, fēcī, factum, to make, do; to suffer (with **abortum**)

falsus, -a, -um, *pf. pass. pple.,* false

fāma, -ae, *f.,* rumor, gossip; reputation, good name

fames, -is, *f.,* hunger

familia, -ae, *f.,* household, family

familiāris, -e, *adj.,* intimate, familiar

familiāris, -is, *m.,* a familiar acquaintance; lover; friend

familiāritās, -ātis, *f.,* familiarity, intimacy

familiās, *archaic gen. of* **familia,** (with **māter**) mistress of the house, matron

far, farris, *n.,* spelt (a species of wheat—a very important crop in antiquity)

farīna, -ae, *f.,* ground corn meal, flour

fas, *indecl., n.,* lawful, permitted

fascia, -ae, *f.,* binding

Fāta, -ōrum, *n. pl.,* Fates

fātālis, -e, *adj.,* deadly, lethal

fateor, -ērī, fassus sum, to confess

favilla, -ae, *f.,* ash, ember

fēcundus, -a, -um, *adj.,* fertile

fēlīcitas, -ātis, *f.,* good fortune

fēlix, -īcis, *adj.,* fortunate, happy

fellō (1), *primary obscenity for to fellate,* to "suck cock"

fēmina, -ae, *f.,* woman

femur, -ōris, *n.,* thigh

ferae, -ārum, *f. pl.,* wild beasts

ferē, *adv.,* barely, scarcely

feriō, -īre, —, —, to strike

fermē, *adv.,* almost, nearly

ferō, ferre, tulī, lātum, to carry, bear, endure; to produce, receive; to say, report

ferox, -ōcis, *adj.,* fierce, savage

ferreus, -a, -um, *adj.,* of iron

fertilitās, -ātis, *f.,* fertility

festīvus, -a, -um, *adj.,* amusing, witty

festus, -a, -um, *adj.,* holy, celebratory

fīcus, -ī, *m.,* fig

fidēs, -eī, *f.,* reliability, trustworthiness; loyalty; promise

fīdus, -a, -um, *adj.,* faithful, devoted, loyal

fīlia, -ae, *f.,* daughter

fīliolus, -ī, *m., diminutive,* little son

fīlius, -iī, *m.,* son

fingō, -ere, finxī, fictum, to shape, devise, create; to compose

fīō, fierī, factus sum (pass. of **faciō**), to be made, become; to be done, happen

flāgitium, -iī, *n.,* shameful action, disgrace

flāmen, -inis, *m.,* a priest (of one particular deity)

flēbilis, -e, *adj.,* to be wept for, worthy of tears

fleō, -ēre, flēvī, fletum, to weep, cry

flōreō, -ēre, -uī, to flourish, thrive; to bloom, be in one's prime

focus, -ī, *m.,* hearth

foedus, -eris, *n.,* treaty, bargain

forās, *adv.,* outside, out of doors

fore = futūrus esse. *See* **sum**

forensis, -e, *adj.,* of the Forum, public

forēs, -um, *f. pl.,* two leaves of a door, door, doors

foris, *adv.,* outside, outside the home; out of doors, in public

forma, -ae, *f.,* beauty; form

formō (1), to set to music

formonsus, -a, -um, *adj.,* beautiful, shapely

formula, -ae, *f.,* principle, formal text

fors, fortis, *f.,* fortune

forsitan, *adv.,* perhaps

fortē, *adv.,* perhaps, per chance

fortis, -e, *adj.,* brave, courageous

fortuitus, -a, -um, *adj.,* accidental

fortūna, -ae, *f.,* fortune, fate

fortūnae, -ārum, *f. pl.,* possessions, property

Forum, -ī, *n.,* the Forum (major public gathering place in Rome)

forum, -ī, *n.,* forum

frangō, -ere, fregī, fractum, to break, break down

frāter, -tris, *m.,* brother

frāternus, -a, -um, *adj.,* of or belonging to a brother

frequentia, -ae, *f.,* crowd

frīgidus, -a, -um, *adj.,* chilly

fructus, -ūs, *m.,* fruit, enjoyment

frūgalitās, -ātis, *f.,* thriftiness

fruor, -ī, fructus sum + *abl.,* to enjoy, experience positively

frustrā, *adv.,* in vain

fugiō, -ere, fūgī, fugitum, to escape, flee

fulcrum, -ī, *n.,* raised end of a couch

fulgeō, -ēre, fulsī, —, to shine

fullō, -ōnis, *m.,* fuller, drycleaner

fulminō (1), to flash fiercely like lightning

fūnus, -eris, *n.,* corpse, dead body; death, funeral; funeral procession

Furiae, -ārum, *f. pl.,* the Furies (the three goddesses of vengeance), avenging spirits

furibundus, -a, -um, *adj.,* full of rage, infuriated

furor, -ōris, *m.,* frenzy, madness

furtim, *adv.,* secretly

futuō, -ere, futuī, *primary obscenity for to penetrate vaginally,* to "fuck"

gallīna, -ae, *f.,* hen

gaudeō, -ēre, gāvīsus sum + *abl.,* to rejoice, take pleasure in

gaudium, -iī, *n.,* joy, delight; pleasure

gemitus, -ūs, *m.,* groan, moan

gener, -ī, *m.,* son-in-law

genius, -iī, *m.,* genius (the divine spirit of a Roman)

gens, gentis, *f.,* nation, tribe, kinship group; race; state, people

genu, -ūs, *n.,* knee

genus, -eris, *n.,* family, stock; kind, sort; type, lineage

Germānī, -ōrum, *m. pl.,* Germans

gerō, -ere, gessī, gestum, to carry, bear, endure; to spend (periods of time)

gignō, -ere, genuī, genitum, to beget, bring forth, produce; **genitus** (substantive), a man born

gladius, -iī, *m.,* sword

glōria, -ae, *f.,* glory

Gracchī, -ōrum, *m. pl.,* the Gracchi (a Roman family name, its most famous members being Tiberius and Gaius)

Graecia, -ae, *f.,* Greece

Graecus, -a, -um, *adj.,* Greek

grandis, -e, *adj.,* lofty, noble

grātia, -ae, *f.,* favor, support; thanks; exemption from (+ gen.)

grātiā, *prep. + gen.,* out of, because of

grātulātiō, -ōnis, *f.,* congratulation

grātus, -a, -um, *adj.,* pleasing

gravis, -e, *adj.,* dignified; serious; heavy, painful; austere, severe

gravitās, -ātis, *f.,* gravity, severity; seriousness, dignity

graviter, *adv.,* harshly; solemnly; reluctantly; sorrowfully

gravor, -ārī, -ātus sum, to feel annoyed at, feel resentment toward

grex, gregis, *m.,* herd, flock, crowd

habeō, -ēre, -uī, -itum, to have, hold; to consider; to own; to keep

habitus, -ūs, *m.,* clothing, dress

hactenus, *adv.,* to this extent

hāmātus, -a, -um, *adj.,* hooked

Hannibal, -alis, *m.,* Hannibal (famous Carthaginian general of the second Punic war, defeated by Cornelia's father)

harēna, -ae, *f.,* sand

Hasdrubal, -alis, *m.,* Hasdrubal (the son of Gisco; Hasdrubal was a military leader of Carthage in North Africa and the father of Sophoniba)

hau = haud, *negative particle,* barely

hauriō, -īre, hausī, haustum, to drink, experience to the full

hem, *expression of surprise or concern,* what's that

hērēs, -ēdis, *m.,* heir

hīc, *adv.,* here

hīc, haec, hōc, *pron.,* this

hilarē, *adv.,* cheerfully, merrily

hinc, *adv.,* from there, from this place

historia, -ae, *f.,* story

historicus, -ī, *m.,* historian

hodiē, *adv.,* today

homō, -inis, *m.,* man, person; human being; individual; people (pl.)

honestus, -a, -um, *adj.,* respectable

honor, -ōris, *m.,* public honor; respect; political office; honor (with **grātia**)

hōra, -ae, *f.,* hour

horridus, -a, -um, *adj.,* rough, shaggy

hortor, -ārī, -ātus sum, to urge, encourage

hortus, -ī, *m.,* garden

hospes, hospitis, *m.,* host, guest, individual who passes by

hūc, *adv.,* over here

hūmānitās, -ātis, *f.,* kindness

hūmānus, -ae, -um, *adj.,* human

hypogaeum, -ī, *n.,* a vault or burial place under ground

iaceō, -ēre, -cuī, -citum, to lie, lie dead

iactō (1), to mention, bring up

iam, *adv.,* now

iānitor, -ōris, *n.,* doorkeeper, porter

iānua, -ae, *f.,* door

ibi, *adv.,* there

idcircō, *adv.,* for that reason

īdem, eadem, idem, *pron.,* the same

identidem, *adv.,* repeatedly, over and over again

ideo, *adv.,* for that reason, on that account

Īdūs, -uum, *f. pl.,* Ides (the 15th day of March, May, July and October; the 13th day of other months)

igitur, *adv.,* and so, therefore, accordingly; consequently; thereafter

ignāvia, -ae, *f.,* neglect of duty

ignis, -is, *m.,* fire

ignoscō, -ere, -nōvī, -nōtum + *dat.,* to forgive, pardon; not to notice, to overlook

ignōtus, -a, -um, *adj.,* unknown, obscure, of no account; stranger (as a noun)

ille, illa, illud, *pron.,* he, she, it; that; famous, well-known (when it follows the noun it modifies)

illim, *adv.,* from that source or quarter

imāgō, -inis, *f.,* ancestral image, funerary mask; image; ghost; bust

impavidus, -a, -um, *adj.,* fearless; **impavide,** *adv.,* fearlessly

impendō, -ere, -dī, -sum, to expend, make useful

imperātor, -ōris, *m.,* military commander, governor

imperium, -iī, *n.,* command, rule; power

imperō (1), to order, command

impetrō (1), to accomplish, succeed (in getting done)

impetus, -ūs, *m.,* attack, sexual assault

impius, -a, -um, *adj.,* irreverent, ungodly, unbelieving

impōnō, -ere, -posuī, -positum, to place on; to place upon or in a place

in, *prep.* + *abl.*, in; *prep.* + *acc.*,
    into, onto
inānis, -e, *adj.*, empty, idle
incertus, -a, -um, *adj.*,
    untrustworthy, doubtful;
    uncertain
incestē, *adv.*, unchastely
incidō, -ere, -cidī, to fall upon,
    meet with; to occur
incipiō, -ere, -cēpī, -ceptum,
    to begin
incolumis, -e, *adj.*, safe,
    uninjured; still alive
indāgō, -inis, *f.*, hunting net,
    group of hunting nets
inde, *adv.*, from there
indicium, -iī, *n.*, proof,
    indication; judgment
indīcō, -ere, -dixī, -dictum, to
    declare publicly
Indicus, -a, -um, *adj.*, Indian
indō, -ere, -didī, -ditum, to
    attach to; to put on
indūcō, -ere, -duxī, -ductum,
    to introduce
indulgeō, -ēre, -dulsī, -dultum,
    to bestow as a favor, grant
ineptus, -a, -um, *adj.*, clumsy,
    unsuited
iners, -ertis, *adj.*, inactive, idle
infācundus, -a, -um, *adj.*,
    ineloquent
inferī, -ōrum, *m. pl.*, the dead
inferiae, -ārum, *f. pl.*,
    offerings to the dead
infernus, -a, -um, *adj.*, from
    the world below
inflectō, -ere, -flexī, -flexum,
    to bend

ingenium, -iī, *n.*, talent,
    intellectual talent;
    cleverness, intelligence;
    clever mind, smart thinking
ingens, -tis, *adj.*, large, huge
ingratiīs, *adv.*, against one's
    will
ingrātus, -a, -um, *adj.*,
    ungrateful, unpleasing
ingredior, -ī, -ingressus sum,
    to enter
inguen, -inis, *n.*, groin, sexual
    organ
inimīcus, -a, -um, *adj.*,
    unfriendly, hostile; inimicī,
    m. pl. substantive, personal
    enemy
inīquus, -a, -um, *adj.*, unfair,
    unjust
initiātiō, -ōnis, *f.*, participation
    in secret religious rites
iniussus, -ūs, *m., only in the
    abl.,* without the orders of;
    without command
inlaesus, -a, -um, *adj.*,
    unharmed
inmortālis, -e, *adj.*, deathless,
    immortal
inops, -opis, *adj.*, without,
    destitute of
inquam, *defective verb,* to say
    (introduces direct speech);
    inquit, he or she says
inquiētō (1), to disturb
inquīrō, -ere, -sīvī, -sītum, to
    inquire or pry into anything
insāniō, -īre, -īvī, -ītum, to
    act like a madman, rave; to
    behave crazily

insānus, -a, -um, *adj.,* crazy, mad

insigniō, -īre, -īvī, -ītum, to mark

insignis, -e, *adj.,* conspicuous, notable, remarkable

insimulō (1), to invent a charge, accuse

insipiens, -ntis, *adj.,* foolish

insistō, -ere, -stitī, —, + *dat.,* to insist upon, press on with

instituō, -ere, -uī, -ūtum, to determine, resolve upon

intactus, -a, -um, *adj.,* chaste, pure

intemperiēs, -ēī, *f.,* madness, outrageous conduct

inter, *prep.* + *acc.,* among, between; during, in the course of an action (idiom)

interficiō, -ere, -fēcī, fectum, to kill, murder

interim, *adv.,* in the meantime, meanwhile

interior, interius, *adj.,* inside, interior

intersum, -esse, -fuī, —, to take part in

interventus, -ūs, *m.,* arrival, involvement

intrō (1), to enter

intrōdūcō, -ere, -duxī, -ductum, to introduce, bring in

introeō, -īre, -īvī, -itum, to enter

invādō, -ere, -vāsī, -vāsum, to go into, invade

inveniō, -īre, -vēnī, -ventum, to come upon, find, discover; to manage to get

invideō, -ēre, -vīdī, -vīsum, to envy, hate

invidia, -ae, *f.,* unpopularity

invidus, -a, -um, *adj.,* envious, jealous

invīsus, -a, -um, *adj.,* hateful

invītō (1), to invite, encourage

invītus, -a, -um, *adj.,* against one's will

invocō (1), to call upon

involvō, -ere, -volvī, -volūtum, to cover, wrap

iocus, -ī, *m.,* pastime, jest; mockery

ipse, ipsa, ipsum, *pron.,* himself, herself, itself; the very

īrātus, -a, -um, *adj.,* angry

is, ea, id, *pron.,* he, she, it; this or that man, woman, thing

iste, ista, istud, *pron.,* that, that of which you speak; one's opponent in court; that dastardly (pejorative)

istic, istaec, istuc, *pron.,* that of yours, that very

istuc, *adv.,* for that reason

ita, *adv.,* in such a manner; so, in this way; thus; in such a way; in this manner

Ītalia, -ae, *f.,* Italy

itaque, *conj.,* and so; therefore

item, *adv.,* likewise, besides

iter, itineris, *n.,* road, journey

iterum, *adv.,* again

iubeō, -ere, iussī, iussum, to order, command

iūcundus, -a, -um, *adj.*,
delightful, enjoyable,
pleasant; pleasurable;
pleasing; cordial

iūdex, -icis, *m.*, juror; judge;
critic

iūdicium, -iī, *n.*, case, trial;
court

iugālis, -e, *adj.*, married, spend
together as a married couple

iūs, iūris, *n.*, justice; law; legal
right; right

iuvat, *impers.*, it is pleasing

iuvenis, -is, *m.*, young man,
youth

iuventus, -ūtis, *f.*, youth, young
men, young persons

iuxtā, *adv.*, beside, near by

Kalendae, -ārum, *f. pl.*, Kalends
(first day of each month)

lābēs, -is, *f.*, defect

labor, -ōris, *m.*, work, toil;
difficulty, trouble, struggle

labōrō (1), to struggle, labor

labrum, -ī, *n.*, lip

lacerō (1), to tear, lacerate

lacrima, -ae, *f.*, tear

lacrimō (1), to weep, cry

lacūnārium, -iī, *n.*, ceiling
panel

laedō, -ere, laesī, laesum, to
injure, harm

laetor, -ārī, -ātus sum, to be
happy, rejoice

landica, -ae, *f.*, clitoris

lānificium, -iī, *n.*, wool
working

lapillus, -ī, *m.*, little stone,
pebble

lār familiāris, lāris familiāris,
m., household divinity

lascīvia, -ae, *f.*, sexual
playfulness

lascīvus, -a, -um, *adj.*, sexually
playful

lassō (1), to exhaust, make weary

latēbrae, -ārum, *f. pl.*, hiding
place

lateō, -ēre, -uī, to hide, lurk

Latīnus, -a, -um, *adj.*, Latin

lātrō (1), to howl

lātrō, -ōnis, *m.*, thief, robber

laudātiō, -ōnis, *f.*, funeral
speech, eulogy

laudō (1), to praise

laus, laudis, *f.*, praise

laxō (1), to release; to withdraw

laxus, -a, -um, *pf. pass. pple.*,
stretched out

lectīca, -ae, *f.*, litter

lectitō (1), to read often, with
eagerness

lectrix, -īcis, *f.*, lectrix (female
slave who reads and
performs writings aloud)

lectulus, -ī, *m.*, *diminutive*,
little couch, bed

lectus, -ī, *m.*, bed, couch

legō, -ere, lēgī, lectum, to
choose, select; to pick up; to
read, read aloud

lēniter, *adv.*, gently, leniently

lēnō, -ōnis, *m.*, pimp, sexual
procurer

lepidus, -a, -um, *adj.*,
charming, witty

levitās, -ātis, *f.,* fickleness, unreliability, irresponsibility

lex, lēgis, *f.,* law

libellus, -ī, *m., diminutive,* little book, book of poetry

libenter, *adv.,* warmly, with pleasure; gladly

līber, -a, -um, *adj.,* free

liber, -rī, *m.,* book

līberī, -ōrum, *m. pl.,* children

lībertās, -ātis, *f.,* freedom, liberty

lībertus, -ī, *m.,* freedman

libet, -ere, libitum est, *impers.,* it pleases

libīdō, -inis, *f.,* passion, lust

liburnica, -ae, *f.,* a light sailing vessel, galley

liceor, -ērī, -licitus sum, to make a bid for

licet, -ere, licuit, *impers.,* it is permitted, allowed; one may or can; although, granted that (+ subjunctive)

līmen, -inis, *n.,* door; threshold; entrance

lingua, -ae, *f.,* tongue

līs, lītis, *f.,* lawsuit

littera, -ae, *f.,* (usually pl.) letter

litterae, -ārum, *f. pl.,* letter, letters

lītus, -oris, *n.,* shore

līvidus, -a, -um, *adj.,* ill-tempered, envious

locus, -ī, *m.* (also n. in the pl.), place, position, location

longinquus, -a, -um, *adj.,* long, lengthy

longus, -a, -um, *adj.,* long, lengthy

loquor, -ī, locūtus sum, to speak

lucerna, -ae, *f.,* lamp

lūgeō, -ēre, luxī, luctum, to mourn, grieve, lament

lūmen, -inis, *n.,* light, lamp, torch

lustrum, -ī, *n.,* a period of five years

lūsus, -ūs, *m.,* erotic game, sport

lux, lūcis, *f.,* light; life, day of life; brilliance, wit

luxuriōsus, -a, -um, *adj.,* self-indulgent, immoderate

māchina, -ae, *f.,* mechanical device

māchinōsus, -a, -um, *adj.,* skillfully constructed to collapse

Magī, -ōrum, *m. pl.,* learned men and magicians (among the Persians)

magis, *adv.,* more, rather

magister, -rī, *m.,* teacher

magistra, -ae, *f.,* (female) teacher

magnō opere, *adv.,* greatly

magnus, -a, -um, *adj.,* great, important, of great weight or importance; large; loud

māiestas, -ātis, *f.,* grandeur, authority

māior, māius, *compar. adj.,* greater, older

malē, *adv.,* badly, unhappily

maledictum, -ī, *n.,* reproach, angry word

malefactum, -ī, *n.,* bad deed

mālō, malle, maluī, —, to prefer

mālum, -ī, *n.,* apple

mālum Scantiānum, mālī Scantiānī, *n.,* the name of a kind of apple

mālum strūtheum, mālī strūtheī, *n.,* the name of a kind of quince, a pear-like fruit used to make preserves

malus, -a, -um, *adj.,* bad, difficult

mandō (1), to commit, hand over, entrust

maneō, -ēre, mansī, mansum, to remain, abide

Mānēs, -ium, *m. pl.,* ghost or shades of the dead; deified souls of the departed

manus, -ūs, *f.,* hand; band

mare, -is, *n.,* sea

marītus, -ī, *m.,* husband

Masinissa, -ae, *m.,* Masinissa (King of Numidia in North Africa, located in what is Algeria and part of Tunisia today)

māter, -ris, *f.,* mother

māternus, -a, -um, *adj.,* of or belonging to one's mother; on the mother's side, maternal

mātrimōnium, -iī, *n.,* marriage; (with **tenēre**) to be one's spouse

mātrimus, -a, -um, *adj.,* who has a mother living

mātrōna, -ae, *f.,* wife, married woman, woman

maximē, *superl. adv.,* to the greatest extent, most, especially

maximus, -a, -um, *superl. adj.,* greatest (superl. of **magnus**)

mecastor, *interjection,* by Castor

medium, -iī, *n.,* the middle

melior, -ius, *compar. adj.,* better

membrum, -ī, *n.,* limb

memor, -oris, *adj.* + *gen,* mindful of

memoria, -ae, *f.,* memory

mendācium, -iī, *n.,* lie, falsehood

mens, mentis, *f.,* mind, frame of mind, state of mind

mensis, -is, *m.,* month

mentula, -ae, *f., primary obscenity for the male organ,* "prick"

mereō, -ēre, -uī, -itum, to deserve, earn

merus, -ī, *m.,* wine unmixed with water

messis, -is, *f.,* harvest, year

metuō, -ere, -uī, -ūtum, to fear

metus, -ūs, *m.,* fear

meus, -a, -um, *possessive pron.,* my

mī = mihi. *See* ego

migrō (1), to depart, be off

mīles, -itis, *m.,* soldier

mīma, -ae, *f.,* mime actress

minae, -ārum, *f. pl.,* threats

minimus, -a, -um, *superl. adj.,* youngest

minister, -trī, *m.*, attendant

ministra, -ae, *f.*, maid-servant, female attendant

minor, *irregular compar. adj. from* parvus, smaller, younger

minus, *compar. adv.*, less, to a smaller degree

minūtiō, -ōnis, *f.*, loss

mīror, -ārī, -ātus sum, to wonder, marvel at; to be astonished at

mīrus, -a, -um, *adj.*, strange

misceō, -ēre, miscuī, mixtum, to mix, combine; to disrupt

miser, -a, -um, *adj.*, wretched, unfortunate, happy

misericordia, -ae, *f.*, mercy, pity

misericors, -cordis, *adj.*, tender-hearted, compassionate

mittō, -ere, mīsī, missum, to send, convey

modo, *adv.*, just now, recently, just recently, lately; modo ... modo *correlative advs.*, now ... now

modus, -ī, *m.*, means, manner, measure

moechus, -ī, *m.*, adulterer

molestia, -ae, *f.*, trouble, distress

molestus, -a, -um, *adj.*, annoying, irksome; troublesome

molior, -īrī, -ītus sum, to undertake, endeavor to do

mollis, -e, *adj.*, sweet, tender

mons, montis, *m.*, mountain

monstrum, -ī, *n.*, evil omen, portent

monumentum, -ī, *n.*, monument, tomb

mora, -ae, *f.*, delay

morior, -ī, mortuus sum, to die

moror, -ārī, -ātus sum, to delay, remain

mors, -tis, *f.*, death

morsus, -ūs, *m.*, bite

mortuus, -a, -um, *adj.*, dead

mos, mōris, *m.*, custom, habit; practice; manner; fashion

moveō, -ēre, mōvī, mōtum, to move; to worry; to bother

mox, *adv.*, then, next

muliebris, -e, *adj.*, of a woman, female; womanish, of or belonging to a woman, womanly

mulier, -eris, *f.*, woman, female, wife

muliercula, -ae, *f.*, *diminutive*, poor little woman

multī, -ae, -a, *adj.*, many

multum, *adv.*, greatly

multus, -a, -um, *adj.*, much, great

mundē, *adv.*, cleanly

munditia, -ae, *f.*, elegance

mundus, -a, -um, *adj.*, clean, neat

mūniō, -īre, -īvī, -ītum, to build (a road)

mūnus, -eris, *n.*, gift, reward

mūtō (1), to change

namque, *conj.*, for indeed

narrō (1), to tell, narrate

nascor, -ī, natus sum, to be
born

nāta, -ae, *f.,* daughter, female
child; girl

nātālis, -e, *adj.,* having to
do with birth; (with **diēs**
understood) birthday

natō (1), to swim

nātūra, -ae, *f.,* nature

nātus, -ī, *m.,* son

naufragium, -iī, *n.,* shipwreck

nāvigium, -iī, *n.,* boat, vessel;
pleasure-boat

nāvis, -is, *f.,* boat

nē . . . quidem, *adv.,* not . . .
even

nē, *conj.,* so that not, lest (after
verbs of fearing); in order
that not, so as not, so as
not to

-ne, *particle* (indicates a
question)

nec opinātō, *adv.,* unexpectedly

nec or neque, *conj.,* nor, and
not, not; neque . . . neque,
neither . . . nor

necessārius, -a, -um, *adj.,*
necessary

necesse, *indecl. adj.,* necessary

necō (1), to kill

nefas, *n., indecl.,* sacrilegious
act, sacrilege; sin; an
impious act

negō (1), to deny

negōtium, -iī, *m.,* business,
task; dealing; occupation,
employment

nēmō, -inis, *m.,* no one, nobody

neptis, -is, *f.,* granddaughter

nēquam, *adj., indecl.,*
worthless, naughty,
licentious

nēquitia, -ae, *f.,* misbehavior,
wickedness; naughtiness,
erotic misbehavior

nēquō, *adv.,* in no way

nesciō quī, quae, quod,
idiomatic phrase, some, one
or another

nesciō quis, quid, *idiomatic
phrase,* some one or other;
something or other

nesciō, -īre, -īvī, -ītum, not to
know, be ignorant

nēve *or* neu, *conj.,* and not, nor,
and that not

nex, necis, *f.,* violent death,
murder

ni, *conj.,* that . . . not
(introducing indirect
prohibitions)

Nīcerōtiānus, -a, -um, *adj.,*
of Nicerotian perfume,
relating to perfume made by
a Niceros

niger, -ra, -rum, *adj.,* black

nīl *or* nihil, *indecl.,* nothing

nimbus, -ī, *m.,* cloud

nimium, *adv.,* too much,
exceedingly; marvelously

nisi, *conj.,* unless, if . . . not,
except

niveus, -a, -um, *adj.,* snowy
white

nō (1), to swim

nōbilis, -e, *adj.,* of noble birth,
celebrated

noctū, *adv.,* at night

nocturnus, -a, -um, *adj.,* night time, at night

nōlō, nolle, nōluī, —, to not want, be unwilling

nōmen, -inis, *n.,* name

nōn tantum . . . sed etiam, *conj.,* not only . . . but also

nōn, *adv.,* not

Nōnae, -ārum, *f. pl.,* Nones (nine days, counting inclusively, before the Ides: seventh day of March, May, July, October; fifth day of the other eight months)

nonne, *interrog. particle,* word introducing a question that expects the answer "yes"

nōs, nostrum *or* **nostrī,** *pron.,* we

noster, -tra, -trum, *possessive adj.,* our, our own

nota, -ae, *f.,* mark

notō (1), to observe, notice; to mark, note, observe; to scare

nōtus, -a, -um, *adj.,* well known, famous; friend (as a noun)

nox, noctis, *f.,* night

nūbō, -ere, nupsī, nuptum, (with **apud** + acc.) to marry, to be married; to be married to

nūdō (1), to bare, expose to view, reveal

nūdus, -a, -um, *adj.,* nude, naked, bare

nullus, -a, -um, *adj.,* no, none, not any

num, *interrog. particle* (word introducing a question that expects the answer "no")

Numa, -ae, *m.,* Numa (legendary second king of Rome)

numerō (1), to number, count; to possess

numerus, -ī, *m.,* number

Numida, -ae, *m.,* inhabitant of Numidia

nummus, -ī, *m.,* coin, money

numquam, *adv.,* never

nunc, *adv.,* now

nundinae, -ārum, *f. pl.,* market-day, business traffic

nuntiō (1), to announce, report; to proclaim

nuntium, -iī, *n.,* message

nuntius, -iī, *m.,* messenger

nupta, -ae, *f.,* wife

nuptiae, -ārum, *f. pl.,* wedding

nuptiālis, -e, *adj.,* having to do with marriage, wedded

nux, nucis, *f.,* nut

Ō, *interjection,* O!

ob, *prep.* + *acc.,* on account of

obitus, -ūs, *m.,* death, demise

obiurgō (1), to scold, rebuke

oblīquus, -a, -um, *adj.,* at an angle, slanting

oborior, -īrī, -ortus sum, to arise; to well up

obruō, -ere, -uī, -utum, to bury; to overwhelm, destroy

obscūrus, -a, -um, *adj.,* dark, obscure

obsecrō (1), to entreat, implore, beseech; to pray (as an interjection)

obsequor, -ī, -secūtus sum, + *dat.,* to comply with, defer to

observātiō, -ōnis, *f.,* requirement, rule

obstringō, -ere, -strinxī, -strictum, to tie up; to place under obligation

obtestor, -ārī, -ātus sum, to call upon as a witness, invoke

obtineō, -ēre, -uī, -tentus, to get hold of, manage

occīdō, -ere, -cīdī, -cīsum, to kill

occultō (1), to hide

occurrō, -ere, -currī, -cursum, + *dat.,* to run towards, meet

octāvus, -a, -um, *adj.,* eighth

oculus, -ī, *m.,* eye

odor, -ōris, *m.,* smell, aroma

offerō, -ferre, obtulī, oblātum, to offer, present

officium, -iī, *n.,* duty; ceremony, a ceremonial observance

ōmen, ōminis, *n.,* omen, portent

omittō, -ere, -mīsī, -missum, not to do, neglect

omnīnō, *adv.,* altogether, utterly

omnis, -e, *adj.,* all, every; whole, the whole

onerō (1), to burden, oppress

opera, -ae, *f.,* labor, effort

operōsus, -a, -um, *adj.,* painstaking, laborious

opīnor, -ārī, -ātus sum, to think, have the opinion

opitulor, -ārī, -ātus sum, + *dat.,* to bring help to

oportet, -ēre, -uit, *impers.,* it is necessary, proper, right

opperior, -īrī, -perītus sum, to await

opsecro = obsecrō (1), to plead, beseech

optineō = obtineō, -ēre, -tinuī, -tentum, to obtain

optiō, -ōnis, *f.,* choice

optō (1), to wish, desire

ōrātiō, -ōnis, *f.,* speech; oration

ordinatīm, *adv.,* in the proper order

ordō, -inis, *m.,* order, rank

orīgō, -inis, *f.,* origin, ancestry

orior, -īrī, ortus sum, to arise, originate, be descended from

ornātus, -ūs, *m.,* adornment, splendor

ornō (1), to decorate, array

ōrō (1), to beg, ask, entreat, plead; to pray to

ōs, ōris, *n.,* mouth, face

os, ossis, *n.,* bone

ostendō, -ere, -dī, -tum, to show, display

ōvum, -ī, *n.,* egg

pactō, *abl., from* **pactum, -ī,** *n.,* means, manner

paene, *adv.,* almost

paenitet, -ēre, paenituit, *impers.,* it causes regret, causes remorse

Palātium, -iī, *n.,* palace
palleō, -ēre, -uī, to grow pale
pallium, -iī, *n.,* bed cover
palma, -ae, *f.,* palm of the hand
pandō, -ere, pandī, passum, to open up; to spread out; **passus, -a, -um,** *pf. pass. pple.,* (of hair) loose, dishevelled
papilla, -ae, *f.,* breast
Pāpius, -a, -um, *adj.,* of or belonging to the Roman family Papius
parābilis, -e, *adj.,* accessible, obtainable
parātus, -a, -um, *pf. pass. pple.,* prepared; acquired, procured; about to happen
parcō, -ere, pepercī, + *dat.,* to spare
parcus, -a, -um, *adj.,* frugal, thrifty
pārens, -ntis, *m. and f.,* parent, mother or father; **parentēs, -ium,** parents
parentō (1), + *dat.,* to perform the rite of appeasement to the dead
pāreō, -ēre, -paruī, —, + *dat.,* to obey
pariō, -ere, peperī, partum, to produce, procure; to give birth to
pariter, *adv.,* equally, together, at the same time
parō (1), to equip, design, prepare
parricīdium, -iī, *n.,* murder of a near relative

pār, pāris, *adj.,* equal, comparable
pars, partis, *f.,* part, portion, area
parum, *adv.,* not sufficiently, not, too little
parvus, -a, -um, *adj.,* small
pascuum, -ī, *n.,* pasture
pater, -tris, *m.,* father
paternus, -a, -um, *adj.,* of or pertaining to a father, paternal, on the father's side
patior, -ī, passus sum, to allow; to bear, endure
patrēs, -um, *m. pl.,* senators
patria, -ae, *f.,* country; native land
patrīmus, -a, -um, *adj.,* who has a father living
patruus, -ī, *m.,* uncle
paulō, *adv.,* by a little, somewhat
pausa, -ae, *f.,* cessation, pause, respite
pax, pācis, *f.,* peace
peccō (1), to commit sexual wrongdoing, misbehave
pectus, -oris, *n.,* mind, breast
pecūlium, -iī, *n.,* private property of a wife, son, daughter, or slave, held with the consent of the husband, father, or master
pecūnia, -ae, *f.,* money
pēdīcō (1), *primary obscenity for to penetrate anally,* to "fuck in the asshole"
pellō, -ere, pepulī, pulsum, to drive, strike; to impress; to capture one's attention

pendō, -ere, pependī, pensum,
  to hang
penetrō (1), to make one's
  way inside, penetrate, gain
  access to
pensum, -ī, *n.*, + habere, to
  care about, have scruples
  about
per, *prep.* + *acc.*, on account of,
  because of; through
peragō, -ere, -ēgī, -actum,
  to go through with,
  accomplish, complete
perarō (1), to write
percontor, -ārī, -ātus sum, to
  question thoroughly
percussor, -ōris, *m.*, assassin
percutiō, -ere, -cussī,
  -cussum, to affect deeply
perdō, -ere, -didī, -ditum, to
  destroy, kill
peregrīnātiō, -ōnis, *f.*, travel,
  journey
pereō, -īre, -iī, -ītum, to
  die, perish; to disappear,
  vanish
perferō, -ferre, -tulī, -lātum, +
  ad + *acc.*, to convey news
perīculum, -ī, *n.*, danger, peril
perlegō, -ere, lēgī, -lectum, to
  read thoroughly
permittō, -ere, -mīsī,
  -missum, to allow
perpōtō (1), to drink heavily
perpudescō, -ere, —, to begin
  to feel very ashamed
persaepe, *adv.*, very often
persequor, -ī, -cūtus sum,
  + *gen.*, to pursue

persevērō (1), to persevere,
  continue
persōna, -ae, *f.*, persona,
  character
persuādeō, -ēre, -suāsī,
  -suāsum, to persuade (to do
  something); to win over
pertinācia, -ae, *f.*, perseverance,
  obstinacy
perturbō (1), to upset, throw
  into disorder, confound; to
  frighten
perveniō, -īre, -vēnī, -ventum,
  to come to, arrive at
perversus, -a, -um, *pf. pass.*
  pple., turned around,
  twisted
pēs, pedis, *m.*, foot
pessimus, -a, -um, *superl. adj.*,
  worst
petō, -ere, -īvī (-iī), -ītum,
  to seek eagerly, aim for; to
  demand
Phaon, -ōnis, *m.*, Phaon (young
  man of Lesbos, loved by
  Sappho)
Phyllis, -idos, *f.*, Phyllis (Greek
  female name)
Pīeridēs, -um, *f. pl.*, Muses
Pietās, -ātis, *f.*, the goddess
  Piety
pirum, -ī, *n.*, pear
placeō, -ēre, -uī, -itum, + *dat.*,
  to please; placuit, *impers.*,
  it was decided, resolved
  (decision of the Senate)
placitus, -a, -um, *pf. pass. pple.*,
  agreeable, pleasing
plāga, -ae, *f.*, blow, strike

plangō, -ere, planxī, planctum, to beat

plēbēs, -ēī, *f.,* the common people

plērumque, *adv.,* very often

plērusque, -raque, -rumque, *adj.,* many, very many

plurimum, *superl. adv.,* very much; most, greatly

plūs, *compar. adv. of* **multum,** more

plūs, plūris, *n.,* more

pluteus, -ī, *m.,* back of a couch

pōculum, -ī, *n.,* cup

poena, -ae, *f.,* punishment

Poenus, -a, -um, *adj.,* Carthaginian, of Phoenician ancestry

pol, *interjection,* by Pollux

polleō, -ēre, —, —, to be powerful, prevail

polluō, -ere, -uī, -ūtum, to defile, degrade, pollute

Pompēius, -a, -um, *adj.,* in honor of the **triumvir** Pompey

pōnō, -ere, posuī, posītum, to place; to put aside

pontifex, -īcis, *m.,* a Roman high priest; **pontifex maximus,** Roman chief high priest

populus, -ī, *m.,* people

porrigō, -ere, -rexī, -rectum, to extend, stretch out

porticus, -ūs, *f.,* colonnade, portico

possum, posse, potuī, —, to be able; to hold power

post, *prep. + acc.,* after, since

posteā, *adv.,* afterwards

posterī, -ōrum, *m. pl.,* descendants

posterius, *adv.,* later

posterus, -a, -um, *adj.,* next; second; following

posthāc, *adv.,* after this; in future, hereafter

postrēmus, -a, -um, *adj.,* the last; **ad postrēmum,** at last, finally

postrīdiē, *adv.,* the next day

postulātiō, -ōnis, *f.,* demand

postulō (1), to demand

potestās, -ātis, *f.,* power; control

potiō, -ōnis, *f.,* drink

potior, potius, *compar. adj.,* more powerful than, preferable to

potissimum, *adv.,* above all; especially

potius, *adv. with* **quam,** rather

praebeō, -ēre, -uī, -ītum, to offer, present; to supply, lend

praeceps, -cipitis, *adj.,* headlong, violent, reckless; impetuous

praecipuē, *adv.,* especially

praeclūdō, -ere, -clūsī, -clūsum, to shut

praecō, -ōnis, *m.,* herald

praedicō (1), to describe

praegnāns, -ntis, *adj.,* pregnant

praemūniō, -īre, -īvī, -itum, to protect

Praenestīnus, -a, -um, *adj.,* from Praeneste (a town near Rome, famous for its nuts and fruits)

praes, praedis, *m.,* surety, bondsman

praesens, -ntis, *pres. act. pple.,* on hand, present

praesentia, -ium, *n. pl.,* present circumstances

praesertim, *adv.,* especially

praestō, *adv.,* on hand, nearby

praestō, -āre, -stitī -stātum, to offer; to furnish, provide; to impart (+ acc.); to offer to (+ dat.); to stand out, surpass

praeter, *prep.* + *acc.,* beyond, outside

praeter, *adv.,* excepting, save only

praeterquam, *adv.,* beyond, besides

praetervehor, -ī, -vectus sum, to pass by

praetexta, -ae, *f.,* the purple-bordered gown worn by free-born males until they assumed the toga

praetextātus, -a, -um, *adj.,* wearing the toga **praetexta** (not yet viewed as an adult)

praetōrium, -iī, *n.,* general's headquarters, tent

prandium, -iī, *n.,* meal, mid-day meal; banquet

precor, -ārī, -ātus sum, to pray, beg, beseech, ask for

prehendō, -ere, -dī, -sum, to take hold of, grasp

premō, -ere, pressī, pressum, to press, overpower, burden

pretium, -iī, *n.,* price

prex, precis, *f.,* prayer; entreaty

prīmārius, -a, -um, *adj.,* leading, first-rate

prīmō, *adv.,* at first, first

prīmum, *adv.,* first

prīmus, -a, -um, *adj.,* first; most valued

prior, -ōris, *compar. adj.,* previous, first

priscē, *adv.,* in an old fashioned manner

prius, *adv.,* first, first of all

priusquam, *conj.,* before

prīvō (1), to deprive

prō, *prep.* + *abl.,* on behalf of, for, representing; in accordance with

probō (1), to approve, justify; to be satisfied with

probus, -a, -um, *adj.,* proper, virtuous, morally upright; respectable

prōcēdō, -ere, -cessī, -cessum, to go forward, go smoothly; to be successful

prōcēritās, -ātis, *f.,* tallness

procul, *adv.,* from a distance

proelium, -iī, *n.,* battle, contest

profectō, *adv.,* indeed, in fact

prōferō, -ferre, -tulī, -lātum, to bring forth; to put off, defer

prōfligō (1), to overwhelm, ruin

prōgeniēs, -ēī, *f.,* descendant

prōgredior, -ī, -gressus sum, to go forward, proceed

prōlābor, -ī, -lapsus sum, to slip forward

promittō, -ere, -mīsī, -missum, to promise, pledge; to send forth

pronepōs, -ōtis, *m.,* great-grandson

prope, *adv.,* nearly

propinquus, -ī, *m.,* close kinsman

propriē, *adv.,* appropriately, properly

propter, *prep.* + *acc.,* on account of

proptereā, *adv.,* therefore, on that account

prorsus, *adv.,* exactly, precisely

prōsequor, -ī, -cūtus sum, to follow after

prosperē, *adv.,* happily, favorably

prōsum, -desse, -fuī, —, to be helpful, beneficial

prōtrahō, -ere, -traxī, -tractum, to drag forward; to prolong, protract; to reveal

prōvincia, -ae, *f.,* province

proximum, -ī, *n.,* vicinity; **in proximo,** nearby

proximūs, -a, -um, *adj.,* next, following

prūdēns, -ntis, *adj.,* far-seeing, wise

prūdentia, -ae, *f.,* prudence, discretion

Pūbliciānus, -a, -um, *adj.,* of or connected with Publicius

publicus, -a, -um, *adj.,* public, affecting the people

pudet, -ēre, puduit, puditum est, *impers.,* it causes shame

pudicitia, -ae, *f.,* chastity, modesty, virtue

pudīcus, -a, -um, *adj.,* modest, chaste, virtuous, pure

pudor, -ōris, *m.,* shame, sense of sexual respectability

puella, -ae, *f.,* young woman, girl; female lover in elegaic poetry; the beloved

puellāriter, *adv.,* in a girlish manner

puer, -ī, *m.,* boy, slave boy; the young (name)

pūga, -ae, *f.,* buttocks

pugiō, -ōnis, *m.,* dagger

pugna, -ae, *f.,* combat, battle

pugnō (1), + *dat.,* to fight; to oppose

pulcher, -ra, -rum, *adj.,* beautiful

pūpula, -ae, *f.,* young girl

pūrus, -a, -um, *adj.,* pure; without dirt

pūsio, -ōnis, *m., colloquial,* little boy, little squirt

putō (1), to think, consider, imagine; to have the opinion

Pylius, -a, -um, *adj.,* of or belonging to Pylos (home of Nestor)

Pyrrhus, -ī, *m.,* Pyrrhus (king of Epirus, an enemy of the Romans)

quaerō, -ere, -sīvī, -sītum, to seek; to ask, inquire

quaesō, (-ere), *mostly in the first person sing., pres. tense,* to seek, ask for; to beg

quaestiō, -ōnis, *f.,* judicial investigation

quaestor, -ōris, *m.,* Roman official charged with supervising state finances

quālis, -e, *interr. and rel. adj.,* what kind, of what sort

quam diū, *adv.,* as long as

quam minimē, *adv.,* as little as possible

quam, *adv.,* how; than (with compar. adjs. and advs.)

quamquam, quanquam, *conj.,* although

quamvīs, *conj.,* although

quandō, *conj.,* when, since; ever (indefinite with **sī**)

quantus, -a, -um, *adj.,* how much, how great, what great; as much as

quārē, *adv.,* therefore, wherefore

quasi, *adv.,* as if, just as, just as if, as it were

quasillum, -ī, *n.,* small wicker basket that holds wool for spinning

quātenus, *adv.,* to what extent, seeing that

quater, *adv., numeral,* four times

quattuor, *indecl. numeral,* four

-que, *conj. added to the end of a word,* and

queō, quīre, quīvī, quītum, *defective verb,* to be able

querēla, -ae, *f.,* argument, quarrel; complaint

queror, -ī, questus sum, to complain, complain about

quī, quae, quod, *rel. pron.,* who, what, which; *at the beginning of a sentence,* he, she, it (coordinating rel.)

quīcumque, quaecumque, quodcumque, *rel.,* whoever, whatever

quid, *adv.,* why?

quīdam, quaedam, quoddam, *indefinite adj.,* a certain

quīdam, quaedam, quiddam, *indefinite pron.,* a certain, a certain one, somebody, something

quidem, *adv.,* moreover, too, also, what is more, indeed, in fact, certainly

quiescō, -ere, -ēvī, -ētum, to rest; to calm down

quīn, *adv. or conj.,* indeed, in fact; how, but that; moreover

quindecim, *indecl. numeral,* fifteen

Quinquātria, -um, *n. pl.,* a festival celebrated in March in honor of Minerva

Quirītēs, -ītium, *m. pl.,* Roman people, body of Roman citizens (in their civilian capacity); citizens or residents of Rome

quis, quid, *indefinite pron.,* anyone, anybody, anything (used with **sī, nisi, nē, num**)

quis, quid, *interrog. pron.,* who, what

quisnam, quaenam, quidnam, *pron.,* who, which, what, pray tell me!

quispiam, quaepiam, quodpiam, *indefinite pron.*, some, any

quisquam, quicquam, *indefinite pron.*, anyone, anybody, anything

quisque, quaeque, quidque, *indefinite pron.*, each, each one

quō, *adv.*, where

quod, *conj.*, because; but; the fact that, that; which

quōmodocumque, *adv.*, in whatever way

quoniam, *conj.*, since, because

quoque, *adv.*, also, even, too

quotannīs, *adv.*, every year

quotienscumque, *conj.*, as often as, whenever

rapiō, -ere, rapuī, raptum, to seize, snatch

rārus, -a, -um, *adj.*, rare, unusual, infrequent, uncommon

ratiō, -ōnis, *f.*, account, reason; means; candidacy

recēdō, -ere, -cessī, -cessum, to withdraw, retreat

recens, -ntis, *adj.*, recent, fresh; newly gathered

recipiō, -ere, -cēpī, -ceptum, to receive, welcome

recitō (1), to recite one's own works in public

reconciliātiō, -ōnis, *f.*, reconciliation

rectē, *adv.*, rightly, properly

rectus, -a-, -um, *adj.*, straight, shapely

recuperō (1), to recover, restore

recurrō, -ere, recurrī, —, to run back, rush back; to return

reddō, -ere, -didī, -ditum, to give, bestow; to report; to render; to restore, bring back

referō, -ferre, -tulī, -lātum, to bring back; to relate, describe, recall

reficiō, -ere, -fēcī, -fectum, to refresh

rēgius, -a, -um, *adj.*, royal, of or belonging to a king

regnum, -ī, *n.*, realm, kingdom

religiō, -ōnis, *f.*, religious observance

relinquō, -ere, -līquī, -lictum, to leave, leave behind, abandon

reliquum, -ī, *n.*, remainder, rest

remissē, *adv.*, gently, mildly

remittō, -ere, -mīsī, -missum, to send back, relax, slacken

removeō, -ēre, -mōvī, -mōtum, to remove, dismiss

renovō (1), to restore; to relight (a torch)

reor, rērī, ratus sum, to realize, think, judge; to suppose, imagine

repellō, -ere, reppulī, repulsum, to reject

repentē, *adv.*, suddenly

repetō, -ere, -īvī, -ītum, to return; to repeat

repleō, -ēre, -ēvī, -ētum, to fill up

rēs pūblica, reī pūblicae, *f.,* Roman state, "the people's concern"

rēs, -eī, *f.,* thing, matter; situation; reality; incident; property; (with **dīvīna**) religious worship

rēscindō, -ere, -scīdī, -scissum, to cut away, annul

resistō, -ere, -stitī, —, to pause on one's journey, stop

resonō (1), to resound, echo

rēspondeō, -ēre, -dī, -sum, to answer, reply

rēspuō, -ere, -uī, —, to reject, refuse

rēstituō, -ere, -uī, -ūtum, to restore, replace; to put back in place

resupīnō (1), to knock flat on one's back, overturn

retardō (1), to impede

rēte, rētis, *n.,* net

revīviscō, -ere, -vixī, —, to come to life, return to life again

rex, rēgis, *m.,* king

Rhodos, -ī, *f.,* the island of Rhodes on the coast of Asia Minor

rīdeō, -ēre, rīsī, rīsum, to laugh

rītus, -ūs, *m.,* ritual

rogō (1), to ask, request

Rōma, -ae, *f.,* city of Rome

Rōmānus, -a, -um, *adj.,* Roman

rōstrum, -ī, *n.,* platform for public speakers in the Roman Forum

ruber, rubra, rubrum, *adj.,* red

rubor, -ōris, *m.,* blush; redness

rubus, -ī, *m.,* bramble

ruīna, -ae, *f.,* falling in, destruction

rumpō, -ere, rūpī, ruptum, to burst, rupture; to break, force a way through; to tear out, pull out

rūs, rūris, *n.,* country, countryside; **rure,** from the country

Sabīnus, -a, -um, *adj.,* Sabine

sacer, -ra, -rum, *adj.,* sacred, holy

sacerdos, -ōtis, *m. or f.,* priest, priestess

sacerdōtium, -iī, *n.,* priesthood

sacrum, -ī, *n.,* a religious ritual, rite

saepe, *adv.,* often

saeviō, -īre, -iī, -ītum, to rage, be violent

saevus, -a, -um, *adj.,* cruel, savage

salūs, -ūtis, *f.,* health; greetings

salūtō (1), to send greetings to (may be abbreviated to *s.*)

salvē, *imperative of defective verb,* hello

salveō, -ēre, to greet

salvus, -a, -um, *adj.,* safe, unharmed, without violation of

sanctitās, -ātis, *f.,* holiness

sanctus, -a, -um, *adj.,* pure, innocent

sānē, *adv.,* certainly, to be sure

sānus, -a, -um, *adj.,* sane, healthy

sapa, -ae, *f.,* new wine

sapiō, -ere, -īvī (-iī), —, to taste, show good taste

Sapphō, -ūs, *f.,* Sappho (famous Greek female poet of the sixth century BCE)

satietās, -ātis, *f.,* state of being glutted (with food)

satis, *adv.,* enough

sauciō (1), to wound

saxum, -ī, *n.,* rock

Scantiānus, -a, -um, *adj.,* Scantianum (the name of a kind of apple, famous in antiquity)

scelerātus, -a, -um, *adj.,* profane, wicked

scelus, -eris, *n.,* crime

scīlicet, *adv.,* naturally, undoubtedly; to be sure, of course

sciō, -īre, -īvī, -ītum, to know, understand

scortum, -ī, *n.,* paid sex worker, one who takes money for sexual favors

scrībō, -ere, scripsī, scriptum, to write

scriptum, -ī, *n.,* writing, something written

Scylla, -ae, *f.,* Scylla

sē *or* **sēsē,** *reflex. pron.,* himself, herself, itself, themselves; the very

sēcessus, -ūs, *m.,* retirement, at leisure; (with **in** + abl.) in the country

secō, -ere, -cuī, -ctum, to cut, scratch

sēcretum, -ī, *n.,* secrecy

sector, -ārī, -ātus sum, to pursue, run after

secundus, -a, -um + *dat.,* a copy of, a duplicate of

secundum, *prep.* + *acc.,* near, by; next to, after; in conformity with

sēcurus, -a, -um, *adj.,* free from, free from care

sed, *conj.,* but

sedeō, -ēre, sēdī, sessum, to sit

sēmita, -ae, *f.,* path, alley

semper, *adv.,* always

senātor, -ōris, *m.,* senator, a member of the Roman senate

senātus, -ūs, *m.,* senate

senecta, -ae, *f.,* old age, long life

senectūs, -ūtis, *f.,* old age

senex, -is, *adj.,* old, aged

senex, -is, *m.,* old man

sensus, -ūs, *m.,* sense; + *gen.,* capacity to perceive by the senses; **sensus aurium,** hearing

sententia, -ae, *f.,* opinion; decision; sentence

sentiō, -īre, sēnsī, sēnsum, to feel, perceive; to observe

sepeliō, -īre, -īvī (-iī), -pultum, to bury

September, -bris, *m.,* September (the seventh month of the Roman year, counting from March)

sepultūra, -ae, *f.,* burial

sermō, -ōnis, *m.,* speech

servīlis, -e, *adj.,* of a slave

serviō, -īre, -iī (-īvī), -ītum, to be in slavery, be a slave

servitūs, -ūtis, *f.,* servitude

Servius, -iī, *m.,* Servius (male *praenomen,* derived from the Latin word for "slave")

servō (1), to save, protect

seu, *conj.,* whether

sevērē, *adv.,* severely, sternly

sevērus, -a, -us, *adj.,* severe, stern

sex, *numeral,* six

sī, *conj.,* if

sīc, *adv.,* so, thus; as follows

siccus, -a, -um, *adj.,* thirsty

sīcut, *conj.,* just as

significō (1), to indicate

signō (1), to sign

signum, -ī, *n.,* signal, war trumpet; sign

silentium, -iī, *n.,* silence

silva, -ae, *f.,* woods, forest

silvāticus, -a, -um, *adj.,* woodland; woodland fruits (n. pl.)

similis, -e, *adj.* + *dat.,* similar

simplicitās, -ātis, *f.,* frankness

simul ac, *conj.,* as soon as, at the same time as

simul, *adv.,* at the same time, together

simul, *conj.,* as soon as

simulō (1), to pretend

sīn, *conj.,* but if, if however

sine, *prep.* + *abl.,* without

singulus, -a, -um, *adj.,* one by one

sinister, -tra, -trum, *adj.,* left

sinō, -ere, sīvī, sītum, to allow, permit

sinus, -ūs, *m.,* lap, embrace

sitis, -is, *f.,* thirst

situs, -a, -um, *pf. pass. pple.,* laid in one's grave

sōlācium, -iī, *n.,* solace, consolation

soleō, -ēre, -uī, -itum, to be accustomed to, be wont to

sollemnia, -um, *n. pl.,* religious festival, ceremony

sollemnis, -e, *adj.,* ceremonial, performed in accordance with the forms of religion

sollicitūdō, -inis, *f.,* anxiety, concern; uneasiness

sollicitus, -a, -um, *adj.,* anxious, worried

sōlus, -a, -um, *adj.,* only, single, alone; sole

solūtilis, -e, *adj.,* that is easily taken apart, collapsible

solvō, -ere, solvī, solūtum, to loosen, unwrap

sonō, -are, -uī, -itum, to sound, make noise

Sophonība, -ae, *f.,* Sophoniba (Carthaginian wife of Syphax, sometimes called Sophonisba; her actual name was Saphanba'al)

sopītus, -a, -um, *adj.,* sleepy

sorbum, -ī, *n.,* the fruit of the sorb-apple (a small brown edible fruit)

sordīdus, -a, -um, *adj.,* low, degrading

soror, -ōris, *f.,* sister

spatior, -ārī, -ātus sum, to walk about in a slow or leisurely manner, stroll

spatium, -iī, *n.,* space

speciēs, -ēī, *f.,* apparition, ghost

spectāculum *or* **spectāclum, -ī,** *n.,* show, sight, view; spectacle

spectō (1), to look at

spernō, -ere, sprēvī, sprētum, to reject

spērō (1), to hope

spēs, -eī, *f.,* hope

splendeō, -ēre, -uī, —, to gleam, be brilliant

st! *expression urging silence,* hush!

stabulum, -ī, *n.,* stable

statim, *adv.,* immediately; then

statiō, -ōnis, *f.,* guard

statua, -ae, *f.,* statue

statuō, -ere, -uī, -ūtum, to decide; to determine; to place

sternō, -ere, strāvī, strātum, to spread, strew, sprinkle

stola, -ae, *f.,* garment worn by a respectable Roman matron

strepītus, -ūs, *m.,* loud noise, din

studiōsus, -a, -um, *adj. + gen.,* concerned with, anxious about

studium, -iī, *n.,* enthusiam for (with objective gen.); love (of)

stultus, -a, -um, *adj.,* stupid

stuprum, -ī, *n.,* illicit sexual act

Stygius, -a, -um, *adj.,* Stygian, of the river Styx in the underworld

sub, *prep. + abl.,* under, beneath

subinde, *adv.,* immediately thereafter, presently

subitō, *adv.,* hastily, quickly, suddenly

submittō, -ere, -mīsī, -missum, to bribe; to make subject or subordinate to

subornō (1), to hire; to incite secretly

subrepō, -ere, -repsī, -reptum, + *dat.,* to creep up on

subsistō, -ere, -stītī, —, to stop, halt

subtīlis, -e, *adj.,* finely ground

subtrahō, -ere, -trāxī, -tractum + *dat.,* to drag away from, remove

suffiō, -īre, -iī, -ītum, to fumigate

suffundō, -ere, -fūdī, -fūsus, to pour in, cause to well up to a surface

suī, sibi, sē, sēsē, *reflex. pron.,* himself, herself, itself, themselves

Sulpicia, -ae, *f.,* Sulpicia (the name of two Roman female poets)

sulpur *or* **sulfur, -uris,** *n.,* sulphur

sum, esse, fuī, futūrus, to be, exist

summoveō, -ēre, -mōvī, mōtum, to move away

summus, -a, -um, *adj.,* highest
sūmō, -ere, sumpsī, sumptum, to take, choose
sumptus, -ūs, *m.,* expense
super, *adv.,* on top of, upon
super, *prep. + acc.,* over; *prep. + abl.,* about, concerning
superbus, -a, -um, *adj.,* arrogant; proud
supercilium, -iī, *n.,* arrogance, haughtiness
superō (1), to surpass
supersum, -esse, -fuī, —, to survive, remain
supervacuus, -a, -um, *adj.,* needless, of no benefit
supplex, -icis, *adj.,* suppliant, pleading humbly; characteristic of a suppliant
supplicium, -iī, *n.,* punishment
supplicō (1), to pray to, venerate
suprēmus, -a, -um, *adj.,* final; (with **officium**) burial, last rites
surgō, -ere, surrexī, surrectum, to rise
suscenseō, -ēre, -suī, -sum, to be angry with
suspīritus, -ūs, *m.,* sigh
suus, -a, -um, *poss. pron.,* his, her, its, their (own)
symphōnia, -ae, *f.,* musical concerts
Syphax, -ācis, *m.,* Syphax (prince of western Numidia during second Punic War, defeated by Scipio Africanus, father of Cornelia)

tabella, -ae, *f.,* wax writing tablet
tabellārius, -iī, *m.,* courier, letter-carrier
taberna, -ae, *f.,* drinking place, bar
tabernāculum, -ī, *n.,* tent
taceō, -ēre, -uī, -itum, to be silent
taeda, -ae, *f.,* torch
taedet, -ere, taesum est, *impers.,* it wearies, tires
tālis, -e, *adj.,* of such a kind, like
tam, *adv.,* so, such, to such an extent, so much
tamen, *adv.,* however, nevertheless
tandem, *adv.,* finally, at last
tangō, -ere, tetīgī, tactum, to touch
tantummodo, *adv.,* only
tantus, -a, -um, *adj.,* so great, so large, so much; such
tegō, -ere, texī, tectum, to cover, hide, conceal
Tēia, -ae, *f.,* Teia (Greek female name)
temerē, *adv.,* rashly, recklessly
temeritās, -ātis, *f.,* recklessness, rashness
tempestīvus, -a, -um, *adj.,* timely, at the right time
temptō (1), to try; to make an attempt upon, attack
tempus, -oris, *n.,* time
tenax, -ācis, *adj.,* stingy
teneō, -ēre, -uī, tentum, to hold, hold on to; to keep; to have

tener, -era, -erum, *adj.,*
delicate, soft, tender

tentīgō, -inis, *f.,* male sexual
tumescence, swelling

tenuis, -e, *adj.,* slender,
delicate

ter, *adv.,* three times

tergō, -ere, tersī, tersum, to
rub clean

terra, -ae, *f.,* land, earth

terrae, -ārum, *f. pl.,* the earth,
the world

terreō, -ēre, -uī, -itum, to
frighten; to terrify

terror, -ōris, *m.,* terror, fright

tertius, -a, -um, *adj.,* third

testāmentum, -ī, *n.,* will

testimōnium, -iī, *n.,* evidence

theātrum, -ī, *n.,* theater

Thyestēs, -ae, *m.,* Thyestes

Tiberis, -is, *m.,* Tiber (river that
runs through Rome)

timeō, -ēre, -uī, —, to fear; to
be afraid

timiditās, -ātis, *f.,* nervousness,
timidity

toga, -ae, *f.,* Roman dress worn
by female prostitutes, as well
as free-born males

togāta, -ae, *f.,* commercial sex
worker (woman dressed
in a **toga** because she
is ineligible to wear the
matron's **stola**)

tolerō (1), to take up the burden
of, shoulder

tollō, -ere, sustulī, sublātum,
to lift, take up; to remove,
take away

Tonans, -ntis, *m.,* the thunderer
(epithet of Jupiter)

torreō, -ēre, torruī, tostum, to
dry up, scorch, burn

tortus, -a, -um, *pf. pass. pple.,*
twisted

torus, -ī, *m.,* bed (as site of
sexual activity or union)

tōtus, -a, -um, *adj.,* all, whole,
entire; complete

tractō (1), to discuss

trādō, -ere, -didī, -ditum, to
hand over, hand down; to
deliver, pass on, transmit

trahō, -ere, traxī, tractum, to
draw; to drag, drag forward;
to reveal

trepidatiō, -ōnis, *f.,* fear;
trembling

trepidō (1), to be in a state of
fear or agitation

trēs, tria, *numeral,* three

tribūnātus, -ūs, *m.,* office of
tribune of the people

tribūnus plēbēī, tribūnī plēbēī,
m., tribune of the people
(a Roman official with the
duty to protect the Roman
people)

triērarchus, -ī, *m.,* captain (of
a boat)

tristis, -e, *adj.,* gloomy, sad; in a
disapproving mood

triumphō (1), to celebrate a
triumph

triumphus, -ī, *m.,* triumph (the
magnificent entrance into
Rome of a general after an
important victory)

tū, tuī, *pron. sing.,* you

tuī, -ōrum, *poss. pron., m. pl.,* your own family

tum, *adv.,* then, in those days

tumeō, -ēre, -uī, —, to swell up

tumultuor, -ārī, -ātus sum, to raise an uproar

tumulus, -ī, *m.,* burial mound, grave

tunc, *adv.,* then

tunica, -ae, *f.,* tunic (male or female undergarment)

tuquidem. *See* tu *and* quidem

turbō (1), to throw into confusion, confuse; to disturb, upset; to disorder

turpis, -e, *adj.,* scandalous, shameless; disgraceful

tūtō, *adv.,* safely

tuus, -a, -um, *poss. adj.,* your, yours (sing.)

ūber, -eris, *adj.,* copious

ubi, *adv.,* when, where, whenever

ūdus, -a, -um, *adj.,* damp, moist

ulcīscor, -ī, ultus sum, to take vengeance on

umbra, -ae, *f.,* shadow, shade

umbrōsus, -a, -um, *adj.,* shady, shadowy

umquam, *adv.,* ever

ūnā, *adv.,* together; at the same time as

unde, *adv.,* whence, from where, from which

undique, *adv.,* everywhere

unguis, -is, *m.,* fingernail

ūnicus, -a, -um, *adj.,* only, unique

ūnus, -a, -um, *adj.,* one

urbānē, *adv.,* courteously, urbanely

urbānius, *compar. adv.,* in a more refined manner, more cultivated manner

urbanus, -a, -um, *adj.,* sophisticated, refined

urbs, urbis, *f.,* city (often to mean "Rome")

urceus, -ī, *m.,* vessel for liquids, pitcher

urgeō, -ēre, ursī, —, to press hard, insist

usque, *adv.,* continuously

ut or utī, *conj.,* + *indicative,* as, when, how (indirect question); + *subjunctive,* that, so that, in order that (purpose clause); so that, with the result that (result clause)

uterque, -traque, -trumque, *pron. and adj.,* each (of two), both

ūtilis, -e, *adj.,* useful, expedient

utīque, *conj.,* and that

ūtor, -ī, ūsus sum, + *abl.,* to use; to socialize with, visit; to employ; to make a speech; (with the acc.) to be in possession of, socialize with, visit

utrimque, *adv.,* on both sides

utrum . . . an, *interrog. conj.,* whether . . . or

ūva, -ae, *f.,* grape; **ūva passa,** dried grape, raisin

uxor, -ōris, *f.,* wife

vacuō (1), to be empty

vādō, -ere, vāsī, vāsum, to go quickly

vagor, -ārī, -ātus sum, to wander

valeō, -ēre, -uī, —, to be well; **valē,** "good-bye"

valvae, -ārum, *f. pl.,* double doors

-ve, *enclitic conj.,* or

vehementer, *adv.,* violently

vel . . . vel, *conj.,* either . . . or

vel, *adv., + superl., denotes the highest possible degree,* the most . . . possible

vēlox, -ōcis, *adj.,* swift

vēlum, -ī, *n.,* curtain

velutī, *adv.,* as if, just as, just as if

venālis, -e, *adj.,* for sale

venditō (1), to sell

vendō, -ere, -didī, -ditum, to sell

venēnum, -ī, *n.,* poison

vēneō, -īre, -iī (-īvī), -ītum, to go to sale, put up for sale; to be sold at auction

venia, -ae, *f.,* pardon, forgiveness, favor

veniō, -īre, vēnī, ventum, to come, arrive

venor, -ārī, -ātus sum, to hunt

Venus, -eris, *f.,* Venus (the goddess of love); **venus,** love, passion, sexual or erotic passion

venustās, -ātis, *f.,* charm, elegance

Venustina, -ae, *f.,* a female name, related to the name of Venus

vēpallidus, -a, -um, *adj.,* deathly pale

verber, -ris, *n.,* whip

verbum, -ī, *n.,* word

vereor, -ērī, -itus sum, to fear, to be afraid

verna, -ae, *m. or f.,* slave born in his/her master's household

vernus, -a, -um, *adj.,* occurring in springtime, spring-like, of or belonging to spring

vērō, *adv.,* but in fact, as for

versor, -ārī, -ātus sum, to be engaged (in)

versus, -ūs, *m.,* verse; verse of poetry

vērum, *adv.,* but

vērus, -a, -um, *adj.,* true

vesper, -eris *or* **-eri,** *m.,* evening

Vestālis, -e, *adj.,* of or belonging to Vesta, Vestal

vestibulum, -ī, *n.,* entrance hall, forecourt

vestigium, -iī, *n.,* track, print

vestis, vestis, *f.,* clothing

vetustus, -a, -um, *adj.,* ancient

via, -ae, *f.,* road, journey

viātor, -ōris, *m.,* traveler, passer-by

vīcīna, -ae, *f.,* female neighbor

vīcīnus, -a, -um, *adj.,* neighboring

vīcīnus, -ī, *m.*, neighbor

victor, -ōris, *m.*, victor; conqueror; champion

victrix, -īcis, *f.*, female conqueror; *as an adj.*, conquering

vidēlicet, *adv.*, of course, to be sure

videō, -ēre, vīdī, vīsum, to see, to seem to

videor, -ērī, visus sum, (passive of **videō**) to seem, be seen as

vigeō, -ēre, viguī, —, to be strong, thrive

vigilō (1), to be unable to sleep, spend the night sleepless

vīgintī, *indeclinable numeral,* twenty

vīlica, -ae, *f.*, housekeeper

vīlicus, -ī, *m.*, overseer or manager of a farm

villa, -ae, *f.*, country house

vīnacia, -ae, *f.*, grape pulp (refuse from wine pressing)

vinclum *or* vinculum, -ī, *n.*, chain, fetter

vincō, -ere, vīcī, victum, to conquer, defeat

vindicō (1), to liberate, lay legal claim to; to avenge; to defend

vīnolentia, -ae, *f.*, drunkenness

vīnum, -ī, *n.*, wine

violentia, -ae, *f.*, violence

violentus, -a, -um, *adj.*, vehement, forcible

vir, -ī, *m.*, man, husband

virgo, -inis, *f.*, virgin; Vestal virgin

viridis, -e, *adj.*, green

virīlis, -e, *adj.*, of or belonging to a man, male

virtūs, -ūtis, *f.*, excellence, strength; courage

vīs, vis, *f.*, force, violence, authority

vīsō, -ere, -sī, -sum, to view, look at attentively

vīta, -ae, *f.*, life

vitium, -iī, *n.*, vice, fault

vītō (1), to escape; (with dat.) to avoid

vituperō (1), to disparage, criticize

vīvō, -ere, vīxī, vīctum, to live, enjoy life

vīvus, -a, -um, *adj.*, living, alive; that has life

vix, *adv.*, scarcely

vocō (1), to call

volō, velle, voluī, —, to wish, want, desire; to mean

voluntārius, -a, -um, *adj.*, of his or her own free will

voluptās, -ātis, *f.*, pleasure

vox, vōcis, *f.*, voice

vulgāris, -e, *adj.*, usual, common

vultus, -ūs, *m.*, face, looks; features

*B*C **LATIN** Readers

Series Editor: RONNIE ANCONA, HUNTER COLLEGE
AND CUNY GRADUATE CENTER

All Other Readers in Series Now Available

An Apuleius Reader
Selections from the
METAMORPHOSES
ELLEN D. FINKELPEARL
(2012) ISBN 978-0-86516-714-8

A Caesar Reader
Selections from BELLUM
GALLICUM *and* BELLUM
CIVILE, *and from*
Caesar's Letters,
Speeches, and Poetry
W. JEFFREY TATUM
(2012) ISBN 978-0-86515-696-7

A Cicero Reader
Selections from Five Essays
and Four Speeches,
with Five Letters
JAMES M. MAY
(2012) ISBN 978-0-86515-713-1

A Latin Epic Reader
Selections from Ten Epics
ALISON KEITH
(2012) ISBN 978-0-86515-686-8

A Livy Reader
Selections from
AB URBE CONDITA
MARY JAEGER
(2011) ISBN 978-0-86515-680-6

A Lucan Reader
Selections from CIVIL WAR
SUSANNA BRAUND
(2009) ISBN 978-0-86516-661-5

A Martial Reader
Selections from Epigrams
CRAIG WILLIAMS
(2011) ISBN 978-0-86516-704-9

An Ovid Reader
Selections from Seven Works
CAROLE E. NEWLANDS
(2014) ISBN 978-0-86515-722-3

A Plautus Reader
Selections from Eleven Plays
JOHN HENDERSON
(2009) ISBN 978-0-86516-694-3

A Propertius Reader
Eleven Selected Elegies
P. LOWELL BOWDITCH
(2014) ISBN 978-0-86515-723-0

A Roman Army Reader
Selections from Literary,
Epigraphic, and Other
Documents
DEXTER HOYOS
(2013) ISBN 978-0-86515-715-5

A Roman Verse Satire Reader
Selections from Lucilius,
Horace, Persius, and Juvenal
CATHERINE C. KEANE
(2010) ISBN 978-0-86515-685-1

A Sallust Reader
Selections from
BELLUM CATILINAE,
BELLUM IUGURTHINUM,
and HISTORIAE
VICTORIA E. PAGÁN
(2009) ISBN 978-0-86515-687-5

A Seneca Reader
Selections from
Prose and Tragedy
JAMES KER
(2011) ISBN 978-0-86515-758-2

A Suetonius Reader
Selections from
the LIVES OF THE
CAESARS *and the* LIFE
OF HORACE
JOSIAH OSGOOD
(2011) ISBN 978-0-86515-716-2

A Tacitus Reader
Selections from
ANNALES, HISTORIAE,
GERMANIA, AGRICOLA,
and DIALOGUS
STEVEN H. RUTLEDGE
(2013) ISBN 978-0-86515-697-4

A Terence Reader
Selections from
Six Plays
WILLIAM S. ANDERSON
(2009) ISBN 978-0-86515-678-3

A Tibullus Reader
Seven Selected Elegies
PAUL ALLEN MILLER
(2013) ISBN 978-0-86515-724-7

 Visit the series website for details and reviews:
www.bolchazy.com/readers